CW00942406

ḤADĪTH LITERATURE

ḤADĪTH LITERATURE

ITS ORIGIN, DEVELOPMENT AND SPECIAL FEATURES

BY

Muhammad Zubayr Siddiqi

Late Professor of Islamic Culture
Calcutta University

Edited and Revised by
ABDAL HAKĪM MURAD

THE ISLAMIC TEXTS SOCIETY

This revised edition first published in 1993 by
The Islamic Texts Society
35 Parkside, Cambridge CB1 1JE, UK

Copyright © The Islamic Texts Society 1993

Reprinted 1996, 2008

British Library Cataloguing-in-Publication Data.
A catalogue record for this book is
available from the British Library.

ISBN: 978 0946621 38 5 paper

ISBN–10: 0946621 38 1 paper

*All rights reserved. No part of this publication
may be reproduced, stored in a retrieval system,
or transmitted in any form or by any means, electronic,
mechanical, photocopying, recording, or otherwise,
without the prior written permission of the Publisher.*

Publication of this volume has been made
possible by the generous support of
Faisal Finance (Switzerland) S.A.

Cover design copyright © The Islamic Texts Society

Printed in Turkey by Mega Printing

CONTENTS

ABBREVIATIONS

EI	*Encyclopedia of Islam* (First edition)
EI[2]	*Encyclopedia of Islam* (New edition)
COPL	*Catalogue of the Arabic and Persian Manuscripts in the Oriental Public Library at Bankipore*
IC	*Islamic Culture*
IQ	*The Islamic Quarterly*
IS	*Islamic Studies*
JASB	*Journal of the Asiatic Society of Bengal*
JRAS	*Journal of the Royal Asiatic Society*
MW	*The Muslim World*
SI	*Studia Islamica*
ZDMG	*Zeitschrift der deutschen morgenländischen Gesellschaft*

EDITOR'S PREFACE

CONTINUED demand for the late Dr Siddiqi's introduction to *Ḥadīth Literature* has encouraged The Islamic Texts Society, distributors of the work in Western countries since 1981, to commission a new edition. This has provided the opportunity to carry out a degree of rewriting and correction of the text, which has also been brought up to date with references to works published since the appearance of the first edition in 1961.

It is to be hoped that in its new guise the work will continue to be of benefit in University courses on Islamic studies, and will, perhaps, serve to resolve a number of obstinate misunderstandings about the nature and provenance of this literature.

A. H. Murad

AUTHOR'S PREFACE

THIS short book exists in order to present to the English-reading public, non-Muslim as well as Muslim, the viewpoint of mainstream Islam with regard to the *Ḥadīth* literature, its origins and evolution, and its criticism by the Muslim doctors. While a number of works on the topic are now available in European languages, several of these represent Orientalist approaches to scholarship which are directed only to a small circle of academics,* while many of the others fail to give the reader an understanding of the normative Muslim viewpoint. Almost all recent studies, moreover, have failed to deal adequately with modern scholarship carried out in the Muslim world itself.

In assembling this book, use has been made not only of contemporary academic works, but also of many original Arabic sources some of which—to the author's knowledge—have not until now been fully utilised. Even the specialist reader, therefore, may perhaps find in this book some important material which may not be available to him or her in any of the conventional European works on the subject.

*For some recent investigations of the Orientalist phenomenon, see in particular R. Olson, A. Hussein and J. Qureishi, *Orientalism, Islam and Islamists* (Brattleboro, 1984CE); E. Said, *Orientalism* (London, 1978CE); A. Abdel Malek, 'L'orientalisme en crise', *Diogenes*, XLIV (1964CE), 130–40; H. Djaït, *Europe and Islam: Cultures and Modernity* (Berkeley, 1985CE), 16–20, 42–73. Note also the (sometimes excessively intense) remarks of the Palestinian diaspora scholar A. Tibawi in his article 'English Speaking Orientalists: A critique of their approach to Islam and Arab nationalism', *MW* LIII (1963CE), 185–204, and reprinted in *IQ* VIII (1964CE), 23–45, 73–88, and published as a monograph (London, 1384/1964). Tibawi later produced a 'Second Critique of English-Speaking Orientalists and their Approach to Islam and the Arabs', *IQ* XXIII (1979CE), 3–54, which was likewise reprinted as a monograph in London in 1979. Arabic readers may also refer to the copious introduction and comments to the Arabic translation of the second edition of *The Legacy of Islam*, published as *Turāth al-Islām* (Kuweit: National Council for Culture, Literature and the Arts, 1398). Critiques of Orientalist views on *ḥadīth* may be found in the two books of M. M. Azami: *Studies in Early Hadith Literature* (Indianapolis, 1978CE); and *On Schacht's Origins of Muhammadan Jurisprudence* (Islamic Texts Society, 1993CE); also the work of the Turkish scholar M. Fuat Sezgin: *Geschichte des arabischen Schrifttums*, volume I (Leiden, 1967CE), and his *Buhârî'nin Kaynakları hakkında araştırmalar* (Istanbul, 1956CE); cf also Muṣṭafā al-Sibāʿī *al-Sunna wa-Makānatuhā fi'l-Tashrīʿ al-Islāmī* (Cairo, 1381), 365–420. Also to be consulted are the works of certain dissident Orientalists such as J. Horovitz, N. Abbott, and J. Robson, set forth in the list of Works Cited at the end of this book. Appendix II of the present work provides a brief assessment of the main Orientalist works in our field. [Editor.]

Some parts of the book have already been published: in *The Proceedings of the All-India Oriental Conference* (1937), pp. 187–206; and in the *Proceedings* of the Idāra-yi Maʿārif-i Islāmiya (Lahore, 1933), pp. 61–71; while an Arabic translation of Chapter 5 was published as part of *al-Mabāḥith al-ʿIlmiyya* at the Dā'irat al-Maʿārif of Hyderabad in 1939.

In 1959, the University Grants Commission of India, together with Calcutta University, provided the necessary funds for the book's publication. I would be failing in my duty if I did not express my gratitude to them for this favour, and likewise to Dr. G. C. Raychaudhury, Registrar of Calcutta University, for his sympathy and keen interest in the publication of this book. I should also express my heart-felt thanks to Dr. S. A. Kamali, a young competent scholar of Arabic, well trained in the modern methods of literary research, who very kindly checked the references in the book. Thanks are also due to Dr. M. W. Mirza of Lucknow, who translated from Turkish a passage from an article by Professor Ahmed Ateş; to Mawlana Mukhtar Aḥmad Nadwi, a keen and critical student of *ḥadīth*, who located for me a number of references to *ḥadīth* works, and also Hajji Muhammad Yusuf, who are respectively Librarian and owner of the Hajji ʿAbdallah Library, Calcutta, for lending me books from their library.

Finally, let me add that if this book stimulates a more active interest in *ḥadīth* literature and Islamic culture amongst young Muslim scholars of Arabic and Islam, I will consider my long years of research to have been amply rewarded.

M.Z.S.

INTRODUCTION

THE history of the origin, development and criticism of *ḥadīth* literature is a subject as important as it is fascinating.

It is important because it serves as an astonishingly voluminous source of data for the history of pre-Islamic Arabia and of early Islam, and for the development of Arabic literature, as well as of Islamic thought in general and Islamic law in particular. It also played a decisive role in establishing a common cultural framework for the whole Islamic world,* and continues to wield substantial influence on the minds of the Muslim community;† an influence which, it seems clear, will continue for the foreseeable future. It is fascinating because it sheds so much light on the psychology of the *ḥadīth* scholars—the Traditionists—the devoutly scrupulous as well as the confirmed forgers, and on many of the key political and cultural movements which germinated and developed in the various regions of the Muslim world throughout its complex history. It portrays a brilliant medieval academic world which gave birth to many European scholarly institutions, including the doctorate and the baccalaureate.‡ It also contains many of the basic ideas now current about democracy, justice among mankind and nations, the condemnation of aggression, and the ideal of global peace. All this, moreover, is linked resolutely to the sacred, to a consciousness of man's exalted meaning and destiny, which seems to mark the Muslims out today more than ever before.

The Muslims (since the Blessed Prophet's lifetime), and European orientalist scholars (for about the last two hundred years), have hence paid close attention to *ḥadīth* and to its ancillary sciences. During the time of the Prophet, the Companions were zealous to learn and recall his words and the incidents of his life. Many of them wrote these '*ḥadīth*s' down, and distributed them for the benefit of their co-religionists. A large number of *ḥadīth*s were

* As has been shown by J. Fück, 'Die Rolle des Traditionalismus im Islam', *ZDMG* XCIII (1939 CE), 1-32.

† Guillaume, *The Traditions of Islam* (Oxford, 1924 CE), 6.

‡ G. Makdisi, *The Rise of Colleges* (Edinburgh, 1982 CE); R. Y. Ebeid and M. J. L. Young, 'New Light on the Origin of the Term "Baccalaureate"', *IQ* XVIII (1974CE), 3–7.

thus collected in the first century of Islam, and were disseminated throughout the vast Islamic empire, partly in writing, and partly as an extensive oral tradition. During the subsequent centuries, efforts were made to compile more or less exhaustive collections of *ḥadīth*s which were considered to be reliable by specific scholarly criteria, and long and arduous journeys were undertaken for this purpose. Thus, partly in the second century after the Prophet's emigration (*hijra*) from Mecca to Medina, but largely in the third, important collections of such *ḥadīth* were compiled and published. As some *ḥadīth* were known to have been forged—some even during the Prophet's lifetime—immense care had to be taken to ensure their credentials. To this end, the Muslim scholars introduced the system of the *isnād*, the chain of authorities reaching back to the Prophet which shows the historical status of a report. This was introduced at an early date, and by the first quarter of the second century was treated as a necessary part of every tradition. In time, too, branches of literature grew up to serve as foundations for the criticism of every individual *ḥadīth*. As the *isnād* alone was not considered to be a sole and sufficient guarantee of a *ḥadīth*'s genuineness, a number of other general principles were laid down as litmus tests for the authenticity of a text. It has hence been generally accepted by the traditionists that the validity of a tradition is sufficiently determined by the rigorous techniques of criticism which have thus been developed by the specialists. All these matters have been touched upon in this book.

Finally, the reader should note that no attempt has been made in this book to deal with the Shīʿī traditions, for the author does not consider himself qualified to undertake such a task.

1

THE EVENT OF THE *ḤADĪTH*

1.1 THE MEANING OF ḤADĪTH

THE Arabic word *ḥadīth* has the primary connotation of 'new', being used as an antonym of *qadīm*, 'old'. From this derived the use of the word for an item of news, a tale, a story or a report—be it historical or legendary, true or false, moral or scandalous, relating to the present or to the past. The word was employed in this sense by the pre-Islamic poets, and by the Qur'ān and the Prophet. Storytellers, also, were called *ḥuddāth*: the purveyors of *ḥadīth*.

This general sense of the word has, as elsewhere in the Arabic lexicon (e.g. *ṣalāt*, *sujūd*, *zakāt*, *taqwā*), been altered under the far-reaching influence of Islam. Since the lifetime of the Prophet himself the Muslims called reports which spoke of his actions and sayings 'the best *ḥadīth*', and, in due course, the word became increasingly confined to such reports.

Not only his Companions, but the Prophet himself appears to have used the term in this sense. When he remarked to Abū Hurayra that he knew his anxiety about *ḥadīth*,[1] he was referring to his own *ḥadīth*. Similarly, ʿUtba had the Prophetic *ḥadīth* in mind when he commented that Ibn ʿAbbās related only two or three *ḥadīth*s in a month.[2] ʿUmar ibn al-Khaṭṭāb meant the *ḥadīth* of the Prophet when he asked his companions not to narrate too many *ḥadīth*s.[3] When ʿAlī instructed, 'When you write down the *ḥadīth*, write it with the *isnād*,' he was referring particularly to the *ḥadīth* of the Prophet.[4]

1.2 ḤADĪTH AND SUNNA

Closely connected to the word *ḥadīth* is the term *sunna*, which, although originally bearing the sense of 'precedent' and 'custom',[5] and used thus in sixteen places in the Qur'ān,[6] was employed by the Muslims for the accepted practice of the community, and, in later years, for the practice of the Prophet only.[7] Some Muslim writers have regarded these philologically unconnected words as wholly synonymous, while others have attempted to draw distinctions between their connotations.[8] Such distinctions, however, have long been theoretical.

1.3 THE IMPORTANCE OF THE ḤADĪTH

Ḥadīth, thus defined, has been the subject of the closest interest among the Muslims since the lifetime of the Prophet. His astonishing career could not have failed to capture the undivided attention of those around him.[9] Having lived a quiet, uneventful life for some forty years, he began one of history's most stirring and transformative movements, which successfully and forever changed the course of human thought and life. At the very beginning of his career as a prophet he struck fearlessly at the root of the firm beliefs and ancient customs of the pagan Arabs. In response, they hated and boycotted him, insulted and injured him, and forced him to leave his home for a distant city. But through his faith in his cause, his tenacity of purpose and the appeal of the simple monotheism he preached, he succeeded in overturning the established prestige of the Quraysh of Mecca, and then returned triumphantly within ten years of his exile, having founded a polity which was destined to measure sword simultaneously and successfully with the well-equipped and trained legions of Persia and Byzantium, and indelibly to influence history and culture down to the present.

The Prophet Muhammad, then, has probably been the most influential single figure of world history. With his spiritual charisma, his straightforward honesty, the eloquence of the book which he brought, and the revolutionary effects of his activities, the eyes of friend and enemy alike were riveted upon him, noting his every act and statement

To his enemies, he was a revolutionary bent upon destroying the whole fabric of their society, whose activities had to be keenly watched if the progress of his mission was to be suppressed. His words must have been the focus for endless reflection, conversation and heated discussion. They watched his movements so closely and carefully that many of his most secretly conceived plans could not escape their watchful eyes. Abū Lahab, one of their most committed leaders, would go to him when he preached his faith to the Arabian tribes, and try to dissuade them from paying any heed to his peaceful sermons.[10] They discovered his plans when his followers were migrating from Arabia to Abyssinia, sending men after them to try and bring about their forced return.[11] They found out that he was secretly speaking to the people of Medina, and they threatened the Medinans with hostility and violence if they continued their friendship with him.[12]

If his enemies took a close interest in his statements and actions, then the interest of his followers was more intense still. They had accepted him as their sole guide and prophet, identifying themselves with him completely in his life for God and his struggle against the Quraysh and the other hostile tribes. Their destiny was bound up with the future of the faith which he had received. His success was theirs. All his actions served them as an ideal, and hence a precedent (*sunna*); every word which he uttered was a law to them, while his moral choices, so different from those of their age, yet so immediate in their impartial wisdom, provided them with a system of personal and social virtue which they tried to follow as faithfully as they could.[13] When he chose a golden ring for himself, his friends put one on also; and when he put it off, gave it away, and wore a silver one instead, they also emulated his example.[14] If he rose at midnight and stood for hours in prayer, his friends wished to do the same, and he himself, fearful for their strength, had to bid them to stop.[15] If he fasted continuously for more than a day, his followers would desire to do the same, and he would have to explain to them that he had his own additional duties which were not incumbent upon them.[16] Zayd ibn Khālid spent a whole night at his door in order to watch him offer his night prayers.[17] Nawwās ibn Samʿān stayed at Medina for a whole year to enquire from the Prophet what was virtue and what was vice.[18] Abū Saʿīd al-Khudrī observed carefully the length of time he remained standing during his afternoon prayers.[19] Ibn ʿUmar even counted how many times he asked pardon of God in one sitting.[20]

The Companions did not simply commit as many as they could of the Prophet's words to memory. Some of them collected them in written books known as *ṣaḥīfas*, which they would use as a basis for lectures, and which were later preserved by their families, and by the next generation of Muslims, the so-called 'Successors' (*tābiʿūn*).[21] After the Prophet's death, when his Companions scattered throughout the new provinces, many of them, and many of the Successors, undertook lengthy and difficult journeys, courting poverty and various hazards, in order to learn and collect as many *ḥadīth*s as they could.[22] With the passage of time, they founded independent scholarly disciplines which would help the community to understand the *ḥadīth* of their Prophet, and to assess its genuineness and source.

This activity has been interpreted as one of the most impressive and original scholarly accomplishments of history. The degree of rigour and perfection to which the Muslims brought the system of *isnād*, the vast literature of *asmāʾ al-rijāl* (names of narrators) which they created as an aid to the formal criticism of the Traditions, the literature on *uṣūl al-ḥadīth* which serves as an aid to their material criticism, and the literature on the *mawḍūʿāt*, which deals with material forged and fabricated in the name of the Prophet, stands today as a remarkable literary and scholarly achievement.

So much veneration and respect did the Companions have for the Prophet that one of them collected some of his perspiration, which was said to have been 'sweeter than musk', and stipulated in his will that it should be sprinkled on his body before it was put into the grave.[23] Others preserved anything that had been touched by him, and used it as a miraculous cure for disease.[24] Still others presented their children to him for his blessing.[25]

Given this intense devotion to the Prophet, inspired by his charisma, holiness and integrity, many Companions made a point of observing his life, and recording for posterity everything that they could. Thus Abū Hurayra kept his constant company for three years, sacrificing all worldly pursuits, in order to see and hear what the Prophet did and said,[26] and regularly devoted a period of time to fixing in his memory the words he had heard.[27] ʿAbd Allāh ibn ʿAmr ibn al-ʿĀṣ physically wrote down everything he heard from the Prophet.[28] ʿĀzib, when asked by Abū Bakr to deliver a message to al-Barāʾ, did not leave his company until he had related to him what he and the Prophet had done when they came out of Mecca and were pursued by the Quraysh.[29] ʿUmar ibn al-Khaṭṭāb, who was living at a distance from Medina and was unable to attend the Prophet every day, made an agreement with one of the Anṣār that they would be present with him on alternate days, and report to each other everything they saw and heard from him.[30] Those Companions who had not been physically present when the Prophet said or did anything made up the deficiency by asking of those who had been present, taking care to ensure the veracity of the intermediary source. In fact, it is said to have been a common practice among the friends of the Prophet that whenever any two of them met, one would enquire from the other whether there was any *ḥadīth* (i.e. news of the Prophet's acts and speech), and the other would tell him what he knew.[31] An extension of this practice seems to have been in vogue among some Muslim scholars even so late as the end of the eighth century of the Hijra: for instance, we are told that one Ismāʿīl ʿAqūlī of Baghdad met with an Ibrāhīm of Aleppo, and asked him, after exchanging the usual greetings, whether he knew any *ḥadīths*. The latter, in his response, recited some *ḥadīths* from the *Ṣaḥīḥ* of Bukhārī, fully equipped with their *isnāds*.[32]

The Prophet himself, conscious of his mortality, attached a good deal of importance to the knowledge of his own *ḥadīth*. He used to ask his Companions to make them as widely known as possible, and take care than nothing should be falsely attributed to him.[33] He encouraged his followers to acquire knowledge (i.e., of the Qur'ān and *Sunna*), and teach it to others.[34] The course of study which he prescribed for the People of the Porch (*aṣḥāb al-ṣuffa*), those ascetics who lived at a porch attached to his house, included the Qur'ān, the *Sunna*, and the art of writing.[35] When appointing state officials he gave preference to those who were learned in the *Sunna* as well as the Qur'ān. Such, for instance, was the case with the appointment of *imāms*[36] and *qāḍīs*, and was probably the case with other appointments also. And in an especially celebrated *ḥadīth*, he asked Muʿādh, when the latter Companion was going out as governor of the Yemen, on what basis he would issue judgements. On the basis of the Qur'ān,' Muʿādh replied. 'Suppose,' said the Prophet, 'that you do not find it in the Qur'ān?' 'Then on the basis of the *Sunna*,' answered Muʿādh.[37]

After the Prophet's death, which signalled the end of direct revelation, the importance of *ḥadīth* inevitably increased. As von Kremer puts it: 'The life of the Prophet, his discourses and utterances, his actions, his silent approval and even his passive conduct, constituted next to the Qur'ān the second most important source of law for the young Muslim empire.'[38] Von Kremer is right in his assessment of the importance of the *ḥadīths* as a source of Islamic law. In reality, however, the role played by *ḥadīth* in the evolution of Arabic literature is far broader than this, for the *ḥadīth*, together with the Qur'ān, have supplied the driving impetus for the creation of many branches of Arabic writing, such as history, geography, anthologies of ancient verse, and lexicography. It would not be an exaggeration to state that the Qur'ān and *ḥadīth* provided the bedrock for all the intellectual and academic enterprises of the Arabs.

In this way, the *ḥadīth* literature originated in the early life of the Prophet of Islam, developed largely through his life, and spread simultaneously with the spread of Islam throughout the new Muslim dominions. The Muslim armies which conquered Syria, Palestine, Persia and Egypt included a large number of the Companions of the Prophet, who carried his *ḥadīth* with them wherever they went.[39] In particular, *ḥadīth* rapidly flourished in Medina, Mecca, Kūfa, Baṣra, Damascus, Fusṭāṭ, Ṣanʿā', and Merv.[40] Even the distant lands of North Africa and Spain received the *ḥadīth*s before the end of the first century.[41] And to the east, the message of the Qur'ān and *Sunna* had been received by India even before the Islamic conquest of Sind towards the end of the first century.[42]

1.4 ASSEMBLING THE ḤADĪTHS

During the first century of Islam, the *ḥadīth*s which had spread in this way through the vast Muslim domains were preserved partly in writing (in the form of laws and letters dictated by the Prophet himself,[43] and as *ṣaḥīfas* ascribed to certain of his Companions),[44] and partly in the memories of those who had associated with him and observed his life. After his death, ʿUmar ibn al-Khaṭṭāb (*regn.* 13–24AH/634–44CE) purposed to collect the *ḥadīth* together. He gave the matter his careful consideration for an entire month, invoking the help of God in coming to a decision, and seeking the advice of his companions. We are told, however, that he was obliged to give up this promising project, for fear that the Qur'ān would be neglected by the Muslims.[45]

The Umayyad caliph ʿUmar ibn ʿAbd al-ʿAzīz (*regn.* 99–101/717–19), in accordance with his pious and saintly nature, initiated and partly carried out the task which his great predecessor—whom he tried to emulate in so many other respects—had conceived.[46] The teaching and collection of *ḥadīth* formed a major part of his plan for the moral regeneration of the Muslim community. He appointed paid teachers to teach the Qur'ān to the ignorant Bedouins, supported teachers and students of *fiqh*, sent instructions to the governor of the Ḥijāz that weekly lectures in *ḥadīth* should be arranged, and sent out men well-versed in the subject to Egypt and North Africa in order to teach the Muslims resident in those parts.[47]

Fearing that the *ḥadīth*s would be lost, he took steps also to bring about their collection. He wrote to a great Traditionist of Medina, Abū Bakr ibn Muḥammad ibn Ḥazm (d.120/737), requesting him to write down all the *ḥadīth*s of the Prophet and of ʿUmar, particularly those he could learn from ʿAmra bint ʿAbd al-Raḥmān, who was at that time the most respected custodian of the *ḥadīth*s narrated by ʿĀ'isha.[48] ʿUmar II is also reported to have asked Saʿd ibn Ibrāhīm[49] and Ibn Shihāb al-Zuhrī[50] to collect *ḥadīth*s in the form of books in order to have these circulated throughout his dominions. According to Abū Nuʿaym's *History of Iṣfahān*,[51] ʿUmar even wrote a circular letter asking the *ḥadīth* scholars living in the various parts of his country to collect in the form of books as many *ḥadīth*s as were available.

The great work initiated by ʿUmar ibn ʿAbd al-ʿAzīz was reinforced by the general spirit of the age, and the process of creating written compilations accelerated. Abū Qilāba (d.104 or 107AH [722 or 725CE]) is said to have 'bequeathed his books'.[52] Makḥūl (d.116/734), who had travelled through Egypt and Syria, and had lived for a while at Medina in order to acquire knowledge in all these places,[53] wrote a book on the *Sunna* which was known to the Baghdad bookdealer Ibn al-Nadīm, author of the famous *Catalogue* (*Fihrist*).[54] The traditionist al-Zuhrī (d.124/742) is stated by Ibn Saʿd to have collected so many *ḥadīth*s that after his death his manuscripts needed several riding-beasts to transport them.[55]

The early students and workers on the *ḥadīth* were followed by many *ḥadīth* specialists (now known as *muḥaddithūn*) who carried on the work begun by their predecessors in various provinces of the Muslim world. Of these major collectors of *ḥadīth*, ʿAbd al-Malik ibn ʿAbd al-ʿAzīz ibn Jurayj (d.150/760) worked at Mecca, Saʿd ibn ʿArūba (d.157/774) in Mesopotamia, al-Awzāʿī (d.159/775) in Syria, Muḥammad ibn ʿAbd al-Raḥmān (d.159/775) at Medina, Zā'ida ibn Qudāma (d.160/776) and Sufyān al-Thawrī (d.161/777) at Kūfa, and Ḥammād ibn Salama (d.165/781) at Baṣra.[56]

As almost all these works are lost, no opinion can be expressed on their plan, method or spirit. But Ibn al-Nadīm, who includes them in his catalogue, gives us a short comment on each. He calls the works of Ibn Jurayj, Ibn ʿArūba, al-Awzāʿī, Ibn ʿAbd al-Raḥmān and Zā'ida ibn Qudāma 'works on the *Sunna*', and says that they are arranged like the books of *fiqh*—into chapters devoted to the conventional *fiqh* problems. They were probably works of the same type as the *Muwaṭṭā'*, the early law manual of Imām Mālik,[57] who might have followed in its general plan the system adopted by some of these earlier writers. Two of the books of Sufyān al-Thawrī, however, which were related by various scholars, were works of a different type. About one of them Ibn al-Nadīm tells us that it resembled the *ḥadīth* works[58]—but this too has been lost.

1.5 THE MUWAṬṬA'

The earliest substantial work connected with our subject which is still extant is the *Muwaṭṭa'* of Imām Mālik (d.179/795), which has been described and analysed by the Hungarian scholar Ignaz Goldziher.[59] Goldziher correctly notes that the *Muwaṭṭa'* is not a work on *ḥadīth* in the same sense in which the *Ṣaḥīḥ* of al-Bukhārī and other later works are. 'It is', he says, 'a *corpus juris*, not a *corpus traditionum*.... Its intention is not to sift and collect the "healthy" elements of traditions circulating in the Islamic world but to illustrate the law, ritual and religious practice, by the *ijmāʿ* recognised in Medinian Islam, by the *sunna* current in Medina, and to create a theoretical corrective, from the point of view of *ijmāʿ* and *sunna*, for things still in a state of flux.'[60]

To prove this theory, Goldziher cites the fact that Imām Mālik includes in his work a large number of *fatwās* and customs current in Medina,[61] without trying to demonstrate them by means of *ḥadīth*; that even in quoting the *ḥadīth*s he has not given the *isnād* in all cases, and that he has not made any mention of such *ḥadīth*s as are of a purely historical character.

These facts serve to demonstrate that the *Muwaṭṭa'* was not intended to serve as a collection of *ḥadīth*s. But it may be said with equal justice that it is not a book of *fiqh* in the same sense in which later books on *fiqh* are said to be works on the subject. It contains a very large number of *aḥādīth al-aḥkām* (legal traditions). According to Zurqānī, as Goldziher has pointed out, it contains 1,710 *ḥadīth*s, of which 600 have *isnāds*, 222 are *mursal*, 613 are *mawqūf*, while 285 stop either at a Companion or a Successor (i.e. are either *mawqūf* of *maqṭūʿ*).[62] According to al-Ghāfiqī, the total number of *ḥadīth*s in the twelve versions of the *Muwaṭṭa'* is 666, out of which 97 differ in the different versions of the book, while the rest are common to all the various recensions.[63] The great difference between Zurqānī's and Ghāfiqī's estimates seems to be attributable to the latter's failure to take into account the versions of the *Muwaṭṭa'* compiled by Shaybānī and others.[64] Originally, however, the number of *ḥadīth*s in the *Muwaṭṭa'* is reported to have been between 4,000 and 10,000, which was reduced by the author himself to about a thousand.[65]

The *Muwaṭṭa'* may be treated as a brief but authoritative collection of legally-oriented *ḥadīth*s. Some Muslim authorities, such as Ibn al-Athīr, Ibn ʿAbd al-Barr and ʿAbd al-Ḥaqq Dihlawī include it in the six canonical collections in place of the *Sunan* of Ibn Māja. The majority, however, do not include it among the six, because almost all the important traditions it contains are included in the *Ṣaḥīḥs* of Bukhārī and Muslim.

On the analogy of the *Muwaṭṭa'*, however, we may reasonably assume that the other '*Sunan* works' compiled before or simultaneously with it also contained a fair proportion of the legal *ḥadīth* material, and might therefore be treated like the *Muwaṭṭa'* as *ḥadīth* works.

1.6 THE LEGAL AND HISTORICAL TRADITIONS

Since the earliest times the Muslims have made a distinction between the legal traditions (*aḥādīth al-aḥkām*) and the purely historical material (*maghāzī*). In the *Ṭabaqāt* of the third century scholar Ibn Saʿd some Companions are described as well-versed in the *fiqh*, while others are noted for their knowledge of the *maghāzī*. It appears that their treatment of the legal material was a good deal more critical and rigorous than their approach to the historical traditions, where they were at times relatively freer. Ṣuhayb, the well-known Companion, stated: 'Come, I will tell you the tale of our battles [*maghāzī*], but I will not relate to you that the Prophet said such-and-such a thing.[66] Al-Sā'ib ibn Yazīd heard Ṭalḥa relate tales of the battle of Uḥud, whereas he did not hear other Companions relate any *ḥadīth* of the Prophet.[67] From these, and similar reports, it appears that the *maghāzī* served the early Muslims as topics for their general conversations. But with the legal traditions they were altogether more careful and scrupulous, as will be seen in the Chapter which follows.

The word *fiqh* itself was sometimes used in the sense of *ḥadīth*. Ibn ʿAbd al-Barr, after relating a *ḥadīth*, points out that here the word *fiqh* is used in the sense of *ḥadīth*.[68] As a matter of fact, Islamic law in its earliest period consisted of little else than these legal traditions (*aḥādīth al-aḥkām*), which either upheld or transformed the current legal practice. It is for this reason that those Companions who are said to have related the largest number of *ḥadīths*, such as ʿĀ'isha, Ibn Masʿūd, and ʿAbd Allāh ibn ʿAbbās, are described as *faqīhs* (scholars of the revealed Law).

None the less, the actual number of legal traditions appears to be quite small. Muḥibb al-Dīn al-Ṭabarī mentions only 1,029, of them in his work *al-Aḥkām al-Ṣughrā*, which is devoted to the legal traditions alone.[69] Al-Ḥāfiẓ ʿAbd al-Ghanī, in his *ʿUmdat al-Aḥkām*, mentions only 500 of them,[70] while Ibn Ḥajar in his *Bulūgh al-Maram* cites about 1,338 of them.[71] It is true that Majd al-Dīn ibn Taymiyya, in his *Muntaqā*, cites a far larger number; but this is due in part to his habit of treating the sayings and acts of the Companions as *ḥadīths*, and sometimes treating various versions of a single *ḥadīth* as independant narrations.[72]

1.7 CLASSIFICATION OF ḤADĪTH TEXTS

The following are the usual categories of *ḥadīth* collections:

(a) *Ṣaḥīfa*. This is a collection of the sayings of the Prophet which were written down by one of his Companions during his lifetime or by their successors of the next generation.[73] Several of these *Ṣaḥīfas* are mentioned by Goldziher, according to whom some are also described as *Rasā'il* and *Kutub*.[74] One such collection, which was assembled by Abū Hurayra and taught and handed down by him to his student Hammām ibn Munabbih, has been edited by Dr Hamidullah of Paris.[75] The most important of them, however, is the *Ṣaḥīfa* which was collected by ʿAbd Allāh ibn ʿAmr ibn al-ʿĀṣ (d.65/684), who gave it the title of *al-Ṣaḥīfa al-Ṣādiqa*.[76]

Ibn al-Āṣ's *ṣaḥīfa* is said to have contained around a thousand traditions.[77] Other *ṣaḥīfas*, too, were often large documents:

> For instance, Ḥumaid al-Ṭawīl, who borrowed and copied the books of Ḥasan al-Baṣrī, gives a very graphic description of a sizeable *ṣaḥīfa* that contained the latter's *ʿilm*, by which is meant his collection of *ḥadīth*. He indicates that it was a roll as thick as a circle made by the joining of a man's thumbs and forefinger, that is, about six inches thick. This was also the size of some of Zuhrī's *ḥadīth* collections.[78]

(b) *Juz'*. This is a collection of *ḥadīths* handed down on the authority of one single individual, be he or she a Companion, or a member of any succeeding generation. The term *juz'* is also applied to collections of *ḥadīths* that were compiled on a specific subject, such as Intention, the Vision of God, and so forth.[79]

(c) *Risāla*. This is a collection of *ḥadīths* which deals with one particular topic selected from the eight topics into which the contents of the *Jāmiʿ* books of *ḥadīth* may generally be classified:

- i Belief.
- ii Laws and rulings (*aḥkām*), also known as *sunan*, which include all the subjects of *fiqh*, from ritual purity (*ṭahāra*) to legacies (*waṣāyā*).
- iii *Riqāq*, that is, piety and asceticism.
- iv Manners (*ādāb*) of eating, drinking, travelling, etc.
- v Qur'ānic commentary (*tafsīr*).
- vi *Tārīkh* and *Siyar*; i.e. historical and biographical matters, which include (a) cosmology, ancient history etc., and (b) the life of the Prophet, and of his Companions and Successors.
- vii Seditions and crises (*fitan*) anticipated towards the end of the world.
- viii The virtues (*manāqib*) and defects (*mathālib*) of various people, places etc.

A *Risāla* may also be known simply as a *kitāb* (book). To this class belong many of the works of late authors such as Ibn Ḥajar, al-Suyūṭī, etc.[80]

(d) *Muṣannaf.* This is a more comprehensive collection of *ḥadīth*s in which the traditions relating to most or all of the above eight topics are assembled and arranged in various 'books' or 'chapters', each dealing with a particular topic. To this class belong the *Muwaṭṭa'* of Imām Mālik, the *Ṣaḥīḥ* of Muslim, and similar works.[81]

(e) *Musnad.* This term, which literally means 'supported', was originally used for such traditions as were supported by a complete uninterrupted chain of authorities going back to the Prophet via a Companion.[82] Later, however, the term came to be used in the more general sense of a reliable and authoritative tradition, being used in this sense as a title for all reliable works of the *ḥadīth* literature, so that works like the *Sunan* of Dārimī and the *Ṣaḥīḥ* of Bukhārī are regularly called *Musnads*. More technically, however, it is reserved for those collections of *ḥadīth*s whose material is arranged according to the names of their original narrating authorities, irrespective of subject-matter. Such are the *Musnads* of Abū Daūd al-Ṭayālisī (d.204/819), Aḥmad ibn Ḥanbal (d.233/847), ʿAbd Allāh ibn Abī Shayba (d.235/849), Abū Khaythama (d.234/844), and a number of others.[83] The collector of a Musnad is known as a *Musnid* or *Musnadī*.[84] The *Musnad* works themselves, however, differ in the detailed arrangement of the authorities who originally related them. In some of them, their names are arranged in alphabetical order. In others, they are arranged according to their respective merit in the acceptance of Islam and in taking part in the early important events of the Prophet's mission. In still others, they are arranged according to the affinity of their tribe to the Prophet.[85]

There are, however, some *Musnad* works which are divided into chapters dedicated to particular subjects; in each such chapter the Traditions being arranged according to the original Companions by whom they were narrated. This plan is followed by the *Musnad* authors Abū Yaʿlā[86] (d.276/889) and Abū ʿAbd al-Raḥmān.[87] These works thus combined the characteristics of the *Musnad* and *Muṣannaf* genres.

It was the intention of some of the *Musnad* compilers to collect all the available traditions reported by the various Companions.[88] The *Musnad* of Ibn al-Najjār is said to have contained the traditions related by all the Companions, but this is no longer extant. The *Musnad* of Ibn Ḥanbal contains more than 30,000 *ḥadīth*s narrated by about 700 Companions.[89] According to Ḥājī Khalīfa, writing on the authority of Ibn Ḥazm, the *Musnad* of Abū ʿAbd al-Raḥmān contained traditions related by 1,300 Companions.[90] There are, however, many *Musnad* works which are devoted to traditions related either by a special group of Companions or by one Companion only.

(f) *Muʿjam.* This is generally applied to works on various subjects arranged in alphabetical order. The geographical and biographical dictionaries of Yāqūt are known as *Muʿjām al-Buldān* and *Muʿjam al-Udabā'*, because they are arranged alphabetically. Such *Musnad* collections of traditions as are arranged alphabetically under the names of the Companions are also known as *Muʿjam al-Ṣaḥāba*. But according to the *ḥadīth* specialists, the term is used technically for collections of *ḥadīth* which are arranged not according to the Companions who reported them, but according to the Traditionists from whom the compiler himself received them. The names of such Traditionists (*shuyūkh*) are arranged alphabetically,[91] and all the traditions received from each *shaykh* are then collected together irrespective of their contents and subject-matter. To this class belong two of the collections of al-Ṭabarānī (d.360/970) and the collections of Ibrāhīm ibn Ismāʿīl (d.371/981) and Ibn Qāniʿ (d.350/960).[92] The largest collection by Ṭabarānī is in reality a *Musnad* work, not a *Muʿjam*, being a *Muʿjam al-Ṣaḥāba*, not a *Muʿjam al-Shuyūkh*.[93]

(g) *Jāmiʿ.* This is a *ḥadīth* collection which contains traditions relating to all the eight topics listed above under the rubric of *Risāla*. Thus, the *Ṣaḥīḥ* of al-Bukhārī, as well as the principal book of al-Tirmidhī, is known as a *Jāmiʿ*. The *Ṣaḥīḥ* of Muslim, by contrast, is not so styled, because although it is comprehensive in most areas, it does not contain traditions relating to all the chapters of the Qur'ān.

(h) *Sunan.* These are collections which only contain *aḥādīth al-aḥkām* (legal-liturgical traditions), and omit material relating to historical, spiritual and other matters. Thus the *ḥadīth* collections made by Abū Daūd, al-Nasā'ī and many other traditionists fall into this class.

(i) *Mustadrak.* This is a collection in which the compiler, having accepted the conditions laid down by a previous compiler, collects together such other traditions as fulfil those conditions and were missed by his predecessor. To this class belongs the *Mustadrak* of al-Ḥākim al-Nīsābūrī, who assembled a large number of *ḥadīth*s which fulfilled the stringent conditions laid down by Bukhārī and Muslim, but were not included by them in their *Ṣaḥīḥs*.[94]

(j) *Mustakhraj.* This is a collection of *ḥadīth*s in which a later compiler collects fresh and additional *isnāds* to add to those cited by an original compiler. To this class belongs the *mustakhraj* of Abū Nuʿaym al-Iṣfahānī on the *Ṣaḥīḥs* of Bukhārī and Muslim. In this book, Abū Nuʿaym gives new *isnāds* for some of the traditions included by Bukhārī and Muslim, thereby reinforcing their authority still further.

(k) *Arbaʿīniyyāt.* As the name indicates, these are collections containing forty *ḥadīth* related to one or more subjects which may have appeared to be of special interest to the compiler. The best-known example is the *Forty Hadith* of al-Nawawī.[95]

Of all these eleven classes, the *Ṣaḥīfas* were the earliest in origin, while the *Muʿjams*, the *Mustadraks*, the *Mustakhrajs* and the *Arbaʿīniyyāt* must have been the latest to appear. The *Juz'* and *Risāla* literature, in the technical sense outlined above, must also have evolved slightly later than the *Muṣannaf* and *Musnad* works. Since the *Sunan* and *Jāmiʿ* types are in reality no more than subdivisions of the *Muṣannaf* works, the only chronological problem is that of the priority of the *Musnad* and *Muṣannaf* works. Addressing this difficulty, Goldziher is of the opinion that the *Musnads* are of earlier origin than the *Muṣannafs*, which originated under the influence of the legal system of the *aṣḥāb al-ḥadīth*.[96] Yet since the collection of traditions was substantially motivated by their legal importance, it seems not unlikely that some of the very earliest collections were arranged according to subject matter, as this related to the Islamic legal, ritual or religious problems—as is also suggested by the title *Sunan* conventionally given to them.

2

THE COMPANIONS

2.1 'COMPANION' DEFINED

THE term *al-ṣaḥāba* or *al-aṣḥāb* (singular, *al-ṣaḥābī* and *al-Ṣaḥīb*, a Companion) is used by the Muslims as a title of honour for those believers who had enjoyed the privilege of having lived in the Prophet's company. The Islamic scholars are not in agreement, however, on the exact qualifications necessary for being a *ṣaḥābī*. Some have held that every Muslim who saw the Prophet was a Companion. Others have thought that only through long association with him could one join this category. The majority of writers, however, have held that the term may be applied to every adult Muslim who associated with the Prophet for any length of time. His near relations, his close friends, his attendants, as well as ordinary Muslims who saw him even once, are generally included within the definition.[1]

It was the Companions who reported the *ḥadīth* corpus from the Prophet. They represent the primal authorities from whom, via the Successors (*tābiʿūn*—their students and associates), are handed down the Traditions of Islam. Upon their reliability and honesty rests to a large degree the trustworthiness of the great mass of *ḥadīth*s collected by the Muslim scholars of the subsequent generations.[2]

2.2 THE NUMBER OF THE COMPANIONS

The exact number of the Companions cannot, of course, be determined. Only once during the early years of Islam was a 'census' taken, when they were found to be 1,525.[3] This census must have been done at about the time of the Treaty of Ḥudaybiya, when the danger to the Muslims was great, and an estimate of their actual strength seemed called for. After that time the number of Muslims grew dramatically, and before the death of the Prophet almost the whole of the Arabian peninsula had accepted Islam.

A large number of these Muslims had seen the Prophet and listened to his orations and sayings. Forty thousand of them were present when he performed the Farewell Pilgrimage at Mecca.[4] The number of all those who ever saw or heard him has been estimated by Abū Zarʿa al-Rāzī at above 100,000.[5]

2.3 THE COMPANION-NARRATORS

Not all these Companions related the *ḥadīth*s of their teacher. The *Musnad* of Abū ʿAbd al-Raḥmān referred to previously, which is said to have been the largest collection of *ḥadīth*s, was said to contain traditions related by only 1,300 Companions.[6] Ibn al-Jawzī, who provides a list of all the Companions who related traditions, gives the names of about 1,060 together with the number of *ḥadīth*s related by each.[7] Five hundred of them are said to have related one *ḥadīth* apiece; a hundred and thirty-two are stated to have handed down two traditions each, eighty have related three each, fifty-two have related four traditions each, thirty-two, five each, twenty-six, six each, twenty-seven, seven each, eighteen, eight each, and eleven, nine traditions each. Sixty Companions are credited with having related 10–20 *ḥadīth*s apiece; the remainder, listed in the table below, have all related twenty or more each.

	NAME OF COMPANION	NUMBER OF ḤADĪTHS
1	Abū Shurayḥ al-Kābī	20
2	ʿAbd Allāh ibn Jarrād	20
3	Muṣawwir ibn Makhrama[8]	20
4	ʿAmr ibn Umayya al-Ḍamrī	20
5	ʿAmr ibn Umayya (another)	20
6	Ṣafwān ibn ʿAssāl	20
7	Saʿd ibn ʿUbāda	21
8	al-Rabīʿ	21
9	al-Sā'ib	22
10	Qurra	22
11	ʿUmayr ibn Rabīʿa	22
12	Umm Qays	24
13	Laqīṭ ibn ʿĀmir	24
14	al-Sharīd[9]	24
15	Rifāʿa ibn Rāfiʿ	24

96	Abū Ayyūb al-Anṣārī	155
97	Muʿādh ibn Jabal	157
98	Muʿāwiya ibn Abī Sufyān	163
99	Ubayy ibn Kaʿb	164
100	Burayda ibn al-Ḥasīb[32]	167
101	Abū Qatāda	170
102	Abū al-Dardā'	179
103	ʿImrān ibn al-Ḥusayn[33]	180
104	ʿUbāda ibn al-Ṣāmit	181
105	Sahl ibn Saʿd	188
106	Maʿd ibn Yamān	225
107	Abū Umāma al-Bāhilī[34]	250
108	Saʿd ibn Abī Waqqāṣ	271
109	Abū Dharr al-Ghifārī	281
110	al-Barā' ibn ʿĀzib	305
111	Abū Mūsā al-Ashʿarī	360
112	Umm Salama, Umm al-Mu'minīn	378
113	ʿAlī ibn Abī Ṭālib	536
114	ʿUmar ibn al-Khaṭṭāb	537
115	ʿAbd Allāh ibn ʿAmr ibn al-ʿĀṣ	700
116	ʿAbd Allāh ibn Masʿūd	848
117	Abū Saʿīd al-Khudrī	1170
118	Jābir ibn ʿAbd Allāh	1540
119	ʿAbd Allāh ibn ʿAbbās	1660
120	ʿĀ'isha Umm al-Mu'minīn	2210
121	Anas ibn Malik	2286
122	ʿAbd Allāh ibn ʿUmar	2630
123	Abū Hurayra[35]	5374

From the above it becomes clear that the great mass of the traditions which have come down to us are related by fewer than three hundred Companions. The *Muwaṭṭa'* of Imām Mālik contains the traditions of only 98 Companions.[36] The *Musnad* of al-Ṭayālisī contains the *ḥadīth*s of some 281 Companions, while the *Musnad* of Imām Aḥmad ibn Ḥanbal includes the *ḥadīth*s narrated by about 700 Companions.[37] The two *Ṣaḥīḥs* of Bukhārī and Muslim contain the material of 208 and 213 Companions respectively, of whom 149 are common between the two great works.[38]

Only 55 have related a hundred or more traditions, and of these, only eleven are responsible for passing down more than five hundred each. Six or seven of the latter, each of whom has reported more than a thousand *ḥadīth*s, are known as the *Mukaththirūn*: the reporters of many traditions.[39]

All these seven Companions enjoyed the privilege of long association with the Prophet, had a tremendous thirst for his *ḥadīth*, and could speak with authority about what he had said and done. They lived for a considerable time after his demise, when the mass of the traditions which they had learnt was handed down to the succeeding generations; whereas the knowledge gathered by the Companions who were either killed in the early battles or died shortly after the death of the Prophet could not spread among the Muslims, and was lost for ever.

The following is a brief guide to some of the most prolific *ḥadīth* narrators.

(a) ʿAbd Allāh (or ʿAbd al-Raḥmān) Abū Hurayra.[40] Abū Hurayra stands at the head of the list of *ḥadīth* transmitters, due to the sheer bulk of his narrations. He had been regarded by the Prophet himself as the most anxious of all Muslims to acquire knowledge of *ḥadīth*. Belonging to the tribe of Daws, an offshoot of the great clan of Azd,[41] he came to Medina in the seventh year of the Hijra, and on being told that the Prophet was at Khaybar, went there and accepted Islam. Since that time, and until the death of the Prophet, he kept his company constantly, attending him and memorising his words during the day, thereby sacrificing all worldly pursuits and pleasures.[42] We are told that he divided his nights into three parts: one for sleeping, one for prayer, and one for study.[43] After the death of the Prophet, he was appointed governor of Baḥrayn for a while during the caliphate of ʿUmar, and acted as governor of Medina under the early Umayyad caliphs.[44] He died in 59/678.

When the Prophet had died, and information about religion and legal judgements had to be sought indirectly, Abū Hurayra (who instructed more than 800 students in *ḥadīth*) poured out the store of knowledge he had so meticulously accumulated. At times he was taken to task for reporting certain traditions which were unknown to other Companions. But he would reply that he had simply learnt what the Anṣār had missed because of attending to their lands and properties, and what the Emigrants had failed to learn because of their commercial activities.[45] Once, when he was taken to task by ʿAbd Allāh ibn ʿUmar for relating a particular *ḥadīth*, he took him to ʿĀ'isha, who bore witness to the truth of what he had related.[46] His knowledge and memory were also tested by Marwān who, having written down some traditions related by him, wanted him to relate the same after a year. He found them to be exactly identical to his earlier narration.[47]

Bearing in mind Abū Hurayra's intense dedication to learning *ḥadīth*, his devotion to the Prophet, and the various tests which were applied to his memory and scholarship by his contemporaries during his life, it appears very unlikely that he himself fabricated any *ḥadīth*.[48] This does not mean, however, that material was not falsely imputed to him at a later date. The fact that he narrated a uniquely large number of traditions itself did make inventing *ḥadīth*s in his name an attractive proposition.[49]

(b) ʿAbd Allāh ibn ʿUmar.[50] The second most prolific narrator of *ḥadīth*, he was the son of the second Caliph. He had accepted Islam simultaneously with his father, and emigrated to Medina with him. He took part in many battles during the Prophet's lifetime, and in the wars in Mesopotamia, Persia and Egypt, but maintained a strict neutrality in the conflicts which erupted among the Muslims following the assassination of ʿUthmān. Despite the immense esteem and honour in which he was held by all Muslims, who repeatedly asked him to become caliph (an offer which he refused), he kept himself aloof from factional strife, and throughout those years led an unselfish, pious life, setting an example of an ideal citizen just as his father had set an example of an ideal ruler. He died in Mecca in the year 74/692, at the age of 87.

ʿAbd Allāh's long association with the Prophet, his kinship with Ḥafṣa Umm al-Mu'minīn, and with certain other Companions, offered him a superb opportunity to learn *ḥadīth*s; and his long peaceful life gave him time and leisure enough to teach and spread *ḥadīth*s among the Muslims who assiduously sought them.

He was renowned for the extreme scrupulousness with which he related *ḥadīth*s. Al-Shaʿbī remarks that he did not hear a single *ḥadīth* from him for a whole year.[51] When he related *ḥadīth*s, his eyes filled with tears.[52] His activities in the service of Islam, his austere life, his straightforward and honest character, and his careful treatment of the *ḥadīth*s, render the material we have from him of the highest value.

(c) Abū Ḥamza Anas ibn Malik.[53] At the age of ten, Anas was presented by his mother, Umm Sulaym, to the Prophet, following his migration to Medina. From that time until the Prophet's death, he was his favourite attendant,[54] and afterwards he was appointed by Abū Bakr as a tax-collector at Baḥrayn. Towards the end of his life he settled at Baṣra, where he died in the year 93/711, at the age of over a hundred.

During the ten years he spent in the Prophet's service, he was able to memorise a large number of his words, of which he later also learnt a good deal from Abū Bakr, ʿUmar, and many other Companions.[55] His knowledge of *ḥadīth* was so copious that his death was regarded as a death-blow to half of the entire mass of traditions.[56]

The traditionists accept him as one of the most reliable narrators of *ḥadīth*.

(d) ʿĀ'ISHA UMM AL-MU'MINĪN. ʿĀ'isha occupies the fourth place among the *mukaththirūn*. She enjoyed the constant company of the Prophet for about eight and a half years.[57] She died in 57/676 at the age of 65.[58]

ʿĀ'isha was naturally endowed with a retentive memory and a developed critical faculty, having memorised a large number of the ancient Arab poems, on which she was a recognised authority. During her lifetime she was also honoured for her expertise in medicine and in Islamic law.[59] Regarding the *ḥadīth*, she had not only learnt a large volume of these from her husband, she also showed a critical appreciation of them, and corrected the mistakes in understanding of many Companions.[60] When, for instance, Ibn ʿUmar related that the Prophet had said that the dead are punished in their graves on account of the wailing of their relatives, she pointed out that the Prophet had said that while the dead are punished in their graves for their sins, their relatives wept for them.[61]

It was on account of her extensive knowledge of *ḥadīth* and Islamic law that even the most important Companions sought her advice on legal problems. A long list of those who related *ḥadīth* on her authority may be found in Ibn Ḥajar's book *Tahdhīb al-Tahdhīb*.[62]

(e) Abu'l-ʿAbbās ʿABD ALLĀH IBN AL-ʿABBĀS. He was born three years before the Prophet's migration to Medina,[63] and was thirteen years old at the time of his death. He was greatly loved by the Prophet, as is apparent from the *ḥadīth*s which concern him. He died in 68/687 at the age of 71.[64]

It appears that despite his youth he learnt a few *ḥadīth*s from the Prophet himself. Ibn Ḥajar (quoting Yaḥyā ibn al-Qaṭṭān) refers to the assertion that Ibn ʿAbbās related only four or ten traditions from the Prophet, and adds that this estimate is incorrect, because the *Ṣaḥīḥs* of Bukhārī and Muslim alone contain more than ten traditions related by him directly from the Prophet.[65] There is, however, no doubt that the number of *ḥadīth*s related by him directly from the Prophet is very small in comparison to what he related via other Companions. These *ḥadīth*s he learnt through years of hard labour: 'If I expected to learn any *ḥadīth* from a Companion,' he remarked, 'I went to his door and waited there, until he came out and said: "Cousin of the Prophet, what brings you here? Why did you not send for me?" And I would reply that it was only proper that I should go to him. Then I learnt the *ḥadīth* from him.'[66]

Ibn ʿAbbās was held in universal awe for his intellectual powers and capacity for memorisation. He was entirely devoted to the study of the Qur'ān and the *Sunna*, and was loved and respected for his scholarship by all the first four Caliphs and his contemporaries. He collected a large body of traditions, which he wrote down in books, and delivered lectures on them to his disciples.[67] His *tafsīr* of the Qur'ān which was handed down by his student Mujāhid is well-known, and has been referred to by numerous later commentators.[68]

Some aspects of his political activity have been criticised severely. But his fame rests on his intellectual attainments, not his politics. The reliability of the *ḥadīth*s which may be proved to extend back in time to him, is unquestionable. Much, however, of what has been attributed to him must have been forged by later narrators.

(f) JĀBIR IBN ʿABD ALLĀH. One of the early Medinan converts to Islam, he was present at the second meeting with the Prophet at Mecca.[69] He took part in nineteen expeditions in the Prophet's company,[70] and died in Medina in about the year 74/693 at the age of 94.[71]

He learnt the Prophet's *ḥadīth* not only from him, but also from many of his important Companions, including Abū Bakr, ʿUmar, and others. He also studied under some of the Successors, including the famous Umm Kulthūm, the daughter of Abū Bakr. He used to teach *ḥadīth* regularly in the mosque at Medina.[72]

(g) ABŪ SAʿĪD AL-KHUDRĪ, Saʿd ibn Mālik. Another early Medinan convert, his father was killed at Uḥud. He himself took part in twelve of the battles fought during the Prophet's lifetime. He died in Medina in 64/683.[73]

Like Abū Hurayra, he had been one of the 'People of the Veranda', those who lived on the porch of the Prophet's dwelling by the mosque in order to dedicate themselves to an austere life of prayer and learning. He learnt the *Sunna* from the Prophet, as well as from his important Companions such as Abū Bakr, ʿUmar, and Zayd ibn Thābit. He was considered the best jurist among the younger Companions.

(h) ʿABD ALLĀH IBN MASʿŪD. He is said to have been one of the first six converts to Islam. He specialised in the interpretation of the Qur'ān, for which he is one of the major early authorities.[74]

(i) ʿABD ALLĀH IBN ʿAMR IBN AL-ʿĀṢ. An early convert to Islam, who had suffered for its cause, had enjoyed the company of the Prophet for many years, and lived long enough after he was gone to transmit the *ḥadīth*s which he had learnt from him. Ibn ʿAmr, although he lived during the period of the civil war, resembled Ibn ʿUmar in keeping himself aloft from factional strife. He was, however, present at the Battle of Ṣiffīn, at the insistence of his father; however he took no active part in it, deeply regretting in later life that he had been present at all.[75]

His interest in perpetuating the way of the Prophet was intense. He wrote down all the Traditions which he had learnt from him, collecting a thousand of them in a *ṣaḥīfa* which he called *al-Ṣādiqa*.[76] When he settled at Mecca, students of *ḥadīth* flocked to him in droves. But as he lived for the most part either in Egypt or at al-Ṭā'if, and since he occupied himself more with prayer than with the teaching of *ḥadīth*, the later generations of Muslims received fewer traditions from him than from Abū Hurayra, ʿĀ'isha and others.[77]

2.4 THE SCRUPULOUSNESS OF THE COMPANIONS

The transformative presence of the Prophet, whose emphasis on honesty and integrity was impressed on all who knew him, together with the Qur'ānic warnings against the practice of wilful scriptural distortion which had brought about the destruction of previous religious communities, created an atmosphere of anxious scrupulousness in the reporting of his words and conduct.[78] Abū Bakr, when Caliph, was concerned to learn *ḥadīth*s, but was careful not to accept the words of those who reported them without an independent witness.[79] He also asked Muslims not to relate traditions which might cause discord among them.[80] ʿUmar, the second Caliph, carefully followed the example set by his predecessor; for instance, he obliged al-Mughīra ibn Shuʿba,[81] Abū Mūsā al-Ashʿarī,[82] ʿAmr ibn Umayya,[83] and Ubayy ibn Kaʿb[84] to produce witnesses to corroborate the traditions they narrated, despite the great esteem in which they were held. He is even said to have briefly imprisoned Ibn Masʿūd, Abu'l-Dardā' and Abū Masʿūd al-Anṣārī because they related too many traditions.[85] His successor ʿUthmān ibn ʿAffān was also careful to report the words of the Prophet with the utmost care,[86] while ʿAlī would not accept any *ḥadīth* until its reporter attested to it on oath,[87] and used to remark that he would rather the sky fell on his head than be guilty of attributing a false *ḥadīth* to the Prophet.[88] Ibn Masʿūd was so cautious in relating traditions that we are told that whenever he recited one he began to perspire nervously, adding immediately that God's Messenger had either said this, or something like it.[89] Al-Zubayr was reluctant to relate *ḥadīth*s, because he had heard the Prophet say that whoever attributed anything to him falsely would be preparing his own seat in hell.[90] Saʿd ibn Abī Waqqāṣ feared that people might add to what he related.[91]

So great was the Companions' fear of committing mistakes when relating the words of the Prophet that many of them refused to relate any *ḥadīth* at all unless it was absolutely necessary. ʿAbd Allāh ibn Masʿūd, for instance, only related two or three *ḥadīth*s in a month.[92] Saʿīd ibn Yazīd once travelled with the erudite Saʿd ibn Mālik from Medina to Mecca, and did not hear him relate a single *ḥadīth*.[93] Al-Shaʿbī lived with ʿAbd Allāh ibn ʿUmar for a whole year, but never heard him relate a single *ḥadīth*.[94] Al-Sā'ib ibn Yazīd reports that he once was together with ʿAbd al-Raḥmān ibn ʿAwf and Ṭalḥa ibn ʿUbayd Allāh, and heard nothing in the way of *ḥadīth*s except Ṭalḥa's account of the battle of Uḥud.[95] Ṣuhayb, too, was always ready to relate historical traditions (*maghāzī*), but otherwise rarely dared to report the words of the Prophet.[96]

2.5 THE CONTROVERSY OVER KITĀBA: THE WRITTEN PERPETUATION OF ḤADĪTHS

Despite this reluctance on the part of some Companions to take part in the process of *ḥadīth* narration, and their extreme scrupulousness, there were some among them who, having learnt the art of writing, wrote down *ḥadīth*s, in some instances during the lifetime of the Prophet himself.[97] ʿAbd Allāh ibn ʿAmr, for instance, requested his permission to do this, and thereafter wrote down whatever he heard from him.[98] His collection, *al-Ṣaḥīfa al-Ṣādiqa*,[99] was seen by Mujāhid, and later came into the possession of ʿAmr ibn Shuʿayb, a great-grandson of ʿAbd Allāh.[100] Likewise, it is said that ʿAlī, the son-in-law of the Prophet, had in his possession a *Ṣaḥīfa* which contained certain laws.[101] Another *Ṣaḥīfa* is said to have been in the possession of Samura ibn Jundab, a document which, according to Goldziher, is identical to his *Risāla* addressed to his son, and which contained many *ḥadīth*s.[102] Jābir ibn ʿAbd Allāh likewise had a *Ṣaḥīfa*, the contents of which were later transmitted by Qatāda.[103] Saʿd is also reported to have had a book from which his son related certain usages of the Prophet.[104] Bukhārī mentions a *ḥadīth* related from the 'book' of ʿAbd Allāh ibn Abī Awfā,[105] while Abū Bakr, the first Caliph, is reported to have collected five hundred *ḥadīth*s, which he later destroyed because he suspected that it contained some *ḥadīth*s related by unreliable people.[106] Ibn ʿAbbās wrote down the *ḥadīth*s which he learnt from Abū Rāfiʿ.[107] He appears to have collected *ḥadīth* in more than one book. Tirmidhī reports in his *Kitāb al-ʿIlal* that some people from al-Ṭā'if brought one of his books to Ibn ʿAbbās, and read it to him;[108] he is also said by Ibn ʿAbd al-Barr to have left at his death so many books that they might serve as a complete load for a camel; these books were later used by his son ʿAlī.[109] It is from these books of Ibn ʿAbbās that al-Wāqidī may have drawn some of his material, as is shown by a passage cited in the *Mawāhib*.[110] Abū Hurayra, too, is said to have written down *ḥadīth*s—probably towards the end of his life. These he showed to

Ibn Wahb[111] and to Umayya al-Ḍamrī.[112] The *Ṣaḥīfa* of Hammām, based on the reports of Abū Hurayra, is of course well-known.[113]

In addition to this kind of report, which establishes that the Companions assembled actual written collections of *ḥadīth*, we also have numerous reports indicating that they regularly wrote down individual *ḥadīth*s that they had learnt or encountered. A report in the *Sunan* of Tirmidhī tells us that one of the Anṣār complained to the Prophet about his weak memory, and was advised by him to take assistance from his right hand—i.e., to write material down.[114] Another Companion, al-Rāfiʿ (also known as Abū Rāfiʿ), secured the Prophet's permission to write down *ḥadīth*s.[115] A certain Abū Shāh, hearing the Prophet's oration in the year of the Conquest of Mecca, asked him to have it written down for him, and his request was granted.[116] ʿItbān ibn Mālik al-Anṣārī liked a *ḥadīth* so much that he wrote it down, so as to possess a physical copy of it.[117]

The Prophet had himself dictated certain laws, with respect, for instance, to the poor-tax,[118] the Prayer and the fast, charity, and blood-money.[119] One such document, containing laws with regard to the revenues which had been sent to officials was found after his death attached to his sword, and in time came into the possession of his successors.[120]

Despite this, however, there are many traditions which forbid the writing down of any scriptural material other than the Qur'ān.[121] Abū Saʿīd al-Khudrī, Zayd ibn Thābit (the Prophet's own scribe), and Abū Hurayra, related traditions to this effect;[122] and many other Companions and Successors are reported to have disliked and discouraged the writing of *ḥadīth*. In particular, there are the names of ʿAlī, Ibn Masʿūd, Ibn ʿAbbās, ʿAbd Allāh ibn ʿUmar, Abū Mūsā al-Ashʿarī, Ibn Sīrīn, al-Ḍaḥḥāk, ʿĀbida al-Madaniyya, Ibrāhīm al-Nakhaʿī, Ibn al-Muʿtamir, al-Awzāʿī, ʿAlqama ibn Qays, ʿUbayd Allāh ibn ʿAbd Allāh, and others.[123] Some such authorities (like ʿAlī and Ibn ʿAbbās), are, as we have already seen, also reported to have written *ḥadīth*s down, and possessed *ṣaḥīfas* and other books. Others (for instance al-Ḍaḥḥāk, Ibrāhīm, and ʿAlqama) are said to have objected to the writing of *ḥadīth*s in book form, but not to making such notes as might serve to help the memory. Others still (such as Ibn Masʿūd and Ibn Sīrīn) are said to have opposed the writing of *ḥadīth* in any form.[124]

The *ḥadīth* analysts have attempted to explain this apparent contradiction in various ways. Ibn Qutayba, in his book *Ta'wīl Mukhtalif al-Ḥadīth* (*Interpretation of Divergent Ḥadīths*) says that either the prohibitive *ḥadīth*s belong to ah earlier period in the life of the Prophet, and are abrogated (*naskh*) by the later ones which carry a permission, or, alternatively, the prohibition was meant only for such Companions as were not well trained in the art of writing, and did not include those who could write proficiently without fear of distortion.[125]

We know, however, that although the art of writing was introduced into Arabia at some time before the birth of the Prophet, and Arabic prose works were not entirely unknown to the Arabs before his day, they were not particularly widespread in Arabia before the advent of Islam. It is said that in pre-Islamic Mecca (the most advanced Arab city), only seventeen people knew how to write.[126] In Medina, where the influence of the Jews (who are said to have been the teachers of the Arabs in this regard) had been considerable, the number of Arabs who could write was less than a dozen, only nine of these being mentioned by name by Ibn Saʿd,[127] who also remarks that writing was a rarity in Arabia before Islam, and that it was considered a great distinction to know it. Such people who combined the knowledge of the art of writing, swimming and archery were known as *al-kāmil*, the perfect.[128] But the contrary opinion was also in the air: we are told, for instance, that Dhu'l-Rumma, the last Mukhaḍram poet of Arabia, concealed his knowledge of this art on account of public opinion against it.[129]

Despite this, new conditions meant that the Prophet encouraged the popularising of this art among the Arabs. Under his guidance, many Muslims who came under his influence at an early age (such as ʿAlī, ʿAbd Allāh ibn ʿAmr, and Ibn ʿAbbās), learnt to read and write. He requested ʿAbd Allāh ibn Saʿīd ibn al-ʿĀṣī of Mecca to teach the people of Medina to write.[130] He was also concerned with female literacy: he asked Shifā' bint ʿAbd Allāh to teach reading and writing to his wife Ḥafṣa.[131] After the Battle of Badr he declared that any prisoner of war who was too poor to pay the required ransom and who knew the art of writing could regain his liberty by teaching Muslim children to write;[132] it was from one of these prisoners of war that Zayd ibn Thābit, the trusted scribe of the Qur'ān, himself learnt to read and write.[133] Neither could it have been without the suggestion of the Prophet that ʿUbāda ibn al-Ṣāmit taught the Qur'ān and the art of writing to some of the People of the Veranda, one of whom presented him with a bow in exchange.[134]

Indirectly, too, the Prophet played a key role in spreading written literacy among the Arabs, by means of establishing a state which wrote down its treaties with the various tribes, its constitution, letters to the various tribal chiefs, orders to officials, and laws for conducting the affairs of state. His immediate successors made reading and writing compulsory in the schools which they established. Thus did Islam inaugurate what can only be described as the most effective literacy programme known to history.

The conclusion is generally drawn that the sayings of the Prophet which discourage the writing of *ḥadīth*, being fewer and weaker than those which encourage it, must have been based either on the generally unfavourable public opinion prevailing in Arabia at the beginning of his career as prophet, or on fears that written *ḥadīth* might become confused with the text of the Qur'ān, about the purity of which he was so scrupulous. But as soon as he discerned that these hazards were at an end, he permitted the written recording of *ḥadīth*. The date of one *ḥadīth* in the *Ṣaḥīḥ* of Bukhārī, which gives to Abū Shāh permission to write down one of his discourses, is dated the year of the Conquest of Mecca, a fact which would favour the view that the *ḥadīth*s which allow the writing of *ḥadīth*s postdate those which indicate a prohibition. The fact of the dictation of certain laws in the later years of the Prophet's life also lends support to this theory. Similarly, the attitude of ʿUmar I towards the collection of *ḥadīth*s shows that the prohibition was not in force during that time. It is reported, too, that ʿUmar intended to collect *ḥadīth*s, and it is extremely unlikely that he would have considered the matter seriously for an entire month as he did, had he been aware of any Prophetic teaching to forbid the writing-down of *ḥadīth* material, particularly since all the Companions appear to have advised him in favour of such a collection; while he explained his final decision against doing so in terms of his fear of the neglect of the Qur'ān rather than any alleged Prophetic prohibition known to him.

Western scholars, too, have held that *ḥadīth*s were written down during the Prophet's life. Goldziher, for instance, writes that:

> It can be assumed that the writing down of the *ḥadīth* was a very ancient method of preserving it, and that reluctance to preserve it in written form was merely the result of later considerations.... Many a Companion of the Prophet is likely to have carried his *Ṣaḥīfa* with him and used it to dispense instruction and edification to his circle. The contents of these *Ṣaḥīfas* were called *matn al-ḥadīth*; those who disseminated these texts named in succession their immediate authorities, and thus the *isnād* came into being.[135]

3

AFTER THE COMPANIONS

May God bless him who heard from us a saying, and preserved it (in his memory) so that he might carry it forth to others; for verily, many a person carries knowledge to a man more learned than himself, and many of those who have carried knowledge have not assimilated it themselves.

Ḥadīth cited by Tirmidhī[1]

3.1 THE SUCCESSORS (AL-TĀBIᶜŪN)

AFTER the death of the Prophet and the inauguration of the vast Islamic polity, the Companions settled in different garrison-towns (*amṣār*) in the various provinces. In these towns they were surrounded by a large number of Muslims who had not known the Prophet, and who were eager to hear reports of his words and deeds from those who had associated with him and had heard his counsels. Abu'l-Dardā' at Damascus, Abū Idrīs at Emesa, Ḥudhayfa at Kūfa, Anas ibn Mālik at Baṣra, Jābir ibn ᶜAbd Allāh, ᶜĀ'isha and others at Medina, and a galaxy of other Companions at other major towns, attracted to themselves large circles of disciples who not only learnt from them the *ḥadīth*s of their master, but also acquired from them the ethos of questing for the Traditions, and their careful cultivation and preservation.

Abu'l-Dardā' had such a crowd of disciples that their multitude resembled the entourage of kings.[2] Muᶜādh ibn Jabal, together with 32 other Companions, related *ḥadīth*s to their disciples at Emesa.[3] Ḥudhayfa delivered lectures on *ḥadīth* to a band of eager disciples in a mosque at Kūfa,[4] while Ubayy ibn Kaᶜb was one of the many Companions who taught *ḥadīth*s to students in the original mosque of Medina.[5]

The early Muslims appear to have been extremely eager to hear the reports of the Prophet's *ḥadīth*s from his Companions. It is related that such a large crowd of them collected round a Companion when he related *ḥadīth*s that he was obliged to climb onto the roof of a nearby house so that he could be heard.[6] Abū Ḥanīfa reports that when he once went to Mecca with his father for the pilgrimage he saw there a large crowd listening intently to a Companion who related to them the *ḥadīth*s of the Prophet.[7]

These enthusiastic disciples of the Companions are known among the traditionists by the honorific title *al-Tabiʿūn*: the Successors, or Followers. They are conventionally divided into several classes according to the ranking of the Companions from whom they learnt and related traditions. Al-Ḥākim has grouped them into no fewer than fifteen classes, of which he explicitly mentions only four. Ibn Saʿd identifies nine classes. But the majority of the later writers on *asmā' al-rijāl* (biographical information on narrators) have classified them into three classes only:

(a) The students of the Companions who accepted Islam before the Conquest of Mecca.
(b) The students of the Companions who embraced Islam after the conquest of Mecca.
(c) The students of such Companions as were not yet adults at the time of the Prophet's death.

Of these Successors, the earliest to die is said to have been Zayd ibn Maʿmar ibn Zayd, who was killed in one of the Persian wars in the thirtieth year of the Muslim era, while the last is said to have been Khalaf ibn Khalīfa, who died in 180AH.[8] Upon them, therefore, devolved the preservation and propagation of *ḥadīth* for over a century, firstly in association with the Companions, and, when the latter had passed away, with the help of their own disciples. The pupils of the Successors are themselves called 'Successors of the Successors' (*atbāʿ al-tabiʿīn*), some of whom are said to have lived until about the end of the first quarter of the third Muslim century,[9] before the end of which almost all the important works of the *ḥadīth* literature were compiled.

3.2 THE TRADITIONISTS' ATTITUDE TO ḤADĪTH

These descending generations shared in common an astonishing zeal for the pursuit of *ḥadīth*. Rich men and women among them sacrificed their wealth for its sake, while the poor devoted their lives to it in spite of their poverty.

We have already seen that so great was the Companions' devotion to the *ḥadīth* that ʿUmar feared that the Qur'ān itself might be neglected.[10]

After the death of the Companions, however, the Successors and their disciples propagated *ḥadīth* with unabated vigour. Ibn Shihāb al-Zuhrī (d.124/741), for instance, 'spent money like water' for the sake of *ḥadīth*; he is said to have been so busy with his books that his wife declared that having three co-wives would be preferable to enduring his love for books.[11] Rabīʿa (d.136/753) spent all he possessed in his search for *ḥadīth*s, and in the end had to sell the beams of the roof of his house and live on the rotten dates which were discarded by the people of Medina.[12] Ibn al-Mubārak spent 40,000 dirhams during his quest for *ḥadīth*s,[13] while Yaḥyā ibn Maʿīn (d.233/847) spent 150,000 dirhams which he had inherited from his father, so that he ended up without even a pair of shoes to wear.[14] ʿAlī ibn ʿĀṣim spent 100,000 dirhams,[15] al-Dhahabī spent 150,000 dirhams;[16] Ibn Rustam, 300,000,[17] and Hishām ibn ʿUbayd Allāh (d.221/835), 700,000 dirhams,[18] all in the search for *ḥadīth*. Al-Khaṭīb al-Baghdādī gave away 200 gold coins to those who devoted their lives to *ḥadīth*.[19] There is no shortage of anecdotes of this type in the books of *asmā' al-rijāl*.

Such of the Traditionists, however, as were not born with silver spoons in their mouths did not abandon their study of the subject in despair. On the contrary, they carried on their pursuit of it with remarkable assiduity. Ibn Abī Dhi'b (d.159/775) for instance, in his thirst for knowledge had to fast uninterruptedly for days and nights on account of his poverty.[20] Abū Ḥātim al-Rāzī, despite his indigence, stayed at Baṣra for fourteen years in order to study *ḥadīth*. During this period he was obliged on one occasion to sell his clothes in order to earn his livelihood.[21] Even al-Shāfiʿī eponymous founder of a great law school, wrote some of the *ḥadīth*s which he had learnt on pieces of bone, which he kept in a bag, because in his student days he was too poor to buy paper.[22] Bukhārī, the famous traditionist, is said to have lived on wild herbs and grasses for three days on one occasion during his peregrinations in search of *ḥadīth*.[23] As a matter of fact, it seems that most of the *ḥadīth* scholars were poor, perhaps because many important theorists of *ḥadīth* science have held that poverty and a readiness to suffer are indispensable conditions for the acquisition of knowledge.[24]

It is scarcely possible to guess at the total number of *ḥadīth*-seekers who flourished during the various periods of Muslim history. Among the Companions, Abū Hurayra is said to have related *ḥadīth*s to over eight hundred students. At Kūfa alone, when Ibn Sīrīn visited that town, there lived some four thousand students of *ḥadīth*.[25] At Medina, more than 300 students were associated with the great Abū Zinād (d.132);[26] and later on, the door of Mālik ibn Anas turned into a rendezvous for a great crowd of students, who sometimes even quarrelled among themselves for a seat near the Imām at his lectures.[27] The discourses of ʿAlī ibn ʿĀṣim on *ḥadīth* were attended, it is said, by more than 30,000 students;[28] those of Sulaymān ibn Ḥarb by 40,000;[29] those of Yazīd ibn Hārūn by 70,000;[30] and those of Abū Muslim al-Kajjī by an immensely large number, of whom only those who used ink-pots for taking down notes were estimated at more than forty thousand.[31]

The attendance of such astonishingly large numbers of people at *ḥadīth* lectures may be better envisaged if we bear in mind some of the techniques of instruction which were commonly used. The most efficient such method, known as *samāʿ* (Hearing), includes *imlāʾ* (Dictation), and consists of the recitation of *ḥadīth*s by the teacher to his students.[32] In order to do this well, the teacher is advised to purify himself of all worldly thoughts, wear clean garments, and appoint some scholars well-versed in *ḥadīth* to keep order among the students and to repeat his recitations to any students who might be sitting too far for his words to carry. The lecturer should stand up, in an elevated place; and he should recite every word of each tradition distinctly, loudly and slowly, so that the students might be able to write it down. The various reproducers should repeat exactly, distinctly, slowly and loudly the words of the lecturer to the nearby students. We are told that Abū Muslim al-Kajjī appointed seven reproducers for the lectures he delivered in Baghdad. At the end of one such lecture, the area vacated by the students was measured, their ink-pots were counted, and after careful calculation it was determined that over forty thousand people had been present.[33]

The number of traditionists who had mastered the subject and were accepted as authorities on it also appears to have been large. At Medina alone, when Imām Mālik went there to study *ḥadīth*, there lived seventy traditionists who had associated with the Companions and had learnt *ḥadīth*s from them.[34] In Baghdad alone there lived some eight hundred shaykhs at the end of the second century AH.

3.3 THE CRISIS OF AUTHENTICITY

The above provides an indication of the great interest which *ḥadīth* scholarship aroused in the classical Islamic world. It was inevitable, however, that not all these students should have been intellectually or morally competent to take up this great task. All the Islamic authorities agree that an enormous amount of forgery was committed in the *ḥadīth* literature.[35] Imām Aḥmad ibn Ḥanbal has said that *ḥadīth* and *tafsīr* have been more affected by forgery than any other branch of literature. The very existence of a copious literature on *mawḍūʿāt* (forged traditions) reminds us of this consciousness.

It is interesting, but not easy, to try to determine the period when forgery in *ḥadīth* began. The Victorian writer William Muir thought that it began during the caliphate of ʿUthmān.[36] It is more likely, however, that it originated during the lifetime of the Prophet himself. His opponents would not have missed the opportunity to forge and attribute words and deeds to him for which he was not responsible, in order to rouse the Arab tribes against his teachings. Ibn Ḥazm, for one, accepts this explanation, and cites one incident which took place in Prophetic Medina. After the *hijra*, he tells us, a man went to an outlying district of Medina and told a tribe living there that the Prophet had given him authority over them. He resorted to this device because he was of a mind to marry a girl who was a member of that tribe, to whom he had proposed marriage before the *hijra*, but who had not consented. The tribe sent a messenger to the Prophet to make enquiries concerning the 'authority' thus asserted in his name. The Prophet told them that the man was a pretender, and had received no warrant for what he did.[37]

During the caliphate of Abū Bakr, too, when apostasy had raised its head, it is not unlikely that some of the apostates should have forged such traditions as suited their purpose; and it may be for this reason that Abū Bakr and ʿUmar were so strict in accepting traditions which were reported to them.[38]

During the caliphate of ʿUthmān, this kind of dishonesty became more common. Some members of the factions into which the community was then divided forged traditions in order to advance their faction's interests. During the first century of Islam, and also thereafter, the various political parties, the heretics, the professional preachers, and even a number of sincere Muslims, all made their contributions to the growing rubbish-heap of false traditions.

As we have seen, during the period following the Prophet's death many Companions were criticised by their friends for their seeming carelessness and want of insight into what they related of the Prophet.[39] Among the Successors and their Successors, with the rise of the 'jarring sects and parties', the number of careless and insincere students and teachers increased markedly. Some of these men and women were careless in their choice of teachers, others made *bona fide* mistakes in relating to their students what they had learnt. Still others, however, made deliberate changes to the text or the *isnād* of certain *ḥadīth*s, and fabricated others from scratch for the sake of personal or sectarian gain, or—more perversely—with the pious intention of calling people to the path of God and the liberating teachings of religion.[40]

In this way there developed among the Muslims a large number of forged traditions, which are conventionally attributed to four categories of people.

(a) Heretics (*zanādiqa*), often of Manichean leanings, who flourished under various banners during early Islamic history, and who wrought havoc by wilfully forging thousands of traditions and propagating them among the Muslim community.[41] 'The *zanādiqa*', remarked Ḥammād ibn Zayd, 'have invented fourteen thousand traditions in the name of the Prophet.'[42] To name only a few, one could cite ʿAbd al-Karīm ibn Abi'l-Awjaʿ, Bayyān ibn Samʿān, and Muḥammad ibn Saʿīd, the first of whom alone had forged some four thousand traditions in the name of the Prophet of Islam.[43] Another heretic who was actually caught, sentenced and executed by order of Hārūn al-Rashīd is said to have confessed to the forgery of a thousand *ḥadīth*s.[44]

(b) The *zanādiqa*, however, proved unable to do much damage to the traditions of Islam, being known and recognised as anti-Islamic. A more malign threat to the integrity of the literature was presented by certain pious Muslims. The various factional and sectarian preachers at both the Shīʿī and Khārijī ends of the political spectrum, and various sycophantic seekers after caliphal favours, proved more dangerous than any outright heretics.[45] These Muslims, with their avowed profession of the faith of Islam, could not be expected to attribute their own forgeries to their own Prophet. Yet the hope of immediate gain has often proved a greater force than truth and scholarship. We are told, for instance, that al-Muhallab (d.83/702), the great general and adversary of the Khawārij, confessed that he had forged traditions against them.[46] ʿAwāna ibn al-Ḥakam (d.158/774) and others who belonged to the Umayyad party concocted pro-Umayyad traditions.[47] Abu'l-ʿAynā' Muḥammad ibn al-Qāsim, likewise, forged *ḥadīth*s which supported the claims of the ʿAlid party.[48] Al-Ṭalqānī (d.310/922), an important member of the Murji'ite sect, forged *ḥadīth*s which justified his sect's doctrines.[49] Ghiyāth ibn Ibrāhīm, a courtier of al-Mahdī, made intentional changes in *ḥadīth* to please the Caliph.[50] Muqātil ibn Sulaymān (d.150/767) expressed to the same caliph his readiness to invent some traditions eulogising al-ʿAbbās, the forefather of the caliph.[51] Muḥammad ibn al-Ḥasan concocted a number of traditions praising ʿĀ'isha and in favour of the Sunnīs.[52] Most of the traditions which extol the virtues of certain individuals, tribes, provinces districts or towns, or a sectarian leader, owe their origin to some of these deliberate forgers, and have been identified by the *ḥadīth* scholars as mere inventions.[53]

(c) The *Quṣṣās* (storytellers). Though much humbler in status than the leaders of parties or sects, these were scarcely less dangerous than the latter for the integrity of the Islamic sources. Their main business at first was to relate moral stories following the morning and evening prayers, to encourage people to do good deeds.[54] Their origin may be traced back to the time of ʿUmar ibn al-Khaṭṭāb, who is said to have permitted either Tamīm al-Dārī[55] or ʿUbayd ibn ʿUmayr[56] to relate edifying tales before the people. Muʿāwiya, founder of the Umayyad dynasty, gave such men the title of 'ordinary storytellers'—i.e., as opposed to the 'special storytellers' who were appointed by the Caliph himself in order to counteract the propaganda of his opponents.[57]

These storytellers, among whom may be included the common street-preachers who held no official position, had to deal with the credulous common people, who appreciated amusing stories and fables more than hard facts. They soon proliferated, spreading through Iraq and Central Asia, and adapted themselves to their audiences, which contained people who found their words more congenial than the learned discourses of the scholars. At a relatively early date[58] they seem to have allowed themselves to degenerate into fablemongers, whose main object was to please their public and extract gold from their pockets. To this end, they invented thousands of such amusing anecdotes as might appeal to the masses, attributed them to the Prophet, and related them publicly. One of them, for instance, related to an audience, on the authority of Aḥmad ibn Ḥanbal and Yaḥyā ibn Maʿīn, that when a man said *lā ilāha illa'Llāh*, God created from each letter a bird with a beak of gold and feathers of pearl. At the end of his sermon, the man was questioned by Ibn Ḥanbal and Ibn Maʿīn, who had been among his listeners, and who objected that they had never related such a tradition. The storyteller tried to silence his critics by making fun of them.[59] Another *qāṣṣ* related to a mosque audience a series of traditions on the authority of Harim ibn Ḥayyān (d.46/666), and when he was challenged by the latter, he claimed that he had been referring to another *ḥadīth* expert by that name. 'As a matter of fact,' said the undaunted storyteller, 'fifteen persons by the name of Harim are present in this very mosque.'[60] Kulthūm ibn ʿAmr al-ʿAttābī once collected a crowd round himself in a mosque, and related to them—with a full *isnād*—a *ḥadīth* saying that he who touched the tip of his nose with his tongue might rest assured that he would never go to Hell. The audience showed their readiness to accept this forgery as a genuine tradition—by trying to ascertain their fate in this way.[61]

So extreme was the self-regard of many *quṣṣās* that not only did they fail to feel ashamed of forging traditions in the name of the Prophet for their own personal gain, but they felt no compunction in attacking other storytellers. A proverb says, 'One storyteller does not love another.' But sometimes in order to do mischief to the people and gain their own ends, two storytellers would work together to forge traditions. In this way, one of them once stood up at the end of a street narrating traditions in praise of ʿAlī, while the other stood up at the other end extolling the virtues of Abū Bakr. Thus did they make money from both the Shīʿa and the Nāṣibīs, and at the end of the day divided the proceeds equally among themselves.[62]

Their activities were so dangerous for the traditions of Islam as well as for the government, that Mālik ibn Anas did not allow them into the mosque at Medina.[63] The best-known traditionists condemned them, and in the year 279/892 their activities were banned in Baghdad.[64]

(d) But perhaps the most dangerous type of *ḥadīth* forgers came from the ranks of the devout traditionists themselves. Their sincerity and love for the traditions of Islam could not be doubted. But it has rightly been observed, by an eminent English writer, that 'everyone kills the object of his love'. Many pious traditionists attempted, unwittingly, to kill the science of Tradition by forging *ḥadīth*s, ascribing them to the Prophet, and spreading them abroad among the Muslim community.[65]

Nūḥ ibn Abī Maryam, who had studied theology with scholars of great repute, was known as *al-Jāmiʿ* on account of his vast and varied learning. He acted as judge at Merv during the reign of al-Manṣūr. He related traditions describing the virtues of the various chapters of the Qur'ān. But when he was pressed for the authorities from whom he had received these traditions, he confessed that he had forged them for the sake of God, and to attract people to His Book.[66] Abān ibn Abī ʿAyyāsh, who was one of the most godly people of his time, was severely censured by Shuʿba ibn al-Ḥajjāj, and more than 1,500 traditions narrated by him on the authority of Anas were found to have no foundation.[67] Aḥmad ibn Muḥammad al-Bāhilī (d.275/888) was generally venerated for his piety, but when Abū Daūd looked into four hundred traditions which were related by him, he found that they were all forged. Aḥmad himself confessed to having forged traditions in order to make the hearts of the people tender and soft (*tarqīq al-qulūb*).[68] Sulaymān ibn ʿAmr was a contemporary of Ibn Ḥanbal, and would fast by day and offer prayers by night, outdoing in this many of his contemporaries. But he is characterised none the less by the critics as a liar and forger of traditions.[69] Wahb ibn Ḥafṣ was generally regarded as a virtuous Muslim: his asceticism was so acute that it is said that for twenty years he did not speak to anyone. Yet none the less, he did not hesitate to forge traditions.[70] These and many other well-intentioned and outwardly pious Muslims, such as Maysara ibn ʿAbd Rabbih the Persian;[71] Aḥmad ibn Ḥarb (d.234/848), the 'man of piety';[72] ʿUbād ibn Kuthayr (d.150/767);[73]

ʿAbd Allāh ibn Ayyūb;[74] Hushaym ibn Bashīr (d.183/799);[75] Ziyād ibn ʿAbd Allāh;[76] and the followers of Muḥammad ibn Karrām al-Sijistānī[77] held that it was permissible to forge traditions in order to attract people to good deeds and warn them against evil.

These four types of forger, then, wrought havoc with the literature. Their activities were often very extensive indeed: we are told that Muḥammad ibn ʿUkkāsha and Muḥammad ibn Tamīm forged more than 10,000 traditions.[78] Abū Saʿīd ibn Jaʿfar forged more than 300 traditions in the name of Abū Ḥanīfa alone.[79] Aḥmad al-Qaysī concocted more than three thousand traditions.[80] Aḥmad al-Marwazī forged more than 10,000.[81] ʿAḥmad ibn ʿAbd Allāh al-Jubarī forged thousands of traditions.[82] Furthermore, a large number of other forgers—like Ziyād ibn Maymūn,[83] Shurayk ibn ʿAbd Allāh,[84] and Ṭalḥa ibn ʿAmr[85]—invented thousands of false *ḥadīth*s, some of which are quoted in sermons and declaimed from the pulpits even today.

3.4 CRITICAL TRADITIONISTS

Despite this process, however, there existed a core of honest and committed scholars who regarded the fabrication of evidence about the Prophet as a sure path to hellfire. Such men and women dedicated their lives to authentic scholarship, carefully ascertaining what was authentic, preserving its purity and genuineness, and propagating it among the community at large. They regarded it neither as a pastime nor a source of income, nor a means of underpinning any particular doctrinal or legal school. For them, knowledge was an end, not a means. As Sufyān al-Thawrī described it, *ḥadīth* for them had become like an infection, against which they could do nothing.[86]

During the early period of Islamic history, when the Companions still lived, an intense scrupulousness was maintained.[87] Among the Successors (*tābiʿūn*), a large number of whom flourished during the second half of the first and the first half of the second Islamic century, Ibn Abī Laylā (20/641–83/702), Rajā' ibn Ḥayawayh (d.112/730), Muḥammad ibn Sīrīn (35/655–115/728), Abū Zinād (d.132/749), Yaḥyā ibn Saʿīd (d.143/760), and an army of others had been intensely honest and strict with regard to the authorities from whom they received the traditions of their beloved Prophet. Ibn Abī Laylā used to say that one could not be credited with knowledge of *ḥadīth* until one was able to reject some of them and accept others.[88] Qāsim, Raja' and Ibn Sīrīn had been scrupulously honest about every word of each *ḥadīth* which they acquired,[89] while the latter declared that *ḥadīth* was religion, and warned that people should be careful about those from whom they received it.[90] Ṭāūs ibn Kaysān of the Yemen counselled students to learn *ḥadīth* from pious people only,[91] while Abu'l-ʿĀliya relates that whenever a seeker after *ḥadīth* went to any traditionist to learn it from him, he enquired first about the piety of his would-be teacher.[92] Al-Zuhrī was of the opinion that the *isnād* was indispensable to a *ḥadīth*.[93] Abū Zinād states that when he went to Medina in order to learn *ḥadīth*, he found there one hundred traditionists who were considered reliable in ordinary matters, but unreliable as teachers of *ḥadīth*, apparently because they did not achieve the high standard of honesty which was expected from the teachers of traditions.[94] Ismāʿīl ibn Ibrāhīm says that only traditions related by people strict in the performance of religion should be considered for acceptance.[95]

The spirit of scrupulous care with regard to choice of teachers among the Successors was imbibed by their students, and kept up by a large number of them throughout the period of their florescence. Among them, Mālik ibn Anas (93–179/711–795), on going to Medina in search of *ḥadīth*, found in the mosque seventy traditionists who had acquired their knowledge directly from the Companions and Successors; but he none the less accepted traditions only from such of them as were demonstrably trustworthy, and whenever he had any doubts about any part of a tradition, he gave up the whole of it as unreliable.[96] He held that one should not accept *ḥadīth*s related by the light-witted, or persons who held erroneous views and propagated them, nor persons who commonly told lies (even if they were not accused of it in connection with *ḥadīth*), or people unfamiliar with the subject matter of the material which they related, however pious, honest and eminent they might appear.[97]

Many of Mālik's contemporaries shared his punctilious care over the authorities from whom they received their material. These contemporaries included Shuʿba ibn al-Ḥajjāj (83/702–160/776), Sufyān al-Thawrī (97/715–161/777), Ḥammād ibn Salama (d.167/783), Ḥammād ibn Zayd (98/716–179/795), ʿAbd Allāh ibn al-Mubārak (121/738–181/797), al-Fuḍayl ibn ʿIyāḍ (d.187/802), Yaḥyā ibn Saʿīd al-Qaṭṭān (120/737–198/813), and many others.

This careful scrutiny of those who related traditions was continued with unabated vigour by a large number of the students of *ḥadīth* in the subsequent generations. Al-Shāfiʿī (156/767–204/819), a student of Mālik, and the founder of one of the most important schools of Islamic law, made a careful inspection of the reliability not only of those from whom he himself received traditions, but also of their authorities.[98] He even rejected the *mursal* traditions of al-Zuhrī.[99] Yaḥyā ibn Maʿīn (d.156/772–233/847) did not include any *ḥadīth*s in his works unless they were supported by thirty independant chains of authority.[100] Ibrāhīm ibn Saʿīd claimed to have included in his collections only such traditions as were supported by a hundred *isnāds*.[101] Aḥmad ibn Ḥanbal's care about his authorities is well-known: even on his deathbed he did not neglect to ask his son to strike off a *ḥadīth* from his great *Musnad* because it was contrary to many more reliable traditions.[102] Al-Bukhārī's scrupulous honesty and exactitude are celebrated, while Muslim's scrutiny of narrators is clearly shown in his advanced introduction to his great work. Abū Daūd al-Sijistānī (200/835–275/910), al-Tirmidhī (d.279/892), al-Nasāʾī (d.302/914), Muḥammad ibn Jarīr al-Ṭabarī (224/839–310/922), ʿAbd Allāh ibn Muḥammad al-Baghawī (214/830–317/929) and a vast number of others, were unquestionably sincere, honest and scholarly in their pursuit and propagation of the Prophetic *ḥadīth*.

Thanks to the precision and rigour of the elite of traditionists, then, the vital core of the *ḥadīth* literature was preserved intact. As Abbott concludes:

> Deliberate tampering with either the content or the *isnāds* of the Prophet's Tradition, as distinct from the sayings and deeds of the Companions and Successors, may have passed undetected by ordinary transmitters, but not by the aggregate of the ever-watchful, basically honest, and aggressively outspoken master traditionists and *ḥadīth* critics.[103]

3.5 THE SCIENCE OF RIJĀL DEVELOPS

Such sincere enthusiasts for the literature were not content with the mere scrutiny of the *ḥadīth* reporters. They also attempted to publicise to the whole Islamic community the character of those reponsible for forgery, or for incompetent and erroneous reporting. During the early period, when Companions still lived, Ibn ʿUmar had not hesitated to point out Abū Hurayra's personal interest in a controversy over field-dogs.[104] Murra al-Ḥamdānī (d.71/690) expressed a desire to kill a man known as al-Ḥārith, who had been fabricating *ḥadīth*, while Ibrāhīm al-Nakhaʿī (d.96/714) warned his pupils about al-Ḥārith, and also asked them to keep away from al-Mughīra ibn Saʿīd and Abū ʿAbd al-Raḥīm, who were liars.[105] Qatāda (d.117/735) pointed out to his students the false presumptions of a contemporary scholar, while the blind Ibn ʿAwn (d.151/768), on being questioned about a *ḥadīth* related to him by Shahr, stressed his unreliability.[106] Sufyān al-Thawrī, Shuʿba, Mālik and Ibn ʿUyayna all instructed people to make the true nature of unreliable narrators known to the public.[107] As a matter of fact, numerous Companions and Successors had criticised various reporters of the traditions; and Shuʿba and Yaḥyā ibn Saʿīd, who are generally said to have been the first critics of the reporters,[108] had only made special efforts with regard to their criticism.[109] Ibn ʿAdī (277/890–360/970), while describing his predecessors in the field of the criticism of *ḥadīth* reporters, mentions the names of Ibn ʿAbbās, ʿUbāda ibn al-Ṣāmit, and Anas (all Companions), together with al-Shaʿbī, Ibn Sīrīn and Saʿīd ibn al-Musayyib (all Successors). He also remarks that the number of critics of *rijāl* in the earliest period was comparatively small because of the small number of weak reporters, and the reduced chances of mistakes and forgeries. When, towards the middle of the second century, less acceptable narrators increased in number, a group of important traditionists discussed the subject, and debated the integrity and reliability of the various reporters.[110]

This core of leading scholars was guided in its pursuit of *ḥadīth* neither by the government and the many sectarian leaders, nor their own personal interests, but 'by the pure love of pure traditions'. The Umayyads and Abbasids made little difference to them. Under the Abbasids, who tried to reconcile them by their outward show of love for religion, the traditionists continued their strict neutrality towards the government of the day and the endlessly warring factions which were competing for power. Of the 'Three ʿAbd Allāhs' who are often considered the pillars of *ḥadīth*, the son of ʿUmar ibn al-Khaṭṭāb took no part in civil strife, and rejected out of hand Marwān's suggestion that he make a bid for the Caliphate.[111] Ibn ʿAbbās held to a strict neutrality in the fight for the caliphate between Ibn al-Zubayr and ʿAbd al-Mālik.[112] ʿAbd Allāh ibn ʿAmr ibn al-ʿĀṣ went to the field of Ṣiffīn at the insistence of his father, but took no part in the battle between Muʿāwiya and ʿAlī, and for the remainder of his days repented of having even gone to the field.[113] Abū Dharr,[114] Muḥammad ibn Maslama,[115] Saʿīd ibn al-Musayyib,[116] Abu'l-ʿĀliya,[117] al-Muṭarrif,[118] al-Ḥasan ibn Yasār,[119] Masrūq,[120] and many other Companions and Successors kept entirely out of politics. Some preferred prison and torture to lending support to any of the warring factions against their own conviction. Saʿīd ibn al-Musayyib, for instance, was flogged by Ibn al-Zubayr, and was put to torture by Hishām ibn Ismāʿīl, who wanted him to declare for ʿAbd Allāh or the sons of ʿAbd al-Malik. Yaḥyā ibn Abī Kathīr (d.129/746) was severely tortured for condemning the Umayyads.[121] ʿUbayd Allāh ibn Rāfiʿ was beaten at the orders of ʿAmr ibn Saʿīd.[122] Imām Mālik was whipped on the orders of al-Manṣūr, because some of his legal judgements did not suit the Caliph.[123] The same caliph ordered the execution of the great Sufyān al-Thawrī.[124]

The unpleasant and heated conversations between al-Aḥnaf ibn Qays and Muʿāwiya,[125] between al-Aʿmash and ʿAbd al-Malik,[126] between Sālim and Sulaymān ibn ʿAbd al-Malik,[127] between Abū Ḥāzim and the same caliph,[128] between al-Ḥasan al-Baṣrī and ʿUmar ibn Hubayra,[129] and between al-Awzāʿī and ʿAbd Allāh ibn ʿAlī,[130] clearly show the highly strained relationship between the orthodox traditionists and the Umayyad and Abbasid potentates. Under the Abbasids, too, many scrupulous and orthodox scholars (such as Abū Ḥanīfa,[131] Sufyān al-Thawrī,[132] and others), continued their attitude of indifference towards the caliphs and their government. Some of these scholars, such as Ibn Ḥanbal,[133] Nuʿaym ibn Ḥammād,[134] Yūsuf ibn Saʿīd,[135] Abū Mushʿir,[136] and others, refused to agree with the Muʿtazilite views of the caliph al-Ma'mūn, and suffered imprisonment and physical punishment. Refusing to compromise with tyrants was a stated principle with them:[137] and hence we discover that very few of the compilers of the great *ḥadīth* collections which are now accepted in the Muslim world were in the pay of the caliphs, or welcomed at their court.

3.6 TRAVELLING (RIḤLA) IN SEARCH OF ḤADĪTH

The Prophet himself recommended travelling in search of knowledge, in a number of sayings which are to be found in several of the important *ḥadīth* collections. Some of the Companions undertook long journeys either to learn a *ḥadīth*, or to refresh their memories of it. Abū Ayyūb, for instance, travelled from Medina to Egypt just for the sake of refreshing his memory on a *ḥadīth* which he—together with ʿUqba ibn ʿĀmir—had learnt from the Prophet himself.[138] Jābir ibn ʿAbd Allāh travelled for a whole month in order to hear from ʿAbd Allāh ibn Unays only one *ḥadīth*, which Jābir had already learnt through another person.[139] Similarly, another Companion went from Medina to Damascus only for the purpose of hearing from the lips of Abu'l-Dardā' a *ḥadīth* which he had already received indirectly from him through one of his friends.[140]

The precepts of the Prophet, and the example of his Companions, also deeply impressed the Successors, who spared no pains in their pursuit of knowledge. They travelled throughout the expanding Islamic world to gather knowledge of as many *ḥadīth*s as possible, and returned home 'like bees laden with honey', to impart the precious store they had accumulated to the crowds of their eager disciples.[141]

Makḥūl (d.112/730) travelled through Egypt, Syria, Iraq and the Ḥijāz, and gathered the knowledge of all the *ḥadīth* which he could obtain from the Companions who still lived in those places.[142] He used to boast that for the sake of knowledge he had 'travelled round the world'.[143] Al-Shaʿbī (d.104/722) said when asked how he had gathered the knowledge of such a voluminous quantity of *ḥadīths*: 'By hard work, long travels, and great patience.'[144] He used to remark that if for the sake of only one word of wisdom anyone travelled from one end of Syria to the furthest corner of the Yemen, he (Al-Shaʿbī) would not consider his journey to have been wasted.[145] Masrūq (d.63/682) travelled so widely for the sake of learning that he was known as 'Abu'l-Safar' ('the traveller'). Saʿīd ibn al-Musayyib (d.94/712) used to travel for days to learn a single *ḥadīth*.[146]

Such journeys became increasingly popular. 'From one end of the Islamic world to the other, from al-Andalus to Central Asia,' says one European scholar,

> wandered diligent men gathering traditions in order to be able to pass them on to their audiences. This was the only possible way of obtaining in their authentic form traditions which were scattered in the most diverse provinces. The honorific *al-raḥḥāla* or *al-jawwāl* is hardly ever absent from the names of traditionists of recognised importance. The title *ṭawwāf al-aqālīm*, wanderer in all zones, is no mere hyperbole for these travellers, who included people who could say of themselves that they had traversed the East and West four times. These men do not travel in all these countries in order to see the world or gain experience but only to see the preservers of traditions in all these places and to hear and profit by them, 'like the bird who alights on no tree without picking at the leaves'.[147]

These seekers of *ḥadīth* gathered their knowledge from every source of which they were aware, and took from each source all that they could extract from it. This is apparent from the large number of teachers which some of them had, and from the considerable periods of time which some of them spent with their preceptors. Abū Isḥāq al-Sabīʿī (d.126/743), for instance, learnt *ḥadīth* from between three hundred and four hundred teachers;[148] ʿAbd Allāh ibn al-Mubārak (d.181/797) from 1,100;[149] Mālik ibn Anas from 900;[150] Hishām ibn ʿAbd Allāh from 1,700;[151] Abū Nuʿaym from 700 or 800;[152] Ibn ʿAsākir from 1,300 traditionists.[153] Al-Zuhrī kept the company of Saʿīd ibn al-Musayyib for ten years.[154] Ḥammād ibn Zayd was with Ayyūb for 20 years;[155] Rabīʿ ibn Anas went regularly to the sessions of al-Ḥasan al-Baṣrī for a similar period.[156] ʿAmr ibn Zirāra associated with Ibn ʿUlayya for 23 years.[157] Ibn Jurayj kept the company of ʿAṭā' for 18 years; while Thābit ibn Aslam studied *ḥadīth* with Imām Mālik for no less than forty years.[158]

Thus, through the energy and scrupulousness of the Successors and the later generations of Muslims, were collected together the reports of the sayings and deeds of the Prophet which had been scattered throughout the length and breadth of the Islamic world. The first organised attempt at their collection, as we have seen, was made at the end of the first century by the caliph ʿUmar ibn ʿAbd al-ʿAzīz. Reports concerning his activities in connection with the collection of *ḥadīth*s are found in many important early works, including the *Muwaṭṭa'* of Imām Mālik, the *Ṣaḥīḥ* of Bukhārī, and the *Ṭabaqāt* of Ibn Saʿd. Although these reports differ of course in certain minor details, the main features of the process are agreed upon by them all.

Once begun, the collection of *ḥadīth*s accelerated rapidly. Within two hundred years almost all the important *ḥadīth* works were assembled, most of which were produced by honest and scrupulous scholars with no attachment to the proliferating political groups and sects, and even less interest in worldly gain. These scholars traced the lives and discussed the characters of all the reporters of traditions, and produced, side by side with their collections of *ḥadīth*, a vast literature on the reporters as an aid to the formal criticism of *ḥadīth*.

4

CATEGORIES OF *ḤADĪTH* COLLECTIONS

4.1 BEGINNINGS

THE origins of the *ḥadīth* literature are to be traced back to the letters, laws and treaties which were dictated to scribes by the Prophet himself. They are likewise to be traced back to numerous *ṣaḥīfas*, documents which were compiled by the Companions and Followers, and to some of which reference has already been made.[1]

The discovery of the *ṣaḥīfa* of Hammām ibn Munabbih, which has been published by Dr. Muhammad Hamidullah, reveals the nature and character of these *ṣaḥīfas*. It proves that they were more than simple memoranda, but were complete records of certain of the sayings of the Prophet, presented in the form familiar to us from the later collections of *ḥadīth*.

Even before the arrival of Islam, Arabic literature possessed some 'books', which introduced a new type of literary spirit among the Arabs.[2] It has already been proved that books were assembled on many branches of Arabic literature during the second half of the first Islamic century.[3] During the reign of Muʿāwiya, ʿĀbid ibn Sharya wrote a book on the pre-Islamic kings of Arabia,[4] which enjoyed some popularity during the tenth century CE.[5] Suḥar ibn al-ʿAbbās, who lived during the reign of the same caliph, wrote a collection of proverbs.[6] Theodocus, a physician at the court of al-Ḥajjāj, wrote some Arabic books on medicine.[7] Abān collected materials for a book on *maghāzī*,[8] while ʿUrwa ibn al-Zubayr, who died towards the end of the first Hijra century, is said to have written a book on the same subject. 'Although nowhere in the older sources,' says one European writer, 'is it said that ʿUrwa composed an actual book on the *Maghāzī*, it is none the less certain that he collected and set forth a series of the most important events in the Prophet's life.'[9] The same collector of *maghāzī* also compiled some books on *fiqh* which he burnt on the day of the Battle of the Ḥarra.[10] It is easy to understand, then, that the Muslims did not neglect the collection of accounts of the words and states of the Prophet, whose example they regarded as divinely inspired.

The early sources of *ḥadīth* fall into three distinct groups. Firstly, there are the books on *maghāzī* (almost synonymous with *sīra*)—such as those of Ibn Isḥāq and others—in which most of the *ḥadīth*s of a historical nature are to be found. Secondly, there are books on *fiqh*, such as the *Muwaṭṭa'* of Imām Mālik and the *Kitāb al-Umm* of Imām al-Shāfiʿī which contain a large number of legal *ḥadīth*s, cited in the context of legal discussions and mingled with other, non-Prophetic, *sunnas*. Finally, there are works which set out to be collections of *ḥadīth* as such. It is these latter which will be dealt with in this Chapter.

4.2 THE MUSNADS

Of all the various types of large *ḥadīth* collections, the *musnads* appear to be the earliest in origin. Yet many of those which are generally ascribed to certain of the early authorities on *ḥadīth* were in fact compiled by later traditionists, who collected *ḥadīth*s which were related to them by, or on the authority of, any one important narrator. Such are the *Musnads* of Abū Ḥanīfa, al-Shāfiʿī, ʿUmar ibn ʿAbd al-ʿAzīz, and others, none of whom is in reality known to have compiled a *musnad* work. The *Musnad* which is generally known as that of Abū Ḥanīfa was compiled by Abu'l-Mu'ayyad Muḥammad ibn Maḥmūd al-Khwārizmī (d.665/1257).[11] The *Musnad* of al-Shāfiʿī was compiled on the basis of his *Kitāb al-Umm* by Muḥammad ibn Yaʿqūb al-Aṣamm (d.246/860).[12] The work known as the *Musnad* of ʿUmar ibn ʿAbd al-ʿAzīz was compiled by al-Bāghandī (d.282/895).[13] The *Musnad* of Abū Daūd al-Ṭayālisī, which is considered to be the earliest *musnad* still extant,[14] was not compiled in its present form by Ṭayālisī himself, but by a traditionist working in Khurasān at a later date.[15]

4.2a THE MUSNAD OF AL-ṬAYĀLISĪ

An old, rare and important manuscript of this work is preserved in the Oriental Public Library of Patna, and has been fully described by Maulawī

ʿAbd al-Ḥamīd in the catalogue of the *ḥadīth* MSS kept at the O.P. Library at Bankipore.[16] The Hyderabad edition of the *Musnad* has been published on the basis of this manuscript.

Abū Daūd Sulaymān ibn Daūd ibn al-Jārūd al-Ṭayālisī, to whom the *Musnad* is generally ascribed, was of Persian origin, and was born in the year 133/750. He studied traditions with more than a thousand scholars of his day, among whom many prominent names stand out, including Shuʿba (in whose traditions Ṭayālisī seems to have specialised), Sufyān al-Thawrī, and others. He had a sharp, retentive memory, and is said to have dictated forty thousand traditions without the help of notes. During his lifetime he came to be accepted as an outstanding authority on *ḥadīth*, and especially on the long *ḥadīth*s, so that students flocked to him from all corners of the Islamic world. His teacher Shuʿba, having heard him discuss certain traditions with his students, confessed that he himself could not do better. Strict traditionists like Ibn Ḥanbal and ʿAlī ibn al-Madīnī accepted Ṭayālisī's authority, and related traditions from him; yet he was none the less not above criticism from some experts, who believed that his memory sometimes failed him. He died in the year 203/813 at the age of 70.[17]

In the present printed edition of the *Musnad*,[18] the work consists of 2,767 traditions related by 281 Companions, whose material is given under their names, which are arranged in the following order: (i) the Four Caliphs (ii) the rest of those who fought at Badr (iii) the Emigrants (iv) the Anṣār (v) the women (vi) the youngest Companions.[19] However, Ṭayālisī, to whom the work is generally ascribed, neither compiled it nor arranged it in its present form. It is rather the work of his student, Yūnus ibn Ḥabīb, who collected together the traditions which he had received from his teacher and arranged them as he saw fit. 'And it was one of the traditionists of Khurasān,' says Ḥājī Khalīfa, 'who collected together the traditions related by Yūsuf [Yūnus] ibn Ḥabīb from Abū Daūd [al-Ṭayālisī].'[20] Ḥājī Khalīfa is right in denying that the *Musnad* was compiled by Ṭayalisī himself; but he seems to be mistaken in attributing it to the students of Yūnus, for internal evidence shows that Yūnus himself was the compiler.[21]

But whoever its compiler might have been, the text clearly shows that he, as well as the authorities from whom he received its contents, had been careful in handling them. Despite its early date, it carried complete *isnāds*.[22] Wherever any doubt exists in the text of a tradition, it has been pointed out. In some cases, various possible readings of certain expressions used in a tradition have been given; in some cases, certain explanatory phrases have been added—care having been taken that these additions might not be mistaken for a part of the text itself.[23] In some cases, it has been pointed out that some of the authorities had doubts with regard to part of the text,[24] but that they dispelled them by referring to some other authorities of their own time.[25] If a tradition has been received through more than one source, the fact is pointed out at the end of the tradition. In some cases where the identity of a narrator is doubtful (because more than one narrator bore the same name), an effort has been made to establish his identity.[26] In some cases the character of some of the authorities is also mentioned.[27] Certain traditions are related from narrators of unknown identity.[28] In some cases attention is drawn to the fact that the tradition had been attributed to the Prophet by some narrators, and only to a Companion by others.[29]

The subject-matters of the traditions contained in the *Musnad* are as varied and numerous as those of any other collection of *ḥadīth*. But those relating to miracles, the personal or tribal virtues of the Companions, and prophecies of future events or sects in Islam, are very few.

The book appears to have enjoyed great popularity until the eighth Islamic century. The Patna manuscript alone bears the names of more than 300 male and female students of *ḥadīth*, who had read it at different periods. Among them are found the names of great traditionists such as al-Dhahabī, al-Mizzī, and others.[30] After the eighth century, for whatever reason, it lost its popularity—so much so that manuscripts of the book have become extremely rare.

4.2b THE MUSNAD OF AḤMAD IBN ḤANBAL

The most important and exhaustive of all the *musnad* works available to us is that of Imām Aḥmad ibn Muḥammad ibn Ḥanbal al-Marwazī al-Shaybānī. His remarkably saintly, selfless life, and his firm stand for his convictions against the tyrannical inquisition and persecution launched by al-Ma'mūn, and continued by al-Wāthiq and al-Mutawakkil, created a halo of sanctity around his great collection of traditions. Despite its great bulk, it survived the vicissitudes of time, and was printed at Cairo in 1896.[31]

Ibn Ḥanbal was descended from the great Shaybānī tribe of the Arabs. This clan had taken a leading role in the early conquest of Iraq and Khurasān, and in the civil wars which erupted between the Hāshimites and the Umayyads, as partisans of the former. Ibn al-Haytham, a Shaybānī chief at Kūfa, was the first in that town to summon people to the side of ʿAlī. Ḥusayn al-Shaybānī was the standard-bearer of the tribe of Rabīʿa at the Battle of Ṣiffīn; and ʿAlī wrote some appreciative verses about his valour.[32] Khālid ibn Maʿmar, also a Shaybānī, had taken a leading part on behalf of ʿAlī in the same battle.[33] The sympathy of the Shaybānīs for the

Banū Hāshim seems to have continued even after the Umayyads were well established on the throne. Khālid ibn Ibrāhīm, who succeeded Abū Muslim as governor of Khurasān, had been one of the *naqībs* of the Abbasids against the Umayyad caliphate.[34] A certain Ḥayyān al-ʿAṭṭār, mentioned by al-Dīnawarī as one of the main early Abbasid propagandists in Khurasān,[35] may be the same Ḥayyān who is mentioned among the forefathers of Ibn Ḥanbal. Certainly, one of Ibn Ḥanbal's progenitors was a general of Khurasān who, according to Patton, fought to overthrow the Umayyads and replace them with the Abbasids.[36]

Ibn Ḥanbal himself was born in Baghdad in 164/780. He was carefully brought up by his pious mother, his father having died young. There he received his early education with the teachers of the day, beginning the serious study of *ḥadīth* at the age of 15 under Ibrāhīm ibn ʿUlayya.[37] After studying with all the major *ḥadīth* experts of the capital, he began to travel in search of knowledge, in the year 183/799. He wandered through Baṣra, Kūfa, the Yemen, the Ḥijāz, and other centres of *ḥadīth* learning, attending the lectures of the traditionists, taking notes, and discussing them with scholars and fellow students, returning finally to Baghdad in around the year 195/810, when he met Imām al-Shāfiʿī with whom he studied *fiqh* and *uṣūl al-fiqh*.[38]

Ibn Ḥanbal appears to have lectured on traditions from an early age. It is said that a large number of students flocked around him in order to hear his lectures on *ḥadīth* in a Baghdad mosque in the year 189/804, when he went there for a short time.[39] He made, however, the service and teaching of the Prophet's message the sole object of his life, and continued thus until 218/833, when a storm of persecution erupted against the orthodox theologians throughout the Abbasid empire.

The caliph al-Ma'mūn, under the influence of his philosophically-minded associates, and perhaps wishing to build an intermediate doctrine which would prove acceptable to both Sunnīs and Shīʿa, publicly accepted the Muʿtazilite creed, including the notion of the created nature of the Qur'ān. When most scholars refused to join him in his conversion, he threatened, and then persecuted them. Many scholars, however—Imām Aḥmad among them—refused to yield. The caliph, who was then at Tarsus, ordered that they should be put in chains and sent to him. Although these orders were carried out, al-Ma'mūn died before his devout prisoners had reached their destination. This, however, proved of little help to them. The Caliph had made a will wherein he asked his successor to carry out his wishes with regard to the propagation of the doctrine of the createdness of the Qur'ān. His two immediate successors, al-Muʿtaṣim and al-Wāthiq, carried out this policy with some fierceness, and did not hesitate to use torture and incarceration to persuade the Muslim scholars of the correctness of the Muʿtazilite system. This *miḥna* (persecution) continued with varying vigour until the third year of the reign of al-Mutawakkil, who, in the year 234/848, put a stop to it, and returned to mainstream Sunnī belief.

The charismatic personality of al-Ma'mūn, and the glamour of his court, seems to have secured the conversion of many Muslim theologians to his views. Even such great traditionists as Yaḥyā ibn Maʿīn and ʿAlī ibn al-Madīnī sought refuge behind the thin veil of *taqīya* (dissimulation). It was Aḥmad ibn Ḥanbal who at this critical juncture proved himself the saviour of Orthodoxy and the Islamic principle of the freedom of faith and conscience. He refused to submit to the dictates of the caliph, attempting to show the fallacies in the reasoning of his adversaries in the public debates, and refused to be impressed by their threats of force, patiently enduring their persecutions. He was kept in a cell for eighteen months; he was whipped by a team of executioners, his wrist was broken, he was badly wounded, and he lost consciousness. None the less, he kept his conscience whole, and emerged from the test with the greatest credit. The prominent Sufi scholar, Bishr ibn al-Ḥārith al-Muḥāsibī, rightly said that God had cast Ibn Ḥanbal into a fire, and he came out like pure gold. Even more impressively, in the eyes of the community, Ibn Ḥanbal showed an unexampled generosity towards his enemies and persecutors, against none of whom he showed any ill-will. He scrupulously refrained from expressing any opinion against Aḥmad ibn Abī Du'ād, who had taken the part of chief inquisitor against him during the *miḥna*.[40]

After the *miḥna* was over, Imām Aḥmad lived for about eight years. Most of this period, we are told, he devoted to teaching, while the rest he spent in prayers and the remembrance of God.[41] He died in 241/855, at the age of 77. Astonishing scenes of sorrow and mourning followed: not only the great metropolis, but even some of the remotest corners of the Islamic world, fell into a slough of despond. His funeral was attended by a vast crowd said to have contained between 600,000 and two and a half million people. It was an event 'the like of which must rarely have been witnessed anywhere'.[42]

Throughout his life Ibn Ḥanbal inspired those who knew him with the exemplary probity and mildness of his character. He always refused pecuniary help, whether large or trivial, from rich princes as well as from poor associates and friends.[43] He boycotted his sons Ṣāliḥ and ʿAbd Allāh because they had accepted stipends from the caliph.[44] He hated luxury,[45] and met his few needs from what he himself earned. Though in his religious beliefs he was extremely firm and principled, yet by nature he was very gentle and anxious not to cause harm to anyone.[46] Honesty and justice were the most admired elements of his character.

Imām Aḥmad's vast and profound knowledge of the traditions, his strictly pious and selfless life, his strong character, his firm and courageous stand for majoritarian Islam against the violence of the caliph, his complete indifference to the court and the courtiers, together with his forceful and inspiring personality, established his reputation as an Imām, and one of the greatest authorities on *ḥadīth* in the Islamic world-community.[47] 'His personality in his lifetime and after his death,' says Patton, 'was a great force in the Muslim world, and it seems yet to be as powerful in its influence as the principles which he enunciated.'[48]

With the exclusion of part of his final years, Imām Aḥmad devoted his entire life to the service of *ḥadīth*, spreading it through the large regiments of his students to every part of the Muslim world, and writing about various theological problems by presenting the relevant proof-texts from the Qur'ān and the *Sunna*. Thirteen of these books are mentioned by Ibn al-Nadīm in his *Fihrist*;[49] while others, such as the *Kitāb al-Ṣalāt*, have also been published in his name.

The most important of his works is without question the *Musnad*. The period of its compilation is unknown; but it is clear from its structure as well as its contents that it must have occupied its compilers' mind for a long time. His main object was not to make a collection of all the strictly genuine *ḥadīth*s, nor those relating to any particular subject or supporting any particular school of thought. Instead, he attempted to collect all the traditions of the Prophet which, by his criteria, were likely to prove genuine if put to the test, and could therefore serve as a provisional basis for argument. Traditions not included in the *Musnad* have no force, he is reported to have said.[50] But he never claimed that all its contents were genuine or reliable. On the contrary, he struck off many traditions from his book; and even when he was on his death-bed, he asked his son to delete a *ḥadīth* from the *Musnad*.[51]

To assemble his work, Ibn Ḥanbal ransacked his own vast store of knowledge, as well as the entire literature available to him on the subject.[52] He sifted 30,000 traditions out of some 750,000 narrated by 904 Companions relating to widely varied subjects, such as *maghāzī*, *manāqib*, rituals, laws, prophecies, and so forth.[53] However, he read out the various parts of his notes to his students, and also to his sons and nephew over a period of 13 years.[54] Although he had wanted to assemble his notes in the form of a *Musnad*, death overtook him, so that the task of arranging the material fell to his son ʿAbd Allāh, who edited his father's notes.[55]

Ibn Ḥanbal was not strict in the choice of his materials and authorities. He included in his notes material which could not by any definition be included as '*ḥadīth*'. Many of the traditions contained in the *Musnad* were later declared by traditionists of a later period to be baseless and forged (*mawḍūʿ*),[56] and many of the narrators relied upon by Ibn Ḥanbal are declared by the authorities on *asmāʾ al-rijāl* to be of dubious worth. Most famous of these is ʿAbd Allāh ibn Lahīʿa (97/715–174/790), over whose credentials a lively controversy continues to rage.[57]

There are, however, many virtues in Ibn Ḥanbal's work. If he receives a *ḥadīth* from more than one narrator, he points out the slightest difference that may exist between them. For instance, in a *ḥadīth* reported to him by Wakīʿ and Abū Muʿāwiya, the former uses the word *Imām*, while the latter uses the word *amīr*, and Ibn Ḥanbal does not fail to point out this discrepancy.[58] In another *ḥadīth*, two earlier narrators differed in the use of *wa* and *aw*; the author of the *Musnad* records the difference, and gives the two versions which were handed down to him.[59] In another *ḥadīth*, the difference in the use of *ilayhi* and *ʿalayhi* is pointed out.[60] If the same narrator reports the same *ḥadīth* with certain differences, it is also pointed out by the Imām; for instance, in a *ḥadīth* narrated by Yazīd ibn Hārūn, the change in his narration from *li-ukhrāhā* to *bi-ukhrāhā* is noted.[61] If any correction or amendment in the text or *isnāds* of a *ḥadīth* was suggested to Imām Aḥmad, he did not fail to make the necessary changes in the manuscript.[62]

Ibn Ḥanbal's son, ʿAbd Allāh (Abū ʿAbd al-Raḥmān), maintained the scrupulous care and thoroughness of his father when editing the material he inherited. He collated the whole of his father's huge but incomplete manuscript with his own notes, which he had taken at his lectures and at the sessions of other traditionists. He also collated it with what he had learnt from him and others during more general learned discussions.[63]

In the case of such *ḥadīth*s as ʿAbd Allāh had heard from his father, but which had been deleted from the manuscript, ʿAbd Allāh points out the change that was made to the book.[64] Where he finds a slip of his father's pen, he corrects it, and reproduces the original in his notes; in some cases, he only points out that there was a mistake in the text.[65] Where he has any doubt about the text of the manuscript, he frankly expresses it.[66] In some cases, he adds explanatory notes as well as numerous *ḥadīth*s taken from other sources.[67] In all these cases, he takes great care to ensure that his own additions will not be mistaken by the reader for parts of the manuscript itself. As a matter of fact, he appears to have taken great care to maintain the integrity of his father's text to the greatest degree possible. He reproduces the words written in the original manuscript in separated letters (*muqaṭṭaʿāt*), adding a note, saying: 'Thus was it written in the manuscript of my father;

but when he read it to us, he pronounced it as one word.'[68]

Ibn Ḥanbal's *Musnad* occupies an important place in *ḥadīth* literature, and has served as an important source for various writers on the different genres of Arabic literature. 'Among the *Musnad* works,' remarks one commentator, 'the *Musnad* of Aḥmad ibn Ḥanbal occupies the most stable position. The great esteem enjoyed by his memory in the pious world of Islam, the piety which hallowed his name and which for a long time served as a magic wand against the most stubborn adversary belonging to the Muʿtazilī school, and stood as a symbol of Orthodoxy, saved his collection of *ḥadīth* from the complete literary eclipse from which most of the works of the type have suffered. It maintained its position in literature for a long period, as the source for a number of important works and compilations'.[69]

Of the numerous scholars and authors who used the *Musnad* as a subject for their commentary or adaptations, or as a source for their own works or compilations, we may mention here just a few. Abū ʿUmar Muḥammad ibn Waḥīd (d.345/956) re-edited the book and added certain supplementary traditions.[70] Al-Bāwartī, the lexicographer (d.499/1155), based his *Gharīb al-Ḥadīth* entirely on this book.[71] ʿIzz al-Dīn ibn al-Athīr (d.630/1234) used it as one of his sources for his biographical dictionary, the *Usd al-Ghāba*.[72] Ibn Ḥajar (d.852/1505) included it among the important works upon which he based his *aṭrāf*.[73] Sirāj al-Dīn ʿUmar ibn al-Mulaqqin (d.805/1402) made a synopsis of it. Al-Suyūṭī (d.911/1505) used it as the basis for his grammatical treatise, *ʿUqūd al-Zabarjad*.[74] Abu'l-Ḥasan ʿUmar ibn al-Hādī al-Sindī (d.1139/1726) wrote a large commentary on it. Zayn al-Dīn ʿUmar ibn Aḥmad al-Shammā' al-Ḥalabī made an epitome of it, which he called *al-Muntaqā min Musnad Aḥmad*.[75] Abū Bakr Muḥammad ibn ʿAbd Allāh re-edited it, arranging the traditions in the alphabetical order of the names of their original narrators.[76] Nāṣir al-Dīn ibn Zurayq prepared another edition of it in the form of a *Muṣannaf*, while Abu'l-Ḥasan al-Haythamī compiled together such of its traditions as were not also found in the six canonical traditions.[77]

The *Musnad* did not only serve as a large mine of materials for Muslim theology and Arabic lexicography, but also, because of the pious personality of its compiler, it acquired a kind of aura of sanctity. This is shown, for instance, by the fact that in the twelfth century a society of devout traditionists read it from end to end in 56 sittings before the tomb of the Blessed Prophet in Medina.[78]

It appears, however, that on account of its large bulk and because of the collection of many better planned and more practical works on *ḥadīth* during the third and fourth centuries, the *Musnad* of Aḥmad grew less popular, and copies of it became more scarce; so that al-Muzanī, one of the leading traditionists of the fourth century, was surprised to learn from a *ḥadīth* student that he had read 150 parts of the book with Abū Bakr ibn Mālik. Muzanī recalled that when he himself had been a student in Iraq that people were surprised to find even one part of the *Musnad* with any traditionist.[79] The scarcity of its manuscripts in modern libraries, therefore, is not a matter for surprise.

4.2c OTHER MUSNAD WORKS

Like al-Ṭayālisī and Ibn Ḥanbal, many other traditionists compiled *musnad* works on the same lines, with certain differences in the details of internal structure. These include Abū Muḥammad ʿAbd al-Ḥamīd ibn Ḥumayd (d.249/863), Abū ʿAwāna (d.317/929),[80] Ibn Abī Shayba (d.235/849),[81] Isḥāq ibn Rāhawayh (d.238/852),[82] al-Ḥumaydī (d.219/834),[83] Abū Yaʿlā (d.307/919),[84] and others.[85]

4.3 THE MUṢANNAF WORKS

Still more important than the *Musnad* works are the collections known as *muṣannaf*.[86] To this genre belong the most important of all *ḥadīth* collections, such as the *Ṣaḥīḥs* of Bukhārī and Muslim, the *Jāmiʿ* of al-Tirmidhī, and also the *Sunan* works such as those of al-Nasāʾī and Abū Daūd. The early *muṣannaf* works are mostly lost: the *Muṣannaf* of Wakīʿ, for instance, is known to us only through references in later works.[87]

4.3a THE MUṢANNAF OF ʿABD AL-RAZZĀQ

The earliest *Muṣannaf* work in existence is the *Muṣannaf* of Abū Bakr ʿAbd al-Razzāq ibn Humām (126/743–211/826), of Ṣanʿāʾ in the Yemen, which has been skilfully edited and published by the Indian scholar Ḥabīb al-Raḥmān al-Aʿẓamī.[88]

We are told that ʿAbd al-Razzāq began the study of *ḥadīth* at the age of twenty. He kept the company of Maʿmar for seven years, learning *ḥadīth* from him, and studied under other leading authorities such as Ibn Jurayj, until he himself became one of the most outstanding *ḥadīth* experts in his day. Many later authorities acknowledge their debt to him, including traditionists like Yaḥyā ibn Maʿīn and Aḥmad ibn Ḥanbal. It is said that after the death of the Prophet, people never travelled in such a large number to meet anyone as they did to ʿAbd al-Razzāq.[89] Later authorities, however, differ over the quality of the material he preserved: some regard it as reliable, while others are less enthusiastic.

Two works by him are mentioned by Ibn al-Nadīm.[90] One of them, the *Kitāb al-Sunan*, is identical with the text now known as the *Muṣannaf*.[91] It is divided in accordance with the *fiqh* classification into various books, in each of which the *ḥadīth*s are disposed according to subject. The final chapter is on *shamā'il*, the very last *ḥadīth* being about the Prophet's hair.[92]

4.3b THE MUṢANNAF OF IBN ABĪ SHAYBA

More exhaustive still, however, is the *Muṣannaf* of Abū Bakr Muḥammad ibn ʿAbd Allāh Ibn Abī Shayba (d.235/849). His grandfather worked as judge of Wāsiṭ during the reign of al-Manṣūr, and his family produced many traditionists.[93] Based at Kūfa, he himself related traditions to leading figures such as Abū Zarʿa, al-Bukhārī, Muslim, and Aḥmad ibn Ḥanbal. His *Muṣannaf*, which is considered an early source of the first importance, has recently been printed in thirteen volumes.[94]

4.3c THE ṢAḤĪḤ OF AL-BUKHĀRĪ

The most important of all *Muṣannaf* works, indeed, of all the *ḥadīth* collections, is of course *al-Jāmiʿ al-Ṣaḥīḥ* of al-Bukhārī.[95] The compiler is said to have questioned more than a thousand masters of *ḥadīth*, who lived in places as far apart as Balkh, Merv, Nīsābūr, the Ḥijāz, Egypt and Iraq. Bukhārī used to seek aid in prayer before recording any tradition, and weighed every word he wrote with scrupulous exactitude. He devoted more than a quarter of his life to the creation of his *Ṣaḥiḥ*, which is generally considered by the Muslims as an authority second only to the Qur'ān.

Abū ʿAbd Allāh Muḥammad ibn Ismāʿīl al-Bukhārī, who was born at Bukhārā in the year 194/810,[96] was of Persian origin. His ancestor, Bardizbah, was a farmer in the vicinity of Bukhārā, who was taken captive during the Muslim conquest of the region. Bardizbah's son, who took the name al-Mughīra, accepted Islam at the hand of al-Yamān al-Juʿfī, the Muslim governor of Bukhārā, and gained from him the *nisba* al-Juʿfī. Al-Mughīra's son Ibrāhīm, the grandfather of our author, had a son called Ismaʿīl, who became a traditionist of great piety and sound reputation. Scrupulous in his habits, he is said to have mentioned on his deathbed that in all he possessed there was not a penny which had not been earned by his own honest labour.[97]

Ismāʿīl died leaving a considerable fortune to his widow and two sons, Aḥmad and Muḥammad, the latter being only an infant at the time. The child who was destined to play such a central role in the development of *ḥadīth* literature was endowed by nature with great intellectual powers, although he was physically frail. He possessed a sharp and photographic memory, and a great tenacity of purpose, which served him well in his academic life.

Like many scholars of his time, al-Bukhārī began his educational career under the guidance of his mother in his native city. Finishing his elementary studies at the young age of eleven, he immersed himself in the study of *ḥadīth*. Within six years he had mastered the knowledge of all the traditionists of Bukhārā, as well as everything contained in the books which were available to him. He thus travelled to Mecca with his mother and brother in order to perform the Pilgrimage. From the Holy City, he started a series of journeys in quest of *ḥadīth*, passing through all the important centres of Islamic learning, staying in each place as long as he needed, meeting the traditionists, learning all the *ḥadīth* they knew, and communicating his own knowledge to them.[98] It is recorded that he stayed at Baṣra for four or five years, and in the Ḥijāz for six; while he travelled to Egypt twice and to Kūfa and Baghdad many times.[99]

Imām Bukhārī's *Wanderjahre* continued for some four decades. In the year 250/864, he came to the great Central Asian city of Nīsābūr, where he was given a grand reception suitable to a traditionist of his rank. Here he devoted himself to the teaching of tradition, and wished to settle down. But he was obliged to leave the town when he declined to accept a request to deliver lectures on *ḥadīth* at the palace of Khālid ibn Aḥmad al-Dhuhalī. From Nīsābūr he travelled on to Khartank, a village near Bukhārā, at the request of its inhabitants. Here he settled down, and died in the year 256/870.

Throughout his life, al-Bukhārī displayed the character of a devout and saintly Muslim scholar. He was rigorous in the observance of his religious duties, ensuring that rather than relying on charity he always lived by means of trade, in which he was scrupulously honest. Once he lost ten thousand dirhams on account of a minute scruple. A good deal of his income, in fact, was spent on helping the students and the poor. It is said that he never showed an ill-temper to anyone, even when there was more than sufficient cause; nor did he bear ill-will against anybody. Even towards those who had caused his exile from Nīsābūr, he harboured no grudge.[100]

Ḥadīth was almost an obsession with Bukhārī. He spared no pains for it, sacrificing almost everything for its sake. On one of his voyages he was so short of money that he lived on wild herbs for three days. But he enjoyed one form of public recreation: archery, in which he had acquired great skill. His amanuensis, who lived with him for a considerable time, writes that Bukhārī often went out to practice his aim, and only twice during his sojourn with him did he see him miss the mark.[101]

Since the very outset of his career, al-Bukhārī showed the signs of greatness. It is said that at the age of eleven he pointed out a mistake of one of his teachers. The teacher laughed at the audacity of the young student; but al-Bukhārī persisted in his correction, and challenged his teacher to refer to his book, which justified the pupil's contention.[102] When still a boy, too, he was entreated by a large group of *ḥadīth* students to give a lecture on the subject. He accepted their request, and a large crowd of students duly gathered at a mosque, and accepted the traditions which he related.[103] Once, when he visited Baṣra, the authorities were notified of his arrival, and a day was fixed for him to lecture. At the lecture, he was able to confine himself only to such traditions as he had received on the authority of the early traditionists of Baṣra, and had none the less been unknown to the audience.[104]

On many occasions al-Bukhārī's learning was put to severe tests, of a kind often favoured by rigorous scholars of the time,[105] and he seems always to have emerged with credit. At Baghdad, ten traditionists changed the *isnāds* and contents of a hundred traditions, recited them to al-Bukhārī at a public meeting, and asked him questions about them. Al-Bukhārī confessed his ignorance of the traditions which they had recited. But then he recited the correct versions of all the traditions concerned, and said that probably his questioners had inadvertantly recited them wrongly. At Samarqand, four hundred students tested al-Bukhārī's knowledge in the same way, and al-Bukhārī succeeded in exposing their interpolations. At Nīsābūr, Muslim, the author of another *Ṣaḥīḥ*, together with others, asked al-Bukhārī questions about certain traditions, and found his answers completely satisfactory. In many scholarly gatherings he successfully identified some of the obscurer early *ḥadīth* narrators in a way which had eluded the other scholars present. These repeated trials and triumphs of al-Bukhārī won him recognition as the greatest traditionist of his time by all the major authorities with whom he came in contact, including Aḥmad ibn Ḥanbal, ʿAlī ibn al-Madīnī, Abū Bakr ibn Abī Shayba, Isḥāq ibn Rāhawayh, and others.[106]

Al-Bukhārī's writings began during his stay in Medina at the age of 18, when he compiled his two earliest books. One of these contained the decrees and judgements of the Companions and the Followers, while the other was made up of short biographies of the important narrators of tradition during his own lifetime.[107] A large number of other collections followed; a list is furnished by his biographers.[108]

The *Ṣaḥīḥ*, known commonly as *Ṣaḥīḥ al-Bukhārī*, is the most important of his books. It is said to have been heard by 90,000 of the author's students, and is considered by almost all traditionists to be the most reliable collection of *ḥadīth*. So venerated is the book that some Muslims use it as a charm through which God overcomes their difficulties;[109] and merely to possess a copy of it has been regarded as a proof against misfortune.[110]

The *Ṣaḥīḥ* may be seen as Bukhārī's life-work: his earlier treatises served him as a preparation for this *magnum opus*, while his later books were little more than offshoots of it. It was to the *Ṣaḥīḥ* that he devoted his most intense care and attention, expending about a quarter of his life on it.[111]

Bukhārī's notion to compile the *Ṣaḥīḥ* owed its origin to a casual remark from Isḥāq ibn Rāhawayh (166–238/782–852), who said that he wished that a traditionist would compile a short but comprehensive book containing the genuine traditions only. These words seem to have fired al-Bukhārī's imagination, and he set to work with indefatigable energy and care. He sifted through all the traditions known to him, tested their genuineness according to canons of criticism he himself developed, selected 7,275 out of some 60,000 *ḥadīth*s,[112] and arranged them according to their subject matter under separate headings, most of which are taken from the Qur'ān, and in some cases from the traditions themselves.

Because al-Bukhārī nowhere mentions what canons of criticism he applied to the traditions to test their genuineness, or tells us why he compiled the book, many later scholars have tried to infer these things from the text itself. Al-Ḥāzimī, in his *Shurūṭ al-A'imma*, al-ʿIrāqī in his *Alfiyya*, al-ʿAynī and al-Qasṭallānī in their introductions to their commentaries on the *Ṣaḥīḥ*, and many other writers on the *ḥadīth* sciences, including Ibn al-Ṣalāḥ, have tried to deduce Bukhārī's principles from the material he presents.

As we have seen, al-Bukhārī's main object was to collect together the sound traditions only.[113] By these, he meant such traditions as were handed down to him from the Prophet on the authority of a well-known Companion, via a continuous chain of narrators who, according to his records, research and knowledge, had been unanimously accepted by honest and trustworthy traditionists as men and women of integrity, possessed of a retentive memory and firm faith, accepted on condition that their narrations were not contrary to what was related by the other reliable authorities, and were free from defects. Al-Bukhārī includes in his work the narrations of these narrators when they explicitly state that they had received the traditions from their own authorities. If their statement in this regard was ambiguous, he took care that they had demonsīrably met their teachers, and were not given to careless statements.[114]

From the above principles, which Imām Bukhārī took as his guide in choosing his materials, his caution is evident. It is important to note, however, that he used less exacting criteria for the traditions which he used as headings for some of his chapters, and as corroboratives for the principal ones. In such cases, he often omits all or part of the *isnād*, and in certain cases relies on weak authorities.[115] The number of 'suspended' (*muʿallaq*) and corroborative traditions in the book amounts to about 1,725.[116]

From this it is clear that Bukhārī's purpose was not only to collect what he considered to be sound traditions, but also to impress their contents on the minds of his readers, and to show them what doctrinal and legal inferences could be drawn from them. He therefore divided the whole work into more than a hundred books, which he subdivided in 3,450 chapters. Every chapter has a heading which serves a a key to the contents of the various traditions which it includes.

It has been aptly remarked that the headings of the various chapters of the *Ṣaḥīḥ* constitute the *fiqh* of Imām al-Bukhārī. These headings consist of verses from the Qur'ān or passages from *ḥadīth*s. In some cases they are in full agreement with the *ḥadīth*s listed underneath them, while in some others, they are of a wider or narrower significance than the traditions which follow; in which case they serve as an additional object of interpretation and explanation of the traditions. In some cases, they are in the interrogative form, which denotes that the Imām regarded the problem as still undecided. In other cases, he wanted to warn against something which might outwardly appear to be wrong and impermissible. But in every chapter heading, al-Bukhārī kept a certain object in view. There are even cases where the headings are not followed by any traditions at all; here al-Bukhārī is intending to show that no genuine tradition on the subject was known to him.[117]

Bukhārī is also being original when he repeats the various versions of a single *ḥadīth* in different chapters. By doing this rather than putting them together in one place, he wanted to bring to light further evidence of the authenticity of the *ḥadīth*s in question, and at the same time to draw more than one practical conclusion from them. Similarly, in including one part of a tradition in one chapter and inserting another part in another chapter, and in introducing the 'suspended' traditions as *marfūʿ* and *mawqūf*, al-Bukhārī has certain specific academic purposes in view, which are explained by the commentators of his *Ṣaḥīḥ*.[118]

It was thus that the *Ṣaḥīḥ*, the work of a great traditionist who combined a vast knowledge of traditions and allied subjects with scrupulous piety, strict exactitude, the painstaking accuracy of an expert editor, and the legal acumen of an astute jurist, rapidly attracted the attention of the whole Muslim community, and became accepted as an authority next only to the Qur'ān. Many Muslim doctors wrote enormous commentaries on it, in which they thoroughly discuss every aspect of the book, and every word of its contents, from the legal, linguistic, contextual and historical aspects. Twelve such commentaries have been printed, while at least another fifty-nine remain in manuscript form.[119]

It would be a mistake, however, to suppose that the *Ṣaḥīḥ* is free of defects, or that the Muslim scholars have failed to criticise it in certain respects. Thus it is generally accepted that like other traditionists, al-Bukhārī confines his criticism to the narrators of traditions, and their reliability, and pays little attention to the probability or possibility of the truth of the actual material reported by them. In estimating the reliability of the narrators, his judgement has in certain cases been erroneous, and the Muslim traditionists have not failed to point this out. Al-Dāraquṭnī (306/918–385/995) tried to show the weakness of some two hundred traditions contained in the book, in his work *al-Istidrāk wa'l-tatabbuᶜ*,[120] which has been summarised by al-Jazā'irī in his *Tawjīh al-Naẓar*.[121] Abū Masᶜūd of Damascus, and Abū ᶜAlī al-Ghassānī have also criticised the *Ṣaḥīḥ*,[122] while al-ᶜAynī in his celebrated commentary has shown the defects of some of its contents.[123]

Despite this, all the Muslim traditionists, including those who have criticised the *Ṣaḥīḥ*, have paid unanimous tribute to the general accuracy, scrupulous care, and exactitude of the book's author. 'In his selections of *ḥadīth*', says the orientalist Brockelmann, 'he has shown the greatest critical ability, and in editing the text has sought to obtain the most scrupulous accuracy.'[124]

4.3d THE ṢAḤĪḤ OF MUSLIM

The position of Bukhārī's *Ṣaḥīḥ* in the literature is not, of course, unrivalled. Another *Ṣaḥīḥ* was being compiled almost simultaneously, which was considered its superior by some, its equal by others, and second to it by most. This was the *Ṣaḥīḥ* of Abu'l-Ḥusayn ᶜAsākir al-Dīn Muslim ibn al-Ḥajjāj ibn Muslim al-Qushayrī al-Nīsābūrī, known as Imām Muslim.[125]

As his *nisba* shows, Muslim belonged to the Qushayr tribe of the Arabs, an offshoot of the mighty clan of Rabīᶜa. His tribe had taken an important part in the history of Islam after the death of the Prophet. Ḥayda of Qushayr is mentioned in the *Iṣāba* as one of the Companions,[126] while Qurra ibn Ḥubayra, another Qushayrī, was appointed by the Prophet as *walī* in charge of the alms of his people.[127] Ziyād ibn ʿAbd al-Raḥmān al-Qushayrī is said to have killed a vast number of Byzantine troopers at the Battle of the Yarmūk, in which he lost one of his legs.[128]

After the great Islamic conquests, various families of Qushayrīs migrated from Arabia and settled in the new provinces, some in the west, and others in the east. Kulthūm ibn ʿIyāḍ and his nephew Balj ibn Bishr, who had served as governors of Ifrīqiya and Spain respectively, settled down in a district near Qurṭuba (Cordoba). Another Qushayrī family made their residence at nearby al-Bīra (Elvira). Others headed east, and settled in Khurasān. Among them was one Zurāra, who served as provincial governor for a time. His son ʿAmr, and grandson Ḥumayd ibn ʿAmr, settled down at Nīsābūr.[129] From them our author was probably descended: the son of al-Ḥajjāj, who was himself a traditionist of no mean repute.[130]

Very little is known about Muslim's early life. It is said that he was born in 202/817, and that having learnt and excelled in the usual disciplines at a precocious age, focussed his attention on *ḥadīth*. In its pursuit he travelled widely, visiting all the important centres of learning in Persia, Iraq, Syria and Egypt. He attended the lectures of most of the great traditionists of his day, including Isḥāq ibn Rāhawayh, Aḥmad ibn Ḥanbal, ʿUbayd Allāh al-Qawārīrī, Shuwayḥ ibn Yūnus, ʿAbd Allāh ibn Maslama, and Ḥamala ibn Yaḥyā. He settled down at Nīsābūr, earning a living from a small business, and devoted the remainder of his time to the service of the Prophetic *sunna*. He died in the year 261/874.

His character is said to have been admirable. His fearless loyalty to the truth is shown by his persistence in associating with Bukhārī despite the political pressures brought to bear on the latter.[131] Like Bukhārī, he adhered to the usual Islamic ethic of refusing to speak ill of anyone.[132]

Like Bukhārī, too, he wrote a good number of books and treatises on *ḥadīth*, and on related subjects. Ibn al-Nadīm mentions five books by him on the subject.[133] Ḥājī Khalīfa adds the names of many other works by him in the same field.[134] In his *Ṣaḥīḥ* he examined a third of a million *ḥadīth*s,[135] from which he selected only about four thousand, which the traditionists unanimously regarded as sound.[136]

Like Bukhārī, Muslim regarded a *ḥadīth* as *Ṣaḥīḥ* only when it had been handed down to him through a continuous *isnād* of known and reliable authorities, was compatible with other material established in this way, and was free from various types of deficiency.[137] He adopted a threefold classification of *ḥadīth*s. Firstly, there were those which had been related by narrators who were straighforward and steadfast in their narrations, did not differ much in them from other reliable narrators, and did not commit any palpable confusion in their reports. Secondly, there were traditions whose narrators were not distinguished for their retentive memory and steadfastness in narrations. Thirdly, there were the *ḥadīths* narrated on the authority of people whom all or most traditionists declared were of questionable reliability. According to Imām Muslim, the first group makes up the bulk of his book; the second is included as corroborative of the first, while the third is entirely rejected.[138]

Because *Ṣaḥīḥ Muslim's* Book of *Tafsīr* is neither complete nor systematic, the work is not considered a comprehensive collection (*Jāmiʿ*) like that of Imām Bukhārī. Despite this, Imām Muslim strictly observed many principles of the science of *ḥadīth* which had been to some extent neglected by al-Bukhārī. He draws a distinction between the terms *akhbaranā* and *ḥaddathanā*, and always uses the former in connection with the traditions which had been recited to him by his own teachers, assigning the latter to what he had in turn read out to them.[139] He was more strict and consistent than al-Bukhārī in pointing out the differences between the narrations of the various *rāwīs*, and in stating their character and other particulars. He also showed greater acumen in the arrangement of traditions and their *isnāds* in his work, and in presenting the different versions of a single tradition in one place.[140] Unlike Imām Bukhārī, he appears not to have committed any mistake or confusion in the text or *isnād* of any tradition.[141] He added a long introduction, in which he explained some of the principles which he had followed in the choice of materials for his book; and which should be followed in accepting and relating traditions.

Upon completing his *Ṣaḥīḥ*, Imām Muslim presented it to Abū Zarʿa of Rayy, a traditionist of great repute, for his comments. Abū Zarʿa inspected it closely, and Muslim deleted everything which he thought was defective, and retained only such traditions as were declared by him to be genuine.[142]

Thus carefully compiled by Muslim, and proof-read by Abū Zarʿa, the *Ṣaḥīḥ* has been acclaimed as the most authentic collection of traditions after that of Bukhārī, and superior to the latter in the details of its arrangement. Some traditionists hold it to be superior to the work of Bukhārī in every respect.[143]

After Muslim, a number of other scholars also compiled *Ṣaḥīḥ* collections, These include Ibn Khuzayma (d.311/923),[144] Abū Ḥātim Muḥammad ibn Ḥibbān (d.354/965),[145] and others. None of them, however, ever gained the recognition and popularity which the Muslim community has accorded the definitive achievements of al-Bukhārī and Muslim.

4.4 THE SUNAN WORKS

The *Sunan* works constitute the richest branch of *ḥadīth* literature. Since the earliest period of Islam, the traditionists attached greater importance to legal and doctrinal reports than they did to accounts of a historical (*maghāzī*) nature, arguing that the precise date of the Prophet's departure from Badr, for instance, was of no practical utility for a Muslim. Attention, therefore, should rather be focussed on topics of relevance to his or her daily life, such as ablutions, prayers, sales, marriages, and so forth.

This emphasis on *ḥadīth*s of a practical nature grew even more pronounced after the second half of the third century. Most of the traditionists, with the exception only of the most ambitious, compiled *ḥadīth* collections of the *sunan* alone. Such are the works of Abū Daūd al-Sijistānī, al-Tirmidhī,[146] al-Nasā'ī, al-Dārimī, Ibn Māja, al-Dāraquṭnī, and a considerable number of others.

4.4a THE SUNAN OF ABŪ DAŪD

This work, which is among the most important of the *ḥadīth* anthologies, is the work of Abū Daūd Sulaymān ibn al-Ashʿath al-Sijistānī, who is said to have examined 500,000 *ḥadīth*s, and selected 4,800 for his book, a labour which occupied him for twenty years.[147]

Abū Daūd was a descendant of one ʿImrān of the Azd tribe, who was killed during the Battle of Ṣiffīn on the side of ʿAlī.[148] Abū Daūd himself was born in 203/817. The biographers dispute the place of his birth: Ibn Khallikān,[149] and, following him, Wüstenfeld, hold that he was born in a village known as Sijistāna in the vicinity of Baṣra, while Yāqūt,[150] al-Samʿānī[151] and al-Subkī[152] think that he was born in the well-known region of Sijistān in Khurasān. There is, in fact, no evidence that a village called Sijistāna ever existed in the Baṣra region.

When his elementary education, which probably took place in his native city, was complete, he joined a school in Nīsābūr when he was ten. There he studied under Muḥammad ibn Aslam (d.242/856).[153] He then travelled to Baṣra,[154] where he received the bulk of his *ḥadīth* training. In 224/838 he visited Kūfa, from which city he began a series of journeys in search of *ḥadīth*, which took him to the Ḥijāz, Iraq, Persia, Syria and Egypt. He met most of the foremost traditionists of his time, and acquired from them a profound knowledge of the traditions which were available.[155]

Abū Daūd's travels regularly took him to the metropolis of Baghdad. Once, while staying in that city, he was visited by Abū Aḥmad al-Muwaffaq, the celebrated commander and brother of the caliph al-Muʿtamid. When Abū Daūd enquired as to the purpose of his visit, al-Muwaffaq replied that his objective was threefold. Firstly, he wished to invite Abū Daūd to reside at Baṣra, which had become deserted on account of the Zanj insurrection, and would, he thought, be repopulated if famous scholars and their students moved there. Secondly, he requested Abū Daūd to give classes to al-Muwaffaq's family. Thirdly, he asked him to make these classes private, so that ordinary students would be excluded. Abū Daūd accepted the first two requests, but expressed his inability to comply with the third. For 'to knowledge all are equal', and Abū Daūd would not tolerate any distinction between rich and poor students. The result was that al-Muwaffaq's sons attended his lectures side by side with anyone else who wished to attend.[156]

This anecdote, preserved for us by al-Subkī, throws light not just on the great reputation enjoyed by Abū Daūd as a scholar and a man of principle, but also on the date of his final settlement at Baṣra. This is unlikely to have occurred before the year 270/883, when the Zanj insurrection was finally crushed. Abū Daūd died at Baṣra in the year 275/888, at the age of 73.

His encyclopedic knowledge of traditions, his photographic memory, his upright character, and his kindliness, are generally recognised by all the traditionists.[157] One of his most celebrated books on traditions and Sacred Law is his *Sunan*, which is not only regarded as the first work of its type in the *ḥadīth* literature, but is generally seen as the best and most reliable. It is divided into books, which are subdivided into chapters.[158]

Although Abū Daūd retained the scrupulous exactitude of his predecessors in reproducing the material which he collected, he differed from them in the criteria of selection. In his *Sunan*, he included not only the *Ṣaḥīḥ* traditions (as Bukhārī and Muslim had done), but also some other accounts that had been classed by other scholars as weak or doubtful. Among the narrators, he relied not only on those who had been unanimously declared acceptable, but also on others who were the subject of criticism from some quarters. This is not necessarily a defect in his book: some critics such as Shuʿba had in fact been overstrict in their criticisms of the narrators.[159] None the less, Abū Daūd collected the most reliable traditions known to him on every subject of the *fiqh*, quoting the sources through which the traditions had reached him, together with the various versions of the accounts in question. He draws attention to the defects of certain of the traditions he cites, as well as the relative value of the variant texts. In the case of the traditions which he believed to be genuine, however, he makes no comments whatsoever; he also has a habit of taking only those parts of long *ḥadīth*s which are relevant to the chapter in which they are included.[160]

The following remarks made by Abū Daūd in connection with some of his traditions give us a general idea of the method and nature of his criticism:

> Abū Daūd says: This is an inauthentic (*munkar*) *ḥadīth*. Certainly, it is related by Ibn Jurayj from Ziyād ibn Saʿd, from al-Zuhrī, from Anas, that he said that the Prophet (upon whom be God's blessings and peace), had put on a ring made of palm-leaf, which he in time discarded. The mistake in this *ḥadīth* is to be attributed to Humām. No other narrator has related it.[161]

About another *ḥadīth* he has this to say:

> This is narrated by Ibn Wahb only. A similar *ḥadīth* has however been related by Maʿqil ibn ʿUbayd Allāh through a chain of narrators.[162]

And in connection with a further *ḥadīth*, after giving two versions of it, he remarks: The account related by Anas is more correct than the other.[163]

At another place, he points out that only the traditionists of Egypt have given an *isnād* for it.[164] To yet another, he adds a note about one of its narrators, Abū Isḥāq, stating that he had learnt only four traditions from al-Ḥārith, and that the present *ḥadīth*, although allegedly told on al-Ḥārith's authority, was not one of them.[165] About the narrators of still another *ḥadīth*, he says: 'Abū Khalīl never heard any *ḥadīth*s from Qatāda,'[166] while elsewhere he remarks: 'This *ḥadīth* has been handed down by several chains of authorities, all of which are inauthentic.'[167]

Containing all the legal traditions which may serve as foundations for Islamic rituals and law, and furnishing explicit notes on the authority and value of these traditions, Abū Daūd's book has generally been accepted as the most important work of the *sunan* genre. 'The *Kitāb al-Sunan* of Abū Daūd,' exclaims its commentator al-Khaṭṭābī, 'is a noble book, the like of which has never been written.' Since the author collected traditions which no-one else had ever assembled together, it has been accepted as a standard work by scholars of a wide variety of schools, particularly in Iraq, Egypt, North Africa and many other parts of the Islamic world.[168]

4.4b THE JĀMIᶜ OF AL-TIRMIDHĪ

The general principles with regard to the criticism of *ḥadīth* which had been adopted by Abū Daūd were further improved upon and followed by his student Abū ᶜĪsā Muḥammad ibn ᶜĪsā al-Tirmidhī, in his *Jāmiᶜ*. This work contains the bulk of the traditions—legal, dogmatic, and historical—which had been accepted by the jurists of the main juridical tendencies as the basis of Islamic law.[169]

Al-Tirmidhī was born at Mecca in the year 206/821. He travelled a good deal in search of traditions, visiting the great centres of Islamic learning in Iraq, Persia and Khurasān, where he was able to associate with eminent traditionists such as al-Bukhārī, Muslim, Abū Daūd and others. He died at Tirmidh in 279/892.[170]

Like Abū Daūd, Abū ᶜĪsā possessed a remarkably sharp and retentive memory, which was severely tested many times. It is related that during an early stage of his travels, a traditionist once dictated to him several traditions which occupied sixteen pages, which, however, were lost by Tirmidhī before he could revise them. He met the traditionist again after some time, and requested him to recite some traditions. The teacher suggested that he would read out from his manuscript the same traditions that he had dictated to Tirmidhī during their previous meeting, and that Tirmidhī should compare his notes with what he heard. Instead of telling the traditionist that he had misplaced his notes, Tirmidhī picked up some blank sheets of paper in his hand, and looked into them as though they contained his notes, while the teacher began to read his book. The latter soon noticed the ruse, and grew angry at the young student's conduct. Tirmidhī, however, explained that he remembered every word of what had been dictated to him. The teacher was reluctant to believe him, and challenged him to recite the traditions from his memory. Tirmidhī accepted this challenge, and proceeded to recite all the traditions without committing a single mistake. At this, the teacher doubted his statement that he had not been able to revise from his notes, and decided to test his student by reciting forty other traditions, and ask Tirmidhī to reproduce them. Without hesitation, Tirmidhī repeated what he heard verbatim, and his teacher, convinced now of the truth of his statement, declared his pleasure and satisfaction at the young man's powers of memory.

Tirmidhī's *Jāmiᶜ*, assembled through the use of this gift, is recognised as one of the most important works of *ḥadīth* literature, and is unanimously included among the six canonical collections of *ḥadīth*. For the first time, the author used the principle of only considering those traditions on which the various rituals and laws of Islam had been established by the ulama of the various schools. Not only did he take great pains to determine the identity, the names, the titles and the *kunya* of the narrators of the traditions he cited; he also attempted to state the degree of their reliability, explaining what use had been made of them by the jurists of the Schools.[171] He adds a note to almost every *ḥadīth*, prefaced with the words, 'Abū ʿĪsā says...'. He then proceeds to state a range of points connected with the tradition. The following examples will show the nature and importance of these notes.

(i) 'It was related to us by Abū Kurayb, who related it from ʿAbda bint Sulaymān from Muḥammad ibn ʿAmr, from Abū Salmā from Abū Hurayra, who said that the Prophet (may God's peace and blessings rest upon him) said that had he not feared causing hardship to his people, he would have enjoined them to brush their teeth with the *miswāk*-brush before every prayer. Abū ʿĪsā says: "This *ḥadīth* has been related by Muḥammad ibn Isḥāq from Muḥammad ibn Ibrāhīm, from Abū Salmā, from Zayd ibn Khālid, from the Prophet (upon whom be peace). And in my view both the traditions of Abū Salmā from Abū Hurayra and Zayd ibn Khālid from the Prophet are genuine, because it has been related to me from Abū Hurayra from the Prophet, through more than one chain of authorities. Muḥammad, however, thinks that the tradition of Abū Salmā from Zayd ibn Khālid is the most correct. On the subject there are [traditions] related by Abū Bakr al-Ṣiddīq, ʿAlī, ʿĀ'isha, Khālid, Anas, ʿAbd Allāh ibn ʿAmr, Umm Ḥabība and Ibn ʿUmar."'[172]

(ii) 'Qutayba, Hannād, Abū Kurayb, Aḥmad ibn Manīʿ Maḥmūd ibn Ghaylān and Abū ʿAmmār have related to us saying that Wakīʿ related to them from al-Aʿmash, from Ḥabīb ibn Abī Thābit, from ʿUrwa, from ʿĀ'isha, that the Prophet (may the blessings and peace of God be upon him) once kissed one of his wives, and then went out to offer prayers without performing ablution. ʿUrwa asked ʿĀ'isha: "Who could this be but yourself?" and ʿĀ'isha laughed. Abū ʿĪsā says: "A similar tradition has been related by many of those who possessed knowledge among the Companions and the Followers, and this is the opinion of Sufyān al-Thawrī and the jurists of Kūfa, who hold that a kiss does not invalidate one's ablution. Mālik ibn Anas, al-Awzāʿī, al-Shāfiʿī, Aḥmad [ibn Ḥanbal] and Isḥāq [ibn Rāhawayh], however, hold that a kiss does indeed invalidate the ablution, and this is the opinion of many learned Companions and Followers. Our people [Mālik, Aḥmad *et al.*] did not follow the *ḥadīth* related by ʿĀ'isha from the Prophet (upon whom be peace) because it did not appear to be genuine to them on account of its *isnād*. I heard Abū Bakr al-ʿAṭṭār of Baṣra quote ʿAlī ibn al-Madīnī, who said that Yaḥyā ibn Saʿīd al-Qaṭṭān declared this tradition to be weak, and said that it was without value. I also heard Muḥammad ibn Ismāʿīl call it a weak tradition, saying that Ḥabīb ibn Abī Thābit never received any traditions from ʿUrwa. Ibrāhīm al-Taymī also related from ʿĀ'isha that the Prophet (upon whom be blessings and peace) kissed her and did not perform ablutions afterwards; but this too is not genuine, because Ibrāhīm al-Taymī is not known to have received this tradition from ʿĀ'isha. As a matter of fact, nothing that has been imputed to the Prophet on this subject can be called 'genuine' ".'[173]

(iii) 'Aḥmad ibn Muḥammad related to us [saying that] ʿAbd Allāh related to us from Fuḍayl ibn Ghazwān from Ibn Abī Nuʿaym from Abū Hurayra, who said that Abu'l-Qāsim [sc. the Prophet], the Prophet of Forgiveness (upon whom be God's blessings and peace), said that he who accused his slave falsely, while his slave was innocent of that which he imputed to him, would be punished on Judgement Day. This is a fair, genuine tradition (*ḥadīth ḥasan ṣaḥīḥ*). On the subject, other traditions are related by Suwayd ibn Muqarrin and ʿAbd Allāh ibn ʿUmar. As for Ibn Abī Nuʿaym, he is ʿAbd al-Raḥmān ibn Abī Nuʿaym, whose *kunya* is Abu'l-Ḥakam.'[174]

The above three examples should suffice to demonstrate the nature of the remarks appended by Tirmidhī to the traditions of his *Jāmiʿ*. These *ḥadīth*s he categorised as either *Ṣaḥīḥ* (Sound), *Ḥasan* (Fair), *Ṣaḥīḥ Ḥasan* (Sound-Fair), *Ḥasan Ṣaḥīḥ* (Fair-Sound), *Gharīb* (Rare), *Ḍaʿīf* (Weak), or *Munkar* (Undetermined).[175] But perhaps the most important feature of the *Jāmiʿ*, so far as assessments of reliability are concerned, is the category of *ḥasan*.

To this class belong most of the traditions on which many of the rites and laws of religion are based. The term had already been used by Bukhārī, Ibn Ḥanbal and others,[176] but rather sparingly, and probably in a loose and non-technical sense. Tirmidhī realised the importance of these *ḥadīth*s as a source of law, defined the term for the first time (in the 'Kitāb al-ʿIlal' of his *Jāmiʿ*), and applied it to those traditions which fulfilled its requirements.

Tirmidhī defines a *ḥasan* Tradition as one that has been related by narrators who are not accused of falsehood, provided it is handed down by more than one chain of authorities, and is not contrary to what has been related by other reliable narrators. Such traditions cannot be termed *Ṣaḥīḥ*, because their soundness is not proven according to the traditional canons. It would be equally wrong to declare them to be entirely unreliable, however, since neither the character of their narrators warrants such a suspicion, nor can it be justified by a comparison with traditions handed down by reliable authorities. Their reliability or otherwise depends on the nature of the particular traditions and the character of their narrators, and must therefore be different in different cases. Some of these traditions may be nearly, although not exactly, as reliable as the Sound traditions, while others may be almost, though not quite, as unreliable as material related by unknown narrators.

To determine this class of traditions and the degree of their reliability, Tirmidhī described some of them as *ṣaḥīḥ ḥasan*, some as *ḥasan*, and others as *ḥasan gharīb*. But he was not quite as consistent in his use of the term *ḥasan*, and many traditionists have criticised him on this account, explaining his inconsistency in various ways.[177]

Despite this, however, the *Jāmiʿ* has sufficient virtues to ensure it a place as a unique work in the literature.

4.4c THE SUNAN OF AL-NASAʾĪ

Another important work in this category is that compiled by Abū ʿAbd al-Raḥmān Aḥmad ibn Shuʿayb al-Nasāʾī, who was born in the year 214 or 215 AH (6 or 7 years after Tirmidhī), at Nasāʾ, a town in Khurasān. Having received his early education in his home province, he travelled at the age of fifteen to Balkh, where he studied *ḥadīth*s with Qutayba ibn Saʿīd for over a year.[178] He travelled widely in pursuit of *ḥadīth*, and settled down in Egypt, when one of his teachers, Yūnus ibn ʿAbd al-ʿAlāʾ, was still living. In 302/914 he went to Damascus, where he found the people holding erroneous views against ʿAlī ibn Abī Ṭālib, due to the past influence of the Umayyads. In order to guide the people, he composed a book on the merits of ʿAlī, and wanted to read it from the pulpit of a mosque. But the congregation, instead of giving him a patient hearing, maltreated him, kicked him, and drove him from the mosque. He died in the year 303/915, perhaps as a result of this incident.[179]

Nasāʾī was recognised as the leading traditionist of his day. ʿAbd Allāh ibn Aḥmad ibn Ḥanbal, Muḥammad ibn Ibrāhīm, ʿAlī ibn ʿUmar and other major traditionists, regarded him thus.[180] His scrupulousness is evident from the fact that in connection with the traditions related by al-Ḥārith, he never used the term *ḥaddathanā* or *akhbaranā*, as he did in the case of those traditions which had reached him via other scholars, for although the materials he acquired from al-Ḥārith were read by the latter in a public class, Nasāʾī had been prohibited from attending, and thus was obliged to hear them by concealing himself at the gate of the lecture hall.

In his large work on *sunan* (which he confessed contained a fair number of weak and dubious traditions), al-Nasā'ī compiled the legal traditions which he considered to be either fairly reliable or of possible reliability.[181] At the request of some of his friends, he also produced a synopsis of the *Sunan*, called *al-Mujtabā*, or *al-Sunan al-Ṣughrā*. This latter work, which he claimed contained only reliable traditions, is now accepted as one of the six canonical collections.[182]

In *al-Sunan al-Ṣughrā*, Nasā'ī entirely ignores the point of view of his contemporary Tirmidhī, who had sought to apply traditions to specific problems, and arranged his book accordingly. Nasā'ī's main object was only to establish the text of traditions and record the divergences between their various versions, almost all of which he quotes *in extenso*, instead of merely referring to them, as Abū Daūd and Tirmidhī had done. In many places, he gives headings to the differences between the various narrators, and mentions the smallest differences between them. This 'pedantry', as Goldziher describes it,[183] is in fact of integral importance to the *muḥaddith*'s art, and is not (as Goldziher thinks) confined to the chapters on rituals alone, but is abundantly present in other chapters. In some cases, after giving the various versions of a *ḥadīth*, Nasā'ī points out that some of them are incorrect. He is known, likewise, for his strictness in assessing and selecting his authorities; in fact, it is said that his canons of criticism were more rigorous than those of Muslim.[184] The book does, however, contain many weak and doubtful traditions related by unknown narrators of questionable credentials.[185]

4.4 d THE SUNAN OF AL-DĀRIMĪ

This is among the earliest sunan works to have come down to us.[186] Its author, Abū Muḥammad ʿAbd Allāh ibn ʿAbd al-Raḥmān (181–255/797–868)[187] was a member of the Arabian clan of the Banū Dārim, an offshoot of the tribe of Tamīm,[188] to which he was probably attached as a *mawlā*. Like many of his contemporaries, he travelled a good deal in search of *ḥadīth*s, and studied under important traditionists such as Yazīd ibn Hārūn and Saʿīd ibn ʿĀmir. Well-known for his devotion to his field, he was also celebrated for his honesty and piety. When offered a post as judge at Samarqand he refused, afraid he might commit an injustice, until he was pressed hard to accept; and he resigned after judging only one case.[189]

The *Sunan* of al-Dārimī has been described as a *musnad* work.[190] This, however, is incorrect, at least if the term be employed in its general sense. Some traditionists have classed it as a *ṣaḥīḥ*; but this, too, is inaccurate, for the book contains many traditions which fail to satisfy the conditions stipulated for sound *ḥadīth*s.

The work contains some 3,550 traditions, arranged in 1,408 chapters according to subject.[191] One special feature of the book is its general introductory chapter in which the compiler presents a number of *ḥadīth*s connected with a range of matters, including certain usages of the Arabs before Islam, traditions connected with the life and character of the Prophet, material related to the written recording of *ḥadīth*s, and the high importance of knowledge. In the main body of the text, Dārimī follows the same plan as the later *sunan* compilers. After citing a group of traditions, he adds notes, in some of which he offers his own opinion on certain problems, identifies some narrators, or criticises their reliability, or draws attention to variant versions of a tradition. These notes, however, are much briefer than those appended to the previously mentioned three *sunan* works.

The book is generally accepted as an important source,[192] and has been regarded by some traditionists as the sixth of the canonical collections.[193] It never, however, attained the position of any of the former three works, because it contains more weak and defective traditions than they do.[194]

4.4e THE SUNAN OF IBN MĀJA

Most *ḥadīth* scholars prefer the *Sunan* of Ibn Māja (209/824–273/886) to the work of Dārimī, including it in the 'Sound Six' collections. Abū ʿAbd Allāh Muḥammad ibn Yazīd (normally known as Ibn Māja, denoting the title of his father, or perhaps his grandfather), was born at Qazwīn. Visiting the important centres of learning in Iran, Iraq, Syria and Egypt, he studied under the great traditionists of his day, and compiled several works in the area of *ḥadīth*, the most important being his *Sunan*. In this work, the author collects four thousand traditions, distributed over 32 books and 1,500 chapters.[195] It is said that after completing the book, Ibn Māja presented it for criticism to Abū Zarʿa, recognised as the most competent *ḥadīth* critic of the day. Abū Zarʿa liked the general plan of the book, and remarked that he expected it to supersede the *ḥadīth* works which then enjoyed general currency. He also said that the number of weak traditions in the book was not large.[196]

Despite this approbation, however, it emerges that the book does in fact include a good many forged traditions. Shaykh ʿAbd al-Ḥaqq of Delhi says that the traditions it contains about Qazwīn—the city in Iran to which Ibn Māja was connected—are forged.[197]

4.4f THE SUNAN OF AL-DĀRAQUṬNĪ

Another *Sunan* work of importance was compiled by Abu'l-Ḥasan ʿAlī ibn ʿUmar (306/918–385/995), generally known as al-Dāraquṭnī on account of his residence in the Baghdad urban quarter known as Dār Quṭn.

Al-Dāraquṭnī rapidly acquired Arabic literature and the Islamic sciences, in particular the Traditions[198] and the Variant Readings *(qirā'āt)* of the Qur'ān. His book on the latter subject is acknowledged as the first work of its type, and its general plan is followed by most later authors. Among his students, who recognised his wide and critical knowledge of *ḥadīth*, were al-Ḥākim al-Nīsābūrī,[199] Abū Nuʿaym al-Iṣfahānī, whose book the *Ḥilya* is said to be the best work of Muslim hagiography,[200] Tammām of Rayy, and the traditionist ʿAbd al-Ghanī ibn Saʿīd. Al-Ḥākim, in particular, who narrates traditions from about 2,000 individuals,[201] remarked that he never met a scholar like Dāraquṭnī, whose knowledge proved encyclopedic whatever subject was broached.[202]

Almost every traditionist who came to Baghdad made a point of visiting him. Abū Manṣūr ibn al-Karkhī, while compiling his own *Musnad*, depended on Dāraquṭnī's help in identifying defective traditions; while Abū Bakr al-Barqānī based a work on *ḥadīth* on notes dictated by Dāraquṭnī to Abū Manṣūr.[203] He likewise rendered material help in the compilation of a *musnad* work by Ibn Hinzāba, the able and learned minister of the Ikhshīdī rulers of Egypt. Having learnt that this *Musnad* was being compiled, Dāraquṭnī travelled from Baghdad to Egypt, where he remained until the work was completed. Throughout this period, Ibn Hinzāba showed him immense deference and respect, and upon completion bestowed upon him rich rewards.[204]

Dāraquṭnī himself compiled many useful works on *ḥadīth* and related subjects.[205] For our purposes, the most useful of these is the *Sunan*, which was recognised as one of the most reliable *ḥadīth* collections—next in importance only to the Sound Six.[206] It was used by al-Baghawī (d.516/1122) as one of the chief sources for his influential *Maṣābīḥ al-Sunna*, which in turn formed the basis for the *Mishkāt al-Maṣābīḥ* of al-Tabrīzī.[207]

In his *Sunan*, Dāraquṭnī adduces traditions he considers reasonably authentic, supplementing them with *isnāds* and alternate versions. Of the very first *ḥadīth*, for instance, he gives five different versions, with five separate chains of authority, some of which he adjudges weak.[208] To some traditions he adds notes, in which he attempts to fix their degree of reliability and the identity of some of their narrators, and assesses their character and reliability. The number of weak traditions in his *Sunan* is fairly large; it is at any rate larger than in any of the *Sunan* works conventionally included in the canonical Six; and has hence not been included among them.

4.4g THE SUNAN OF AL-BAYHAQĪ

After Dāraquṭnī came Abū Bakr Aḥmad ibn al-Ḥusayn of Bayhaq, a group of villages near Nīsābūr. Bayhaqī was born in 384/458, and studied tradition under more than a hundred eminent traditionists of his time, including the above-named al-Ḥākim al-Nīsābūrī, of whom he became the most eminent pupil. Having excelled in the various Islamic sciences, Bayhaqī soon became a remarkably prolific author, producing several hundred books on *ḥadīth* and Shāfiʿī law, some of which are said to be unparallelled in the history of the literature.[209] His two *Sunan* works, of an unusual length and thoroughness, are particularly revered.[210] His reputation as a traditionist and a jurist attracted the attention of the learned of Nīsābūr, who invited him to their city and requested him to read one of his books to them. He died in the year 458/1065.[211]

4.4h THE SUNAN OF SAʿĪD IBN MANṢŪR

Less well-known, but earlier than all the *sunan* works so far mentioned, is the *Sunan* of Abū ʿUthmān Saʿīd ibn Manṣūr ibn Shuʿba (d.227/841).[212] Born at Merv and brought up in the city of Balkh, he wandered throughout a large part of the known world, finally settling at Mecca.

Ibn Manṣūr learnt traditions from a range of prominent experts including Imām Mālik, Ḥammād, Abū ʿAwāna and others, and in turn instructed another group of luminaries such as Muslim, Abū Daūd, and Aḥmad ibn Ḥanbal, all of whom spoke of his scholarship in terms of the highest veneration.[213] His *Sunan*, in which he is said to have had great confidence, appears to have been compiled towards the end of his life.[214] It contains a large number of traditions received from the Prophet through only three intermediaries.[215]

4.4i THE SUNAN OF ABŪ MUSLIM AL-KASHSHĪ

The *nisba* of Abū Muslim Ibrāhīm ibn ʿAbd Allāh al-Kashshī, who died in 282/895, has been explained as a reference either to his forefathers, or to his place of residence (a village called Kashsh located in Khuzistān).[216]

The latter interpretation seems to be supported by the fact of his prominent participation in a number of battles fought in the area.

After studying traditions under Abū ʿĀṣim al-Nabīl, Abū ʿAwāna and others, he visited Baghdad, where he delivered lectures on *ḥadīth*. These soon attracted a remarkably large number of students, so many, in fact, that his voice was not audible to them all, and seven men had to be appointed to repeat his words to various parts of the audience.[217] Like the work of Ibn Manṣūr, his work on *sunan* is said to have contained many reports transmitted through only three narrators.[218]

4.5 THE MUʿJAM WORKS

Although the *Muʿjam* works never acquired the esteem accorded the collections of *Sunan*, many were compiled and are still extensively used. The best known are the *Muʿjams* of Abu'l-Qāsim Sulaymān ibn Aḥmad ibn Ayyūb al-Ṭabarānī, who is generally known by his *nisba*.

Ṭabarānī was born in Tiberias, then a flourishing Muslim city, in 260/873. On his academic travels, he visited most of the important centres of learning in Syria, Egypt, the Ḥijāz, Iraq and Iran, acquiring traditions from about a thousand narrators. He finally settled at Iṣfahān in 290/902, where a pension was fixed for him.[219] There he lived a quiet and saintly life for 70 years, teaching *ḥadīth* and compiling a number of books on the subject, dying at last in 360/970 at the age of one hundred.

Of his works, a list of which is provided by al-Dhahabī,[220] the most important are his three *Muʿjams*. The largest of these, commonly known as *al-Muʿjam al-Kabīr* (*The Great Muʿjam*), is in fact a *Musnad* work.[221] It contains about 25,000 traditions which have been collected together under the names of the various Companions by whom they are narrated, the names being presented alphabetically.[222] The 'Medium' *Muʿjam* (*al-Muʿjam al-Awsaṭ*) is in six volumes, and contains the rare traditions narrated to the compiler by his teachers, whose names, together with their traditions, are set out, again alphabetically. The author took great pride in this work, which, although it contains a number of weak traditions, demonstrates his wide knowledge of the subject. Finally, there is Ṭabarānī's *Lesser Muʿjam* (*al-Muʿjam al-Ṣaghīr*), which, according to his own statement, was his first *Muʿjam*, and which contains only one tradition narrated by each of his teachers.[223]

Although these are the best-known works of the type, many other *muʿjam* works were compiled, some of which are listed by Ḥājī Khalīfa.[224]

4.6 THE TRADITIONAL RANKING OF ḤADĪTH COLLECTIONS

The works of *ḥadīth* literature have been grouped by the traditionists into four classes, according to their authority and importance.

I. To the first category belong the works which are considered the most reliable. These are (i) the *Muwaṭṭa'* of Mālik; (ii) *Ṣaḥīḥ al-Bukhārī*, and (iii) *Ṣaḥīḥ Muslim.*[225] The latter two of these works include almost all the traditions contained in the *Muwaṭṭa'*, and hence most major traditionists did not include it in the six canonical collections. These three books have been generally accepted as authentic since the lifetime of their authors: the *Muwaṭṭa'* was declared by Imām al-Shāfiʿī to be the most authentic book after the Qur'ān,[226] while the *Ṣaḥīḥ* of al-Bukhārī was, as described earlier, received by 90,000 students from the author himself, and was accepted as reliable by important traditionists of the time, such as Abu'l-Ḥasan ibn al-Qaṭṭān[227] and others.[228] The *Ṣaḥīḥ* of Muslim, too, did not take long to receive the general approbation of the traditionists.

II. To a second category belong the four *Sunan* works, which, together with the two *Ṣaḥīḥs*, are known as *al-Kutub al-Sitta* (the 'Six Books'). The tendency to associate some of the *Sunan* works with the two *Ṣaḥīḥs* appears, as Goldziher recognises,[229] to have begun sometime in the middle of the fourth century, when Saʿīd ibn al-Sakan[230] announced that the two *Ṣaḥīḥs* of al-Bukhārī and Muslim, and the two *Sunans* of Abū Daūd and al-Nasā'ī, were the foundations of Islam. After a period of time the *Jāmiʿ* of al-Tirmidhī was added to the above four books, and the five together were given the title of *al-Uṣūl al-Khamsa.*[231]

It is not easy to determine when the *Jāmiʿ* of al-Tirmidhī received the general recognition of the traditionists. Ibn Ḥazm, whose list of reliable *ḥadīth* works is still extant,[232] directed some criticism against the book, because it contained traditions related by the questionable figures of al-Maṣlūb and al-Kalbī.[233] But it is probable that the general recognition of al-Tirmidhī's *Jāmiʿ* preceded that of the work of Ibn Māja, which was added to the five books for the first time by Muḥammad ibn Ṭāhir, who died around the beginning of the sixth century (505/1113). None the less, it has been pointed out that throughout the sixth century pride of place was denied Ibn Māja by the traditionists. Razīn ibn Muʿāwiya (d.535/1140), in his compendium of the Six Books (*Tajrīd al-Ṣiḥāḥ al-Sitta*), Ibn al-Kharrāṭ (d.581/1185), and al-Ḥāzimī (d.584/1184) did not recognise the *Sunan* of

Ibn Māja as a canonical collection. It was just a century after the death of Muḥammad ibn Ṭāhir that the book was again recognised as one of the six collections of *ḥadīth*: by ʿAbd al-Ghanī (d.600/1203), in his *al-Kamāl fi maʿrifāt al-rijāl*, by Ibn al-Najjār (d.643/1245) in his *Rijāl al-Kutub al-Sitta*, by Najīb al-Dīn ibn Ṣayqal (d.672/1273) in his collection of traditions, by Shams al-Dīn ibn al-Jazarī (d.711/1311) in his work on the subject, and by al-Mizzī (d.742/1341) in his *Tuḥfa*. It may, therefore, be assumed that it was from the seventh century that the Six Books became generally recognised as the most reliable collections of *ḥadīth*.[234]

Among these six books, however, although the position of al-Bukhārī and Muslim was always supreme, the place of the *Sunan* of Ibn Māja always remained doubtful. Abū ʿUmar ʿUthmān ibn al-Ṣalāḥ (d.643/1245), and after him al-Nawawī (d.676/1277) and Ibn Khaldūn (d.808/1405) recognised only five books, and excluded Ibn Māja from this elite category.[235] The other works included in the Six have been accepted by all the leading scholars of the Muslim East and West, as the most authentic works, and were included in the various selections of the best ten collections of *ḥadīth*.

The following principles appear to have guided the traditionists in their choice of these six works:

(i) Their compilers had laid down certain clear principles for the selection and assessment of the *ḥadīth* they chose.
(ii) They mostly contained sound or fair traditions, and any weak material was usually indicated as such.
(iii) The material they contained had been carefully assessed and checked by the leading authorities in different parts of the Islamic world, and furnished with extensive commentaries which clarified their virtues and demerits.
(iv) They had been used as a basis for the establishment of legal and theological positions.

III. To a third category belong such *Musnads*, *Muṣannafs*, and other collections as had been compiled before or after the *Ṣaḥīḥs* of al-Bukhārī and Muslim, contained reliable as well as unreliable material, and had not been thoroughly examined by the traditionists or used as source texts in books of law and doctrine. Works of this type include the *Musnads* of ʿAbd ibn Ḥumayd and al-Ṭayālisī, and the *Muṣannaf* works of ʿAbd al-Razzāq, Ibn Abī Shayba, and others.

IV. A fourth category contains collections of *ḥadīth*s made by compilers who in the later period collected traditions which were not found in the collections of the early anthologists. Much such material was spurious. The *Musnad* of al-Khwārizmī may be included in this class.

V. According to some authorities,[236] there exists a fifth category of *ḥadīth* works, which contain such traditions as are declared by the Muslim doctors to be unreliable or definitely forged.

5

SOME SPECIAL FEATURES OF THE LITERATURE

EVERY type of literature develops certain features keyed to its particular nature and content, the character of the people who cultivate it, and the distinctive social, political or historical conditions in which it originates and flourishes. *Ḥadīth* literature is no exception to this rule. Its hero, the Prophet of Islam, and the movement launched by him, captured the attention of all the people of Arabia, friends and enemies alike. His actions and words were minutely observed: his opponents made use of them in their planning, while his supporters attempted to emulate him scrupulously in everything he did and said.

This intense interest did not cease upon his death; in fact, it intensified. When it was no longer possible to ask the Prophet about questions of religion, spiritual effort, and the moral life, the Muslims were obliged to turn either to the Qur'ān, which they had intact, or, where no detailed guidance was identified in the Sacred Book, to their recollections of the teachings of the Prophet. The capacious memories of the Arabs, which had already proved their worth in preserving the ancient poetry of their people, were now pressed into the service of the new revelation, to preserve for posterity the teachings of the Messenger who had 'brought them out of the shadows into light'. The present Chapter describes some of the more remarkable features of this endeavour.

5.1 THE ISNĀD SYSTEM

Each tradition found in every *ḥadīth* collection until the third century of the *hijra* includes the chain of the narrators who transmitted it—from the Prophet, a Companion, or a Follower, down to the compiler himself.

The traditionists called this chain an *isnād*, or 'authority'. They attached great importance to it, and considered it an indispensable part of every tradition. In order to ascertain the relative value of the various *isnāds* and their different classes, they produced a vast literature on the biographies of the transmitters and developed a system which was almost scientific in its precision and rigour.[1]

Recent European scholars have regularly attempted to discover the origins of the *isnād* system, but without reaching any very consistent results. Leone Caetani[2] and Joseph Horovitz[3] were the first European orientalists to address this problem.[4] Caetani, writing in an age of chauvinism, was convinced that the *isnād* could not have originated among the Arabs. The wild desolation of the Arabian steppe, and the restive character of the primitive, ignorant, uncivilised and Semitic Arabs were not congenial to the development of a rigorous scholarly tradition.[5] But even if the theory of Caetani, based squarely on prejudice rather than fact, were acceptable, it would only prove that the system of *isnād* did not originate with the Arabs. From whom, then, did it emanate? The Italian orientalist does not give an example of its use by any other people.

David Margoliouth, in his series of lectures on the Arab historians, only remarks, *en passant*, that the Greeks and Romans rarely used any thing akin to the *isnād* system.[6]

Horovitz goes slightly further. Giving several instances from Jewish literature, he successfully demonstrates that the *isnād* was known to the Jews before the Arabs. He also endeavours to show that its use in Jewish literature can be traced back 'as early as the Mosaic period, and by Talmudic times its chain assumed enormous length, the subject-matter being of the most varied nature.'[7]

The main conclusions, however, of Horovitz's minute researches, had already been dealt with by the widely-read Ibn Ḥazm of Spain (364–456/994–1064).[8] Describing in detail the various forms of transmission from the Prophet to later generations, he identifies six categories of transmission:

(i) Transmission from the Prophet to future generations through an overwhelming number of persons, Muslims and non-Muslims of every generation, by parallel narration, without any difference of opinion between them.
(ii) Unanimous transmission by all learned Muslims of every generation since the time of the Prophet.
(iii) Transmission from the Prophet by reliable persons of known identity and established reliability of every generation, each of them stating the name

of his authority.

(iv) Transmission by any one of the three classes of transmitters just mentioned, not from the Prophet, but from a person belonging to the generation following him, the earliest transmitter being silent about the source of his information.

(v) Transmission by any of the various classes of persons mentioned above, from the Prophet himself, but having in the chain of narrators a person who is known either to be a liar, or careless in his statements, or whose reliability has been questioned.

(vi) Transmission by a chain of transmitters similar to that of the first three classes, but stopping either at a Companion or a Follower, or at any Imām after them, who did not make any reference to the Prophet in his statement.

After dealing with these classes of transmission, some of which overlap with each other to some extent, Ibn Ḥazm makes some remarks about their use by the Christians and the Jews. He states that the first three classes of transmission are entirely absent from Christian as well as Jewish literature. According to him, these two religions are based on the Torah and the New Testament; and the *isnād* of the former does not go back to Moses, but rather stops short of him by many generations, while the latter is ultimately based on the testimony of five persons, the reliability, and even the identity, of whom has been questioned. The first three classes of *isnād*, Ibn Ḥazm says, are a unique feature of Islamic literature. The last three classes, however, are, according to him, found in Christian as well as in Jewish literature. The first (iv above) is particularly frequent in Jewish literature; whereas only one example of it (viz. the law relating to the impermissibility of divorce) is to be found in Christian literature. The last two classes of *isnād*, he observes, are found abundantly among the Christians and the Jews. He also cites certain details of the differences between the forms of transmission found in Islamic literature, and those used by the Christians and the Jews.

It is interesting to note further that an *isnād* system was used by the Indians long before Islam.[9] An occasional use, for instance, can be found in ancient Hindu, Buddhist and Jain literature. In the great epic, the *Mahabharata*, we read: 'Vysda composed it, Ganesa served as a scribe, and the work was handed down by Vaisampayana, who communicated it to the king Janamejaya. Sauti, who was present at the time, heard it and narrated it to the assembly of sages.'[10] The *Purāṇas* also contain some short *isnāds* of this type. The *Sutras* (exegetical works on Vedic literature) contain brief chains mentioning some of the transmitters through whom they have been handed down. In the *Sānkhāyana Āraṇyaka*[11] and the *Brhada-āraṇyaka* Upanishad[12] long lines of successive teachers of the text are given. In the first case, we get a list of eighteen teachers, while in the latter, the longest of several lists contains twenty-seven names.

In early Buddhist literature, no chain of authorities is attached. The text is almost always introduced with the common formula: 'Thus I heard, once the lord sojourned at...'.[13] But in the later literature, long chains of transmitters are frequent—particularly in such Sanskrit-Buddhist texts as are preserved in Tibetan translation. The colophon of the *Sadanga-yoga*, for example, contains the following sequential chain of narrators:

> Buddha Vajradhara: Nagarjuna: Nagabodhi: Aryadeva: Chandrakirti: Sakyaraksita: Ratnamitra: Dharmabhadra: Gunamati: Manjusrijnana: Amoghasri: Viramati: Vijayakirti: Varaprajnadhar-mabhadra: Sribhadra: Dharmapala: Sakyadhraja: Vagisvarakirti: Ratnakirti: Vanaratna: Dharmabuddhi.

We are also told that the last mentioned of these transmitters, who came from Eastern India, translated the text from Sanskrit into Tibetan, by order of the master of Ron, with the assistance of a Tibetan scholar from Stag-tshan (Tibet).[14]

However this may be, a question more important than the originality of the *isnād* system is that of determining the time when it first began to be applied to *ḥadīth*. Caetani again holds that al-Zuhrī (d.124/741) was the first to do this, and that it was further developed by his pupils, including Mūsā ibn ʿUqba (d.141/757) and Ibn Isḥāq (d.151/678). According to Caetani, then, the institution was first developed in Islam during the first half of the second century AH.[15] On the other hand, Horovitz is of the opinion that the first appearance of *isnāds* was not later than the last third of the first Muslim century.[16] After adducing a series of facts to demonstrate this theory, he says: 'Isnād in its primitive form was then—somewhere about the year 75AH—already established, and one has no right, merely because it appears only incidentally in the letters, to deny to ʿUrwa[17] without further consideration, those *aḥādīth* supplied with statements of authorities for which he stands as sponsor.... Isnād was, indeed, already customary in his [Urwa's] time, but it was not yet an absolute necessity.'[18]

Joseph Schacht, however, contests this judgement, and suggests that there is no reason to suppose that the regular practice of using *isnāds* is older than the beginning of the second century AH.[19] Although he quotes the well-known remark of Ibn Sīrīn about the beginning of the *isnād* institution: 'People used not to ask about *isnāds*, but when the civil war (*fitna*) occurred, they began to say: "Name your narrators!"'[20] he interprets the word *fitna* as a reference to the civil war which began with the killing of the Umayyad caliph Walīd ibn Yazīd in 126AH.[21] Taking into consideration the date of Ibn Sīrīn's death (110AH), Schacht regards the remark attributed to him as spurious. Yet Robson disagrees, pointing out that his interpretation of the term *fitna* here is arbitrary: it could refer to almost any of the earlier periods of confusion, and is most likely to denote the struggle between ʿAlī and Muʿāwiya.[22] Robson goes on to conclude that it is during the middle of the first century of Islam that one could first expect to discern anything resembling an *isnād*.[23] He is followed in this verdict by Abbott, who presents a substantial body of evidence, backed up with recently unearthed papyrus material, to show that *isnāds* were in use at this time.[24]

This debate among Western scholars does little more than confirm that the problem of assigning a definite date to the first appearance of the *isnād* defies easy resolution. There is no doubt, none the less, that the period fixed for this by Horovitz, Robson and Abbott is very close to what is claimed by the early traditionists themselves. Ibn Sīrīn, in the account disputed by Schacht, is reported to have said that at first, people did not enquire about *isnāds*, but since the Sedition (*fitna*), they began to ask for it. The *fitna* here is claimed by Muslims (and, as we have seen, Robson) to refer to the civil war between ʿAlī and Muʿāwiya, which erupted in the year 35AH; an event which is conventionally referred to by this term. But there are other indications, which, if genuine, would suggest an even earlier provenance. ʿAlī himself is reported to have advised students: 'When you write down a narration, write it with the *isnād*.'[25] We likewise find reports of Abū Ayyūb al-Anṣārī, himself a Companion, transmitting *ḥadīth*s from the Prophet not directly but via Abū Hurayra.[26] And, as Azami has pointed out, it was only natural that the Companions,

> in informing their colleagues, would have used sentences like 'The Prophet did so and so' or 'The Prophet said so and so'. It is also natural that anyone gaining information at second-hand, when reporting the incident to a third man, would disclose his sources of information and give a full account of the incident.[27]

From these facts, and from the intense caution with which the important Companions treated the memory of the Prophet, it may legitimately be inferred that the system of *isnād* was considered a necessary part of *ḥadīth* well before the century was out.

But whenever it originated, there is no doubt that having adopted the system, the Muslims came to consider the *isnād* as an indispensable part of the *ḥadīth*s. They developed it, and gave it a firm foundation by introducing the chronological method, assembling biographies of the transmitters, and by establishing various canons for determining the value of its different classes. The ancient Indians, so far as is known, never made any attempt at a rigorous and consistent treatment of the *isnād*, nor are they known to have developed the chronological method. Neither does the early literature of the Jews reveal any use of the chronological method, something which renders their '*isnāds*' valueless. 'In the Talmudic literature', says Professor Horovitz, 'there is no idea of chronological method, and the oldest extant work attempting such an arrangement was composed after 885 AD—more than a century later than the earliest Islamic work on *isnād*-critique.' 'From this fact,' he goes on, 'and from the fact that the important Jewish works [of this period] had been composed in the Islamic dominions, it may be inferred that this historical interest was due to the Islamic influence.'[28]

The Muslims not only gave a scientific form and basis to the system of *isnād*, but also tried to make a comparative study of the various *isnāds* deployed in the literature, with a view to establishing their relative value. It is said that Aḥmad ibn Ḥanbal, Ibn Maʿīn, and Ibn al-Madīnī once gathered together with some other traditionists and debated which was the most authentic of all *isnāds*. One said that it was the *isnād* Shuʿba-Qatāda-Saʿīd-ʿAmir-Umm Salāma. Ibn al-Madīnī held that it was Ibn ʿAwn- Muḥammad-ʿUbayda-ʿAlī. Ibn Ḥanbal declared that it was al-Zuhrī-Sālim-Ibn ʿUmar.[29] Al-Bukhārī, however, was of the opinion that the best *isnād* was Mālik-Nafiʿ-Ibn ʿUmar. This *isnād* later prolonged itself through the names of al-Shāfiʿī and Ibn Ḥanbal, making it one long chain extending from Imām Aḥmad up to Ibn ʿUmar. This *isnād* was dubbed the 'Golden Chain'.[30]

Ibn Maʿīn, however, considered ʿUbayd Allāh-Ibn ʿUmar-Qāsim-ʿĀ'isha to be the best *isnād*, and called this a 'chain of pure gold'.[31] Many other traditionists preferred other chains. The consensus among later traditionists, however, was that it is impossible to qualify any *isnād* as the best of all. The judgement of the various authorities must refer to the traditions accepted on the authority of a particular Companion or Follower, or to the traditionists of a particular place.[32]

Once it had been introduced into the literature, the *isnād* system was not only continued for four centuries or more,[33] but was also applied to the *ḥadīth* collections themselves and on works on the other Islamic disciplines. Partly in order to reduce the risk of forgery and interpolation, every teacher of every book on *ḥadīth* or a related subject at every period of the history of the literature, gave his students the names of the teachers via whom he had received it from its original author, each of them stating that he read the whole, or a part of it (which had to be specified), with his own teacher. The certificates of competency of students to teach from a book of *ḥadīth* granted them by their teachers contain not only the statement of the fact that they read it with them, but also the name of their own teachers of the book, and other teachers of their teachers up to its author. Such certificates, called *ijāza*, are the essential qualification of an authentic Muslim scholar.

The practice of retaining the *isnāds* of important books must have been introduced at the time the books themselves were compiled. Dr. Ṣalāḥ al-Dīn al-Munajjid, the world's leading authority on the *ijāza* institution, has traced it back to the fourth century, giving an interesting example.[34] Here are a few other instances of books with their own *isnāds*, belonging to an even earlier period.

(i) A copy of a collection of *ḥadīth*s (said to be *Ṣaḥīḥ Muslim,* part XIII) dated 368AH, and preserved in the Municipal Library, Alexandria (no.836B).
(ii) A copy of the *Kitāb Gharīb al-ḥadīth* by Abū ʿUbayd al-Qāsim ibn Sallām (154–223/770–837), copied at Damascus in 319AH, and the reading of which has been traced back to the author in whose presence the original manuscript was read—a fact recorded on the authority of Abū Sulaymān Muḥammad ibn Manṣūr al-Balkhī.[35]
(iii) The most important of all such manuscripts is the fragment of a book on *maghāzī* by Wahb ibn Munabbih. It is preserved among the Schott-Reinhardt Papyri, and has been described by C. H. Becker.[36] It is dated Dhu'l-Qaʿda 229, July 844), and bears on its top the *isnād* up to its author.

The practice of specifying the *isnād* was of immense value in preserving the integrity of books in an age in which printing was unknown, and the creation of spurious and distorted works was a relatively straightforward task. In modern times, however, with the arrival of the printing press and the consequent proliferation of identical copies, it has perhaps been rendered less necessary. Human nature, however, is conservative, and the old orthodox norms still survive. No scholar, however competent, is supposed to have the right to teach a *ḥadīth* work for which he has not received the necessary permission from a competent teacher, who must, moreover, himself have been authorised by his own teacher. But this institution, while academically less indispensable than it used to be, still has the merit of maintaining the Islamic disciplines as organic and continuing traditions which represent a living link to the past.

According to the classical traditionists, the *isnāds* of books had to be recorded on their manuscripts also. They held that it was advisable for students to write on their copies of a book, after the Name of God (the *basmala*), the names of their teachers together with their *kunya* and their *nisba*, and the names of the teachers of their teachers right back to the author of the book. Above the *basmala*, or on the first page of the manuscript, or at any other prominent place in it, such as the margin, should be inscribed the names of the other students who read the book in the same class together with the owner of the manuscript, and the places and dates at which the various parts of it were read.[37]

These notes are found on the generality of the manuscripts which are still preserved in the world's great libraries. The manuscripts of the *Musnad* of al-Ṭayālisī,[38] of the *Sunan* of al-Dārimī,[39] of *al-Mashīkha maʿ al-Takhrīj*,[40] of the *Kitāb al-Kifāya*,[41] of the four volumes of the *Tārīkh Dimashq*,[42] and of many other *ḥadīth* works, in the O. P. Library of Bankipore; and the manuscripts of the *Sunan* of Abū Daūd[43] in the State Library at Berlin, are only a few instances of this; an enormous number of other manuscripts of this type may be seen in the other libraries containing Islamic material scattered around the globe. Of course, there are also manuscripts which contained only a few or even none of the detailed notes mentioned above. These tend to be defective manuscripts from which the parts, usually at the beginning, which contain these notes have been lost; alternatively, they are low-grade manuscripts copied by common scribes for the use of laymen, rather than being destined for specialists in the subject.

This practice appears to have been current among the traditionists since the second century of the *hijra*. Ḥafṣ ibn Ghiyāth (d.194/809), the well-known judge, is said to have decided a case on the basis of this usage. Al-Fuḍayl ibn ʿIyāḍ (d.187/802), the well-known traditionist and Sufi, is said to have forbidden the traditionists from refusing to issue students with their certificates when they deserved them. Al-Zuhrī (d.124/741) is also credited with this view.[44]

This scholarly practice, which has proved of immense value in enabling us to construct an image of the early *ḥadīth* science and the milieu in which it flourished, seems to be unique in the world's literary history, just as the Islamic *ḥadīth*s themselves are unique in employing a thorough and systematic method of source identification. Greek, Latin, Hebrew and Syriac manuscripts rarely if ever supply us with such a wealth of information about a book's provenance and use.

The *isnād* system, while originating in connection with the *ḥadīth* literature, was in due course extended by the Arab authors to many other genres, including geography, history, and prose fiction.[45] 'There are works', says Margoliouth,

> of which the subject-matter is so frivolous that one marvels at the trouble taken by the author to record the name of each transmitter and the date and place at which he heard the narrative; an example is the *Maṣāriᶜ al-ᶜUshshāq* of al-Sarrāj, a collection of cases wherein men and women are supposed to have died of love, where the author records with minute accuracy the date at which he heard the story and gives similar details of the transmitters.[46]

5.2 ACADEMIC PROCEDURES

The imperative of preserving the legacy of the Prophet, whose teachings and example underpinned the Islamic way of life, obliged the *ḥadīth* scholars to be almost obsessively accurate. There were certainly numerous forgers of *ḥadīth*; but these remained marginal and despised, and had little to do with the literature as such. Those who were mainly responsible for its development strove to be as exact as possible. While some remained faithful only to the message presented in a *ḥadīth*, without attaching the highest importance to the exact words used, others tried to be faithful to the words as well as the ideas. They reproduced each word and letter, energetically avoiding the least deviation from what they themselves had received. Al-Khaṭīb al-Baghdādī, in several chapters of his *Kitāb al-Kifāya*, shows how exact some traditionists had been with regard to every word and letter in a *ḥadīth*.[47] Ibn ᶜUmar, for instance, did not like to change the order of words in a phrase even when it did not affect the meaning in the slightest. Mālik ibn Anas tried to be exact about each and every letter, while Ibn Sīrīn did not approve of making corrections to a *ḥadīth* even in cases where it was certain that a reporter had made an error.[48]

The care and exactitude of the leading traditionists is further illustrated by the principles which they established for the method of acquiring knowledge, and the associated duties of teachers and students. These principles had been discussed in detail since the second Islamic century, and are explained in the various works on the *ḥadīth* sciences (*ᶜulūm al-ḥadīth*).

The first problem in the theory of *ḥadīth* instruction is that of the age at which it may be commenced. The traditionists of Kūfa fixed this at the age of twenty; those of Baṣra, the age of ten; and those of Syria, the age of thirty. According to a majority of the later traditionists, however, the study of *ḥadīth* may be commenced at the age of five.[49]

In any case, the study of *ḥadīth* should be preceded by that of Arabic grammar and language, so that mistakes arising from pure linguistic ignorance could be detected or avoided.[50] ʿAbd Allāh ibn al-Mubārak, the famous traditionist of Merv, spent more money on learning the Arabic language than on traditions, attaching more importance to the former than the latter, and asking the students of *ḥadīth* to spend twice as long on Arabic studies than on *ḥadīth*. Ḥammād ibn Salama is said to have remarked that he who takes to *ḥadīth* without knowing grammar is like an ass which carries a sack without corn. Al-Aṣmaʿī held that someone who studied *ḥadīth* without learning grammar was to be categorised with the forgers of *ḥadīth*;[51] and similar remarks are credited to Shuʿba and al-ʿAbbās ibn al-Mughīra.[52] Sībawayh, the great grammarian, took to the study of grammar only because Ḥammād ibn Salama had pointed out that he had made a mistake over the text of a *ḥadīth*.[53]

Having learnt these preliminary subjects, the student should purge his mind of all worldly considerations. He should nurture good character, seek the help of God in all his efforts, and strain every nerve towards the acquisition of knowledge, not for his own aggrandisement, but in order to benefit the community. He should begin his study with the best teachers of his town, and carry it on by making journeys to other centres of academic excellence, and by acquiring the knowledge of the greatest exponents of the field. He should not, however, concern himself with gathering the greatest possible number of *ḥadīth*s, but should instead hear and write them down, understand them fully, be aware of their strength or weakness, their theological importance and implications, the proper significance of the words used in them, and the character of those through whom they have been handed down.

The following account, by Qāḍī ʿIyāḍ of Ceuta (d.544/1149), gives an interesting portrait of the decorum and sobriety which characterised the traditional *ḥadīth* lesson:

> One of the rights of the scholar is that you should not be persistent when questioning him, nor gruff when answering him. Neither be importune if he is tired, nor catch hold of his robe when he rises to depart. Do not point to him, or spread abroad some private information about him, or speak ill of anyone in his presence. Do not seek out his failings; when he slips, wait for him to recover and accept his apology. You must revere and esteem him, for the sake of God. Do not walk in front of him. If he needs anything, you should make haste to serve him before the others. You should not find his long company tedious, for he is like a date-palm that you are sitting beneath, waiting for a windfall. When you arrive, greet him in particular,

> and all who are present. All this should be for the sake of God; for a learned man receives more reward from God than someone who fasts, prays, and fights in God's path, and when he dies, a hole appears in Islam which remains until the Day of Judgement, unless it be filled by a successor who is his like. The seeker of knowledge, moreover, is accompanied by the Angels of Heaven.[54]

Of the technical aspects of learning *ḥadīth*, the traditionists have mentioned the following eight forms of instruction:

I *Samāʿ*. Under this procedure, the student attends the lectures of a traditionist, which may take the form of a simple narration of the traditions, or be accompanied by their dictation (*imlā'*), either from memory or from a book.[55]

II *Qirā'a*. Here the student reads to the traditionist the traditions which have been narrated or compiled by the latter. Alternatively, one may hear the traditions while they are recited by another student to a traditionist—on condition that he is attentive to what is recited, or compares his own copy to what is being recited.[56]

III *Ijāza*. This is to obtain the permission of a scholar to narrate to others the traditions compiled by him. This may be granted in different ways, some of which are recognised by the majority as valid, while others are rejected.[57]

IV *Munāwala*. This is to obtain the compilation of a tradition together with his permission to narrate its contents to others; a procedure recognised as valid by most authorities. If it takes place without his permission, most scholars regard it as unsound.[58]

V *Mukātaba*. This is to receive certain written traditions from a scholar, either in person or by correspondence, with or without his permission to narrate them to others.[59]

VI *Iʿlām al-Rāwī*. The declaration of a traditionist to a student that the former received certain specified traditions or books from a specified authority, without giving the student permission to narrate the material concerned.[60]

VII *Waṣīya*. To obtain the works of a traditionist by his will at the time of his death.[61]

VIII *Wijāda*. To find certain traditions in a book, perhaps after a traditionist's death, without receiving them with any recognised authority.[62]

The first two of these methods are recognised by the traditionists as the preferable techniques for the transmission of knowledge. The rest are dismissed as invalid by some, and accepted on various conditions by others.

None the less, the student who gains his knowledge of *ḥadīth* by any one or more of the above methods will not be recognised as a traditionist unless he also acquires the necessary information about the life and character of the narrators, and the degrees of the reliability of the various traditions, and other connected matters. Such of them as combine all these and other qualities are known as *muḥaddith*, or *ḥāfiẓ*, according to the degree of perfection they have obtained.[63]

Students of *ḥadīth* who have mastered the above conditions and information, as well as ancillary subjects, may deliver lectures on the subject, once, twice, or three times a week, if their intention is exclusively the propagation of knowledge. Before going to their lectures, they should bathe, perform their ablutions, and put on clean, pure garments. They should locate themselves in a prominent and elevated place, and deliver lectures while standing. They should keep perfect order during their lectures, and appoint assistants to repeat their words to students sitting at a distance.

Lectures should be preceded by recitations from the Qur'ān, praises of God, and prayers for His Prophet, the fountainhead of knowledge. After this, the lecturer should recite and dictate traditions, narrating one tradition from each of his teachers, giving preference to the short ones which have theological or legal importance, specifying all their narrators and the method by which he received them, introducing them with expressions particularly suited to the traditions received by the different methods. If his teacher had read out the traditions to him, he should begin with the word *ḥaddathanā* ('he related to us'), or *akhbaranā* ('he informed us'), and so on, according to the standard convention. If he or any of his fellow-students read out the traditions to his teacher who heard it, he should begin with the words *qara'tu ʿalā* ('I read out to'), or *quri'a ʿalayhi wa-anā asmaʿ* ('it was read out to him, while I heard'). In the case of the *ijāza*, he should begin by saying, 'I found it in the handwriting of such-and-such a person', or 'I found it in his book' or 'in his own handwriting', and so on.

Lectures may be delivered either from memory—which is preferable—or from books, on condition that these be written either by the lecturer himself, or any other person of reliable character; and provided further that the reliability of the manuscripts is absolutely proved to the lecturer. In case the lecturer finds any discrepancy between the contents of the manuscript and what he remembers, or between his own version of a tradition and that of other traditionists, he should point this out to his students. In case the lecturer narrates certain traditions in a *non-verbatim* form, he must be well-versed in the subject, so that he may be certain that the change in expression would cause no change in his meaning. He should also add at the end of every *ḥadīth* such words as might show that the words used in it were his own. In case he finds any mistake in the text of a *ḥadīth*, he should narrate it first in its corrected form, and then specify the form in which it was related to him. If he has received a tradition from more than one narrator, in different words conveying the same idea, he should narrate it, giving the name of every narrator and pointing out that the expressions used were by certain narrators, whom he should also name. In case he has received a part of a tradition from one narrator, and another part from another, he should point this out to his students. If there had been any negligence on the part of the lecturer when he received a tradition, which might have affected his knowledge, he should not fail to bring such negligence to the attention of his audience. In short, it is a duty of the *ḥadīth* lecturer to convey the material to his students exactly as he himself received it, and to add his own comments on it, in such words as could not be mistaken for a part of the tradition. He is not permitted to make the least alteration, even, for instance, by changing the phrase *Rasūl Allāh* ('the Messenger of God') into *Nabī Allāh* ('the Prophet of God'). He should finish his discourse by relating instructive and attractive, historical and humorous stories which encourage his hearers towards faith, righteousness, kindness, and good manners.[64]

Although the emphasis in Islamic culture has always been on carefully memorised information, for 'he who has not memorised a fact, does not know it', the traditionists have also tried to maintain a comparable level of care and exactitude in writing their material down. For this they established a range of principles and conditions, to eliminate as far as possible the possibility of mistaken information being transmitted by the writers and readers of *ḥadīth*.

Students of *ḥadīth* who choose to record them in writing must use clear, distinct and bold letters, each letter being so written as not to be liable to confusion with any other letter. Dots of pointed letters are to be correctly placed, and those without them are to be made distinct with additional signs (which are thoroughly discussed in the works of *ʿulūm al-ḥadīth*). Special attention is to be paid to rare and archaic words and proper names, which in addition to the text are to be noted on the margin in distinct separate letters. Such expressions as ʿAbd Allāh should be completely written on one and the same line. The various traditions are to be separated from one another by small circles in which dots may be put after the manuscript has been compared with its original copy. The soundness of sound traditions, and the defects of defective ones, are to be indicated by special signs. If, for instance, the chain of authority of a tradition is broken, or if any part of it contains any obvious or hidden defect, these points should be clearly marked.

Once the manuscript is completed, it should be carefully compared with the original; and all mistakes of commission and omission rectified. All omissions should be put down on the right hand margin, to which a line should be drawn from the word in the text after which the missing part should fall. The mistakes of commission should be either struck out or erased. It is, however, preferable to pen through them in such a way as to keep them legible, while showing that they are deleted.

In the text of his manuscript, the writer should always follow a particular version of a book or individual tradition. Differences in other versions and associated criticism may be noted clearly in the margin.

Students who write down traditions at the dictation of their teachers are required to be extremely vigilant and precise in their writing, and in putting dots wherever they might be necessary. They are also obliged to put down in a prominent part of the manuscript the names of their teachers together with other particulars about them, the names of all the fellow-students who attended these lectures, and the time and place when and where the discourses were delivered.[65]

The above are only the more important of the detailed requirements for the learning, teaching and recording of traditions, which have been discussed by the specialists since the second century of the *hijra*, with the most exhaustive, minute details, which remind us yet again of the care and precision which they sought to maintain at every stage of the process of the transmission of *ḥadīth*.

5.3 SCHOLARS AND THE STATE

While almost all of Arabic literature developed under the encouraging patronage of the caliphs and their courtiers, so that almost every literary figure 'basked in the sunshine of their generosity', the scholars of *ḥadīth* were generally either ill-treated by those who reigned in the name of the Islamic religion, or, in their pious stoicism, were given to rejecting and refusing favours if these were ever offered to them. None of the compilers of the important and authoritative collections of *ḥadīth* received any post, purse or privilege from the caliphs or their officials. Almost the whole of the orthodox mainstream of this literature evolved as a result of the spontaneous religious enthusiasm of the Muslims, and paid little attention to the caliphs and their representatives.

Throughout the reign of the Umayyads (with the exception of the devout rule of ʿUmar ibn ʿAbd al-ʿAzīz, who did assist in the *ḥadīth* compilation process), the strict traditionists had been either hostile or neutral towards the state. Ibn ʿUmar, ʿAbd Allāh ibn ʿAmr, Ibn ʿAbbās, Ibn Sīrīn, Ibn al-Musayyib, al-Ḥasan al-Baṣrī, Sufyān al-Thawrī, and other pivotal traditionists, had all adopted this attitude. 'Since the death of Saʿīd', says Goldziher, 'the pious traditionists disliked the state of affairs under this rule. They became indifferent to the tyrannical government, and passively resisted it.' 'In return', he adds, 'they were hated and despised by the ruling circles.'[66] These austere and devout men and women believed and declared that association with the rulers was a source of sin.[67]

There were other early traditionists, however, who did enjoy some degree of patronage from the Umayyad regime, and often refused to consider it as sinful to help the rulers of the day. Most of them did not, however, overstep certain limits, nor did they forge traditions in their favour. Among this type may be included traditionists such as ʿUrwa ibn al-Zubayr, Rajā' ibn Ḥayawayh, and Muḥammad ibn Muslim al-Zuhrī, all of whom enjoyed limited patronage from the caliphs, but at the same time retained their academic independance.[68] Some traditionists criticised them for this co-operation, but their veracity and reliability have never been seriously questioned by any of them. For instance, while Goldziher claimed that al-Zuhrī was a forger of traditions in favour of the Umayyads,[69] Horovitz has shown that this claim is false and tendentious.[70] In fact, al-Zuhrī at times enraged some of the caliphs by quoting traditions against their interests, and sticking to these traditions in spite of the fury of his patrons.[71] It is none the less true, however, that some supporters of the Umayyads did overstep the limits of proper co-operation: ʿAwāna ibn al-Ḥakam, for instance, forged and tried to propagate traditions in their favour. Such activities, however, were easily detected by their more pious contemporaries.

During the reign of the Abbasid caliphs, who tried to win over the pious Muslims by adhering to an outward show of religious commitment, the attitude of the various classes of traditionists towards the state continued to be largely unchanged, despite the fact that this period witnessed the evolution of the great achievements of the science of *ḥadīth*. Some traditionists, such as Mālik ibn Anas and Aḥmad ibn Ḥanbal suffered considerably under the Abbasid order.[72] Others, such as al-Bukhārī, were annoyed by officials.[73] Imām Muslim was wholly indifferent to their blandishments. In fact, none of the compilers of the important *ḥadīth* anthologies received or expected any help or encouragement from these caliphs.

6

THE BIOGRAPHICAL DICTIONARIES

WE have seen that every *ḥadīth* consists of two parts: the *isnād* (the chain of its transmitters), and the *matn* (text). Each of these two parts is of equal importance to the traditionist. The latter, as the report of an act or statement of the Prophet, helps to build up a picture of his teachings and thus forms a basis for Muslim beliefs and rites; while the former represents the 'credentials' of the latter. The traditionists, therefore, treat and consider traditions with one and the same *isnād* and different texts, as well as traditions with identical texts and differing *isnāds*, as entirely independent traditions.

To check the *isnād* it is essential to know the life and career as well as the character and scholarship of all the individuals named. And in order to understand the exact significance of the *matn*, and to test its soundness, it is necessary to know the meaning of the various expressions it contains, especially those which appear rare or obsolete, and also to learn its relation to the *matn* of other traditions, some of which may be either corroborated or contradicted by it.

The Muslim community has thus developed several ancillary branches of literature, which are summarised in famous works such as those of Abū Muḥammad al-Rāmhurmuzī (d.360/970), Abū Nuʿaym al-Iṣfahānī (d.430/1038), al-Khaṭīb al-Baghdādī (d.403/1012), al-Ḥākim al-Nīsābūrī (d.405/1014), Ibn al-Ṣalāḥ (d.643/1245), and many others. The number of such ancillary sciences is conventionally put at a hundred, and each of them is said to be important enough to warrant treatment as an independant branch of knowledge.[1] Some are concerned only with the *isnād* of the traditions; others relate to the *matn*, while still others deal with both together. We propose here to deal with only two of these disciplines, and briefly discuss their evolution and influence on the literature.

6.1 ASMĀ' AL-RIJĀL

(Biography and Criticism of *ḥadīth* Narrators.)

One of the richest and most important branches of the literature deals with the biography of *ḥadīth* narrators. Under the rubric of this science are included all the works which deal with (a) the chronology; (b) the biography; (c) the criticism of the narrators of traditions or of any class of narrators, or with any such aspect of their life as may help to determine their identity and reliability.

A. *Chronology.*

The consideration of chronology commenced and developed at a comparatively early date; although opinions differ as to the exact time when Muslims first began to employ it. According to some authorities, dates were introduced into official correspondance by the Prophet himself in the fifth year of the *hijra*, when a treaty was concluded between him and the people of Najrān.[2] But it is more generally held that this was done by ʿUmar ibn al-Khaṭṭāb, acting on the unanimous advice of a congregation of important Muslims, in the sixteenth or seventeenth year of the *hijra*.[3] The same far-sighted caliph followed a chronological principle in the award of military pensions (*dīwān*) to the various groups of Muslims according to their priority in accepting the faith, a principle which was already accepted by the Community as a basis of great distinction. Its use assumed greater importance on account of the need to interpret the historical verses of the Qur'ān, and of the determination of the dates of revelation of the legal verses, in order to determine which had been abrogated and which remained in force.

The Muslims followed the lunar calendar, which had been adopted by the Arabs long before the advent of Islam. Originally, however, the Meccans had followed a solar calendar, as is evident from their division of the year according to seasons, and from the names of some of the months.[4]

In *ḥadīth* science, chronology was an important expedient. 'Whenever you have a doubt about the veracity of a narrator,' remarks Ḥafṣ ibn Ghiyāth (d.160/776), 'test him by means of the years' (i.e. his birth and death dates). Sufyān al-Thawrī is said to have declared: 'When the narrators forged traditions, we used the *tārīkh* (chronology) against them'.[5] Ḥassān ibn Ziyād observed, 'We never used against the forgers any device more effective than the *tārīkh*.'[6]

It is clear, then, that chronology had been used as early as the second century in order to test the statements made by narrators. Some examples of this are cited by Imām Muslim in the introduction to his *Ṣaḥīḥ*; others are plentifully found in the works of *asmā' al-rijāl.*

B. *Biography.*

The composition of biographical works properly equipped with chronological information began before the end of the first century of the *hijra.*

Horovitz has shown that Abān (d. between 86 and 105AH), the son of the caliph ʿUthmān; ʿUrwa ibn al-Zubayr (26–94/646–712); and Shurayḥ (who is said to have been born in 20AH, and lived more than 100 years) had collected a good deal of material relating to the biography of the Prophet. Soon after them, Wahb ibn Munabbih wrote a book on *Maghāzī*, a fragment of which is preserved at Heidelberg.[7] Wahb was followed by numerous biographers of the Prophet during the second and third centuries. The fragment, and the texts of extant biographies, reveal a thorough use of the chronological system by their authors.

C. *Criticism of Narrators.*

A general critical appraisal of the reliability of the narrators, based on knowledge of their life and character, as an aid to determining the veracity of *ḥadīth* reports, seems to have been customary before the period when the *isnād* became long enough to admit the application of the chronological method. Ibn ʿAdī (d.365/975), in the introduction to his book *al-Kāmil fī ḍuʿafā' al-rijāl*, gives a general survey of the development of narrator criticism from its beginnings down to his own time. According to him, narrators were criticised and assessed by Ibn ʿAbbās, ʿUbāda ibn al-Ṣāmit, and Anas (all Companions); and by al-Shaʿbī, Ibn Sīrīn and Ibn al-Musayyib (who were Successors). It did not, however, become common until the next generation, for the simple reason that the events narrated were recent, and the narrators were for the most part reliable. In the next generation, when the narrators of doubtful veracity grew in number, narrator criticism grew in importance. About the middle of the second century, therefore, we find al-Aʿmash, Shuʿba and Mālik criticising a large number of narrators, declaring some to be weak or unreliable. At around the same time flourished two of the greatest critics in this field: Yaḥyā ibn Saʿīd al-Qaṭṭān (d.198/813) and ʿAbd al-Raḥmān ibn Mahdī (d.198/813), whose verdict on the narrators' reliability or otherwise was widely accepted as final. Where they differed in their opinion about a narrator, the traditionists used their own knowledge and discretion. They were followed by another generation of critics, such as the great Yazīd ibn Hārūn.[8]

Chronology, biography and criticism, then, were applied together in assessing the worth of *isnāds*. Having realised their importance, the traditionists compiled, before the end of the second century, independent works dealing with the narrators in chronological order. 'Such registers of the narrators of tradition', says Otto Loth, 'as had been chronologically arranged and in which every Muslim traditionist in general received a definite place, had been already in common use among the traditionists as indispensable handbooks in the second century.'[9]

Nevertheless, it is not easy to determine the precise period at which the works of *asmā'* began to be compiled. Ibn al-Nadīm mentions two books called *Kitāb al-Tārīkh* in his section dealing with works about jurists and traditionists. One of these is by the great Ibn al-Mubārak, while the other is by al-Layth ibn Saʿd (d.165–75/781–91), a senior disciple of Imām Mālik.[10] These authors had little interest in history as such; and their works are not included in the section of the *Fihrist* devoted to historical works; and it would seem probable, therefore, that they are early works of *asmā'*. Horovitz is correct in his opinion that the earliest work on the subject was composed about the middle of the second century.[11] Also important was the *Tārīkh al-Ruwāt* of Yaḥyā ibn Maʿīn (158/774–233/847).[12] Other products of the second century include such works as the *Kitāb al-Ṭabaqāt*, *Kitāb Tārīkh al-Fuqahā'*, *Kitāb Ṭabaqāt al-Fuqahā' wa'l-Muḥaddithīn*, *Kitāb Tasmiyat al-Fuqahā' wa'l-Muḥaddithīn*,[13] *Kitāb Ṭabaqāt man Rawā ʿan al-Nabī*, by al-Wāqidī and Haytham ibn ʿAdī, both of whom died at the beginning of the third century, and whose works served as important sources for the later writers on the subject, such as Ibn Saʿd (d.230/844), Ibn al-Khayyāṭ (d.240/854),[14] and others.[15]

As all the early works on *ḥadīth* have been lost, it is impossible to determine their general plan and the nature of their contents. But from the later works which were based on them, and which still exist, and also from the general tendencies discernable among the traditionists of that time, it may be inferred that their contents consisted mainly of: (a) short descriptions of the genealogies and dates of birth and death; (b) some biographical matters; and (c) a brief critique of their reliability, backed up with the opinions of important authorities and contemporaries. These are the main features of the contents of the *Ṭabaqāt* of Ibn Saʿd, an immensely important work which will be described later in this Chapter; and these matters, as we have seen, had received serious attention from the *ḥadīth* experts before the end of the second Islamic century.

The compilation of the *ḥadīth* narrators' biographies, thus begun in the second century, was continued with great enthusiasm in the centuries that followed. In the third century, not only various specialists in the subject, such as Ibn Saᶜd, Ibn al-Khayyāṭ, and Ibn Abī Khaythama (d.279/892), but also almost every traditionist of repute compiled simultaneously with his collection of traditions, some biographical material relating to his authorities. All the compilers of the six standard *ḥadīth* collections wrote one or more important books on the biography of the narrators of traditions.[16] Other traditionists also, such as Ibn Abī Shayba (d.235/849) and ᶜAlī ibn al-Madīnī, wrote books of this type.

During the fourth and succeeding centuries, such compilations continued to be produced in bulk throughout the Islamic world. The Ḥijāz, Syria, Iraq, Iran, Egypt, North Africa, Spain and India all produced numerous biographers of the traditionists.

This genre naturally helped the growth of more general biographical literature in the Arabic language. During this same period, works were compiled which presented biographies of poets, grammarians, physicians, saints, jurists, judges, calligraphers, lovers, misers, idiots, and almost every other human type. 'The glory of the Muhammadan literature', says Sprenger, 'is its literary biographies. There is no nation, nor has there been any, which, like them, narrated the life of every man of letters.'[17] And according to Margoliouth: 'The biographical literature of the Arabs was exceedingly rich; indeed it would appear that in Baghdad when an eminent man died, there was a market for biographies of him, as is the case in the capitals of Europe in our time.... The literature which consists in collected biographies is abnormally large, and it is in consequence easier for the student of the history of the caliphate, to find out something about the persons mentioned in the chronicles than in any analogous case.'[18]

The enormous scale of these biographical dictionaries may be suggested by the large number of people whose biographies they contain. Ibn Saᶜd's *Ṭabaqāt* gives us the biographies of more than four thousand traditionists. Al-Bukhārī's *Tārīkh* deals with more than 42,000, while al-Khaṭīb al-Baghdādī, in his *History of Baghdad*, offers short but carefully honed biographies of 7,831 persons. Ibn ᶜAsākir, in his eighty-volume *History of Damascus*, collects a far larger number, while Ibn Ḥajar, in his *Tahdhīb al-Tahdhīb*, and al-Dhahabī, in his *Mīzān al-Iᶜtidāl*, summarise the biographical notices on 12,415 and 14,343 narrators of tradition respectively. These figures, which may be easily augmented from other works, are sufficient to show the magnitude of biographical literature in Arabic, a resource which offers a detailed portrait of a remarkably literate society.

The works on *asmā'* differ greatly in their scope, plan, and detailed contents, according to the main object of their compilers. Some contain extremely short notices on a particular class of narrators; such is the *Ṭabaqāt al-Ḥuffāẓ* of al-Dhahabī,[19] and various other works on weak or unreliable narrators. Others record only names, *kunyas*, and *nisbas*; to this class belong the various works on *al-Asmā' wa'l-Kunā*,[20] and the well-known *Kitāb al-Ansāb* of al-Samʿānī.[21] Still others contain biographical details of all narrators who lived in or visited any particular town: examples include the *Tārīkh Baghdad* of al-Khaṭīb al-Baghdadī, the *Tārīkh Dimashq* of Ibn ʿAsākir, and others.[22] Some deal exclusively with reliable or unreliable narrators: the *Kitāb al-Kāmil fī Ḍuʿafā' al-Rijāl* of Ibn ʿAdī[23] and Nasā'ī's *Kitāb al-Ḍuʿafā' wa'l-Matrūkīn*[24] are examples.[25] Some restrict themselves to offering biographies of narrators used in particular collections of traditions, or in a group of collections. To this class belong a large number of works which deal with the lives of the narrators on whom al-Bukhārī or Muslim, or the authors of all the six standard works, have relied.

Works on *asmā'* may therefore be divided into two broad groups: general and specific.

6.1 a GENERAL WORKS

These are works which contain biographies of all narrators, or at least of all the important ones among them who were known to the author. Most early books on the subject belong to this category: for instance, the *Ṭabaqāt* of Muḥammad ibn Saʿd, the three *Histories* (*Tārīkh*) of al-Bukhārī, the *Tārīkh* of Aḥmad ibn Abī Khaythama, and many other works on the *asmā' al-rijāl*, which were compiled during the third century of the *hijra*, and which try to include all the well-known narrators.

6.1 b THE ṬABAQĀT OF IBN SAʿD

The earliest of all these is the *Kitāb al-Ṭabaqāt al-Kabīr* (*Great Book of Classes*) by Ibn Saʿd. The life of its author has been well summarised by two distinguished German orientalists, Loth[26] and Sachau;[27] whose account is briefly summarised in the following paragraphs.

Abū ʿAbd Allāh Muḥammad ibn Saʿd ibn Manīʿ al-Zuhrī belonged to a family of Babylonian slaves of the family of the great traditionist ʿAbd Allāh ibn ʿAbbās, who had granted them their freedom. Born at Baṣra, then a great centre of *ḥadīth* learning, Ibn Saʿd was attracted by the charms of Tradition, in the pursuit of which he himself travelled to Kūfa, Mecca and Medina, where he must have stayed for a considerable period. At last, he came to Baghdad, the greatest centre of intellectual activity in his time. Here he came into close contact with al-Wāqidī, one of the early Arab historians. He worked as al-Wāqidī's literary assistant for some time, thereby acquiring his soubriquet *Kātib al-Wāqidī* ('Wāqidī's Scribe'). Gaining a reputation at Baghdad as a traditionist and historian in his own right, Ibn Saʿd soon attracted a band of students, who sat at his feet and studied these subjects with him. One of the most prominent of them was the great historian al-Balādhurī, who in his later career borrowed a great deal from Ibn Saʿd in his important work *Futūḥ al-Buldān*. Ibn Saʿd died in 230/844.

Ibn Saʿd, who possessed immense erudition coupled with an enthusiasm for his subject, was also a great bibliophile, at a time when the possession and collection of books had become something of a fashion among the Muslims. Al-Khaṭīb al-Baghdādī says: 'He possessed vast learning, knew a great number of Traditions—for which he had a great thirst—narrated a good many of them, and collected a large number of books, particularly rare ones, and texts on *ḥadīth* and *fiqh*.'[28] 'Of the collections of the works of al-Wāqidī', he adds, 'which were in the possession of four persons during the time of Ibn Saʿd, his was the largest.'

Ibn Saʿd made good use of his literary resources in compiling his own works. Two of these, the *Ṭabaqāt* and the *Kitāb Akhbār al-Nabī*, are mentioned by Ibn al-Nadīm,[29] while a third, a smaller edition of the *Ṭabaqāt*, is mentioned by al-Nawawī[30] and others, but is not known to exist today.

Ibn Saʿd's *Kitāb Akhbār al-Nabī* constitutes only one part of the *Ṭabaqāt*. It was compiled and completed by the author, but was handed down to posterity by his student, al-Ḥārith ibn Muḥammad ibn Abī Usāma (186–282/802–896).

The *Ṭabaqāt* was completely planned and compiled by Ibn Saʿd, but was not completed by him. He appears, however, to have read whatever he had written of this book to his student Ḥusayn ibn Fahm (211–289/826–901), who is reported to have been a keen student of traditions and of the biographies of the narrators.[31] Ibn Fahm completed the book according to the plan of its author, added to it his short biographical notice as well as notices of certain other narrators whose names had already been included by the author in the general plan of his work, and read it to his own students.

Both of these two books of Ibn Saʿd were received from his two students by some of their common disciples. One of these, Aḥmad ibn Maʿrūf al-Khashshāb (d.322/933) combined them into one book of enormous dimensions,[32] and read it out to his students. One of these students, Abū ʿUmar Aḥmad ibn ʿAbbās (generally known as Ibn Ḥayawayh, 295–382/907–992), who is celebrated for his interest in the works on the early history of Islam and for the preservation of the early historical and biographical works of the Arabs, edited the whole work without making any change in its text.[33] His student, al-Jawharī (363–454/973–1062), handed it down to posterity. Through him are traced back to the author all the extant manuscripts of this great work. All these manuscripts preserve the author's original arrangement of the contents. On the basis of all the various known manuscripts of Ibn Ḥayawayh's edition, the great *Book of Classes* was edited by an enthusiastic band of German scholars, and was published by the Prussian Academy of Sciences.[34]

In this printed edition, despite various lacunae, we find a detailed biography of the Prophet, and biographical notices for about 4,300 narrators of the various generations down to 238/852, as follows:

Vol I part i (ed. E. Mittwoch). Genealogy of the Prophet, and his biography down to his migration to Medina.

Vol I part ii (ed. E. Mittwoch and E. Sachau, 1917). Biography of the Prophet after the *hijra*, and various related topics.

Vol II part i (J. Horovitz, 1909). The Prophet's campaigns.

Vol II part ii (J. Schwally, 1912). Sickness and death of the Prophet. Elegies written on his death by various poets. Biographies of the jurists and Qur'ān readers who lived in Medina during the Prophetic period, and just after his death.

Vol III part i (ed. E. Sachau, 1904). Biographies of the *Muhājirūn* who took part in the Battle of Badr.

Vol III part ii (ed. J. Horovitz, 1904). As III/i above.

Vol IV part i (ed. J. Lippert, 1906). Biographies of early converts who did not take part at Badr, but had migrated to Abyssinia, and later took part in the Battle of Uḥud.

Vol IV part ii (ed. J. Lippert, 1908). Biographies of other Companions who converted to Islam before the conquest of Mecca.

Vol V (ed. K.V. Zettersteen, 1905). Biographies of the *Tābiʿūn* (Successors) who lived at Medina.[35]

Vol VI (ed. K.V. Zettersteen, 1909). Biographies of the Companions, and other jurists and Traditionists, who settled and lived at Kūfa.

Vol VII part i (ed. B. Meissner, 1918). Biographies of the Companions and other jurists and traditionists who lived at Baṣra.

Vol VII part ii (ed. E. Sachau, 1918). Biographies of the Companions and other jurists and traditionists of Baṣra, Baghdad, Syria, Egypt, North Africa, etc.

Vol VIII (ed. C. Brockelmann, 1904). Biographies of the women narrators, including the Companions and the Successors.

Vol IX/i (E. Sachau, 1921). Index of personal names which are the subject of notices.

Vol IX/ii (E. Sachau, 1928). Index of places, tribes, Qur'ānic verses, *ḥadīth*, and poetry.

Vol IX/iii (E. Sachau, 1940). Index of all personal names.

No precise plan has been followed within all the articles of the work. However, those on the Companions are long, and generally contain their genealogy both on the paternal and maternal side, the names of their wives/husbands and children, the time of their conversion to Islam, the part taken by them in the important events of the Prophet's career, the dates of their death, and other matters connected with their habits and lives which the traditionists considered to be of importance. Of course, the reader is very often disappointed with regard to important biographical details which he may naturally expect. But at the same time, he often comes across important historical insights which he may not have anticipated. All these details, however, are entirely wanting in the articles on the later narrators, which do not exceed one or two sentences. Many of them are completely blank, from which fact it has rightly been inferred that these parts were meant by Ibn Saʿd to serve as notes to be developed at some later date, although he died before completing the work.

As Sachau remarks, Ibn Saʿd shows impartiality and honesty, thoroughness, minuteness, objectivity and originality.[36] Just as despite his status as a *mawlā* of the Hashimites he took no part in their political activism, so in his articles on the various figures of Islam he gave no expression to his personal relation to or prejudice for or against anyone, and merely recorded in a simple style all he knew and considered important about them. His thoroughness is abundantly shown by his constant reference to the various versions of an event as well as to the differences among his authorities. His objectivity is illustrated by the absence of irrelevant material, while his originality is displayed in his sub-classification of the narrators according to the various provinces in which they dwelt, and the general citing of the *isnāds* of the various versions of an event before describing them, and their entire omission in some places.[37] Sachau compares him to Plutarch—the main difference (other than length) being due to the fact that Plutarch formed the last link in a long chain of biographers whose contributions to the art he had inherited, whereas Ibn Saʿd had been one of the pioneers in the field.

Be this as it may, the *Ṭabaqāt* of Ibn Saʿd is one of the earliest extant works of *asmāʾ al-rijāl*, containing biographical data on most of the important narrators of the most important period in *ḥadīth* history. As a rich mine of many-sided information about early Islamic history, it may be considered not only one of the most important works of its type, but also one of the most significant works in Arabic literature as a whole. Since the beginning of the fourth Muslim century, it has been used as a source by a large number of authors, including al-Balādhurī,[38] al-Ṭabarī,[39] al-Khaṭīb al-Baghdādī, Ibn al-Athīr, al-Nawawī,[40] and Ibn Ḥajar,[41] while the prolific Egyptian scholar al-Suyūṭī prepared an epitome of it. As a general biographical dictionary of narrators is appears always to have occupied a unique position among works on *asmāʾ al-rijāl*. Other works of *Ṭabaqāt* dealt only with particular classes of narrators.

6.1c THE KITĀB AL-TĀRĪKH OF AL-BUKHĀRĪ

Ibn Saʿd's *Ṭabaqāt* was soon followed by works by al-Bukhārī, who claimed to possess at least some biographical information about every narrator of Traditions. He compiled three books on the history of narrators. The largest of these, *al-Tārīkh al-Kabīr* (*The Great History*), is said to have contained the biographical notices of more than forty thousand narrators. No complete manuscript, however, is known to exist. Only various parts of it are preserved in certain libraries, and on the basis of these the Dāʾirat al-Maʿārif press at Hyderabad prepared and published the standard text of the book (1361–62).[42]

6.1d AL-JARḤ WAʾL-TAʿDĪL OF IBN ABĪ ḤĀTIM AL-RĀZĪ

This author (d.327/939) followed the example of Bukhārī's *al-Tārīkh al-Kabīr* in including all the narrators known to him, together with such significant information as he could acquire concerning their capacities in *ḥadīth*, followed by his own verdict on each individual. Although ordered alphabetically (by first letter only), Companions are found first under each letter. For each figure the author provides the father's name, the *kunya*, and his tribal or locational name (*nisba*), his best-known teachers and pupils, the cities where he lived, some of his written works, and, where possible, the date of his death. The work has been printed in eight volumes in Hyderabad (1360-73), together with its important methodological introduction, known as *Taqdimat al-Maʿrifa*.[43]

6.2 BIOGRAPHICAL DICTIONARIES OF PARTICULAR CLASSES OF NARRATORS

Almost simultaneously with the general biographical dictionaries of narrators, there began the compilation of those of particular categories of them. The most important of these are: (a) those containing the biographies of the Companions; (b) those containing the biographies of the narrators who lived in or visited any particular town or province; and (c) those containing the biographies of the narrators who belonged to individual schools of law.

6.2a BIOGRAPHICAL DICTIONARIES OF COMPANIONS

These constitute the vital core of the *asmāʾ* literature. It appears, however, that no independent book of this type was written before the third century, when al-Bukhārī compiled a work[44] which must for the most part have been based on the *Sīra/Maghāzī* literature, the numerous monographs relating to important events in early Muslim history, Traditions containing information about Companions, and the earlier, more general works on *asmāʾ*.

Bukhārī was followed by a great number of authors. These included Abū Yaʿlā Aḥmad ibn ʿAlī (201/816–307/919), Abu'l-Qāsim ʿAbd Allāh al-Baghawī (213/828–317/929), Abū Ḥafṣ ʿUmar ibn Aḥmad (known as Ibn Shāhīn, 297/909–385/995),[45] Abū ʿAbd Allāh Muḥammad ibn Yaḥyā ibn Manda (d.301/913),[46] Abū Nuʿaym Aḥmad ibn ʿAbd Allāh (336/947–403/1012),[47] Ibnʿ Abd al-Barr (368/978-463/1070) (of Cordoba and Lisbon, the greatest traditionist of his time in the West),[48] Abū Mūsā Muḥammad ibn Abī Bakr (501/1107–581/1185), and many others.

On the basis of the works of Ibn Manda, Abū Nuʿaym, Abū Mūsā and Ibn ʿAbd al-Barr, the historian and traditionist ʿIzz al-Dīn Ibn al-Athīr (555/1160–630/1230), compiled his *Usd al-Ghāba*, a dictionary of Companions in which the sources are compared and used with discrimination.[49] In his introduction, Ibn al-Athīr defines the term *ṣaḥābī*, provides a short sketch of the life of the Prophet, and then sets out in alphabetical order the biographies of 7,554 Companions. In each article, he tries to give the

Companion's name, *kunya*, genealogy, and certain biographical facts. When he differs from his predecessors, he discusses the matter at length, gives reasons for his position, and explains the reasons for his predecessors' mistakes. Despite its many repetitions, the *Usd* is widely appreciated as a solid authority on the subject, and has been summarised by several *ʿulamāʾ*, including al-Nawawī, al-Dhahabī, and al-Suyūṭī.[50]

Ibn al-Athīr's work was followed in the ninth century of the *hijra* by a more comprehensive work, *al-Iṣāba fī tamyīz al-Ṣaḥāba*, by Shihāb al-Dīn Abu'l-Faḍl ibn ʿAlī ibn Ḥajar al-ʿĀsqalānī (773/1371–852/1448).[51] Born in Old Cairo, he lost both parents when still an infant, and was brought up by one of his relatives, who worked as a merchant. Despite great disadvantages, the orphan excelled in his studies, and soon acquired a knowledge of history, Sufism, doctrine, and *tafsīr*, devoting particular attention to *ḥadīth*. For ten years he sat at the feet of the great traditionist Zayn al-Dīn al-ʿIrāqī (725/1351–806/1404), who had reintroduced the old system of *imlāʾ* (dictation) of *ḥadīth*s.[52] Ibn Ḥajar in time served as professor at a number of educational institutions, and worked as a judge—a post he accepted after refusing it several times.

He left behind him some 150 books, some of which are incomplete. The *Fatḥ al-Bārī*, a great commentary on *Ṣaḥīḥ al-Bukhārī*, is sometimes described as the work by which the Muslims scholars repaid the accumulated debt they owed to Imām Bukhārī. In his *Iṣāba*, Ibn Ḥajar assembles the results of the labours of all his distinguished predecessors in the field of biographies of the Companions, criticising them in certain cases, and adding to them the results of his own research. He divides his book into four parts, including 12,267 people, of whom 1,522 were women:[53]

Part I. Persons directly or indirectly cited as Companions in any tradition, sound, good or weak.

Part II. Persons still young when the Prophet died, but who were born during his lifetime in the family of a Companion, who may hence be considered Companions themselves.

Part III. Persons known to have lived both before and after the advent of Islam, but who are not known ever to have met the Prophet. These are not classified as Companions, but are included because they were their contemporaries.

Part IV. Persons wrongly cited as Companions in other dictionaries.

6.2b BIOGRAPHICAL DICTIONARIES OF THE NARRATORS OF A TOWN OR PROVINCE

Another sizeable genre of biographical dictionaries of *ḥadīth* narrators consists of works written according to places or provinces where they lived or which they visited.[54] Not only almost all the provinces, but almost every important town, had several biographers who collected the lives of every important traditionist or literary figure who was associated with it. Mecca, Medina, Baṣra, Kūfa, Wāsiṭ, Damascus, Antioch, Alexandria, Qayrawān, Cordoba, Mawṣil, Aleppo, Baghdad, Iṣfahān, Jurjān, Bukhārā, Merv, and other places: all had their local historians and biographers of their men of letters.[55]

Many of these provincial historians dealt with the political history of their regions. Many others treated the lives of their literary figures. Still others wrote supplements to earlier regional works, bringing them up to date; some works of this type extend into modern times.

6.2c THE HISTORY OF BAGHDAD BY AL-KHAṬĪB AL-BAGHDĀDĪ

One of the most important works in this class is al-Khaṭīb al-Baghdādī's *Tārīkh Baghdad*, which is also the earliest biographical dictionary of literary figures, mainly traditionists, who either belonged to, or delivered lectures in, the great capital.[56]

Al-Khaṭīb al-Baghdādī (392/1002–463/1071), whose full name was Abū Bakr Aḥmad ibn ʿAlī, was the son of a preacher in a village near Baghdad. He began the study of *ḥadīth* at the age of eleven, and in due course travelled to acquire it in Syria, the Ḥijāz, and Iran, soon becoming an authority on both *asmā'* and *ḥadīth*. He lectured on these fields in Damascus, Baghdad and elsewhere, until some of his own teachers, recognising his merit, became his pupils. Finally he settled and taught in Baghdad, where his authority on *ḥadīth* was recognised by the caliph al-Qā'im, and his minister Ibn Maslama, who ordered that no preacher should include in his sermon any *ḥadīth* that was not approved by al-Khaṭīb al-Baghdādī.

His life in the metropolis was not uneventful. During the revolt of al-Baṣāṣīrī (450/1058), when Ibn Maslama was killed, he was forced to leave the city and wander in Syria for several months; and when after the execution of the rebel he returned to Baghdad in 451, he found himself persecuted by the Ḥanbalites on account of his having deserted their teachings and joining the Shāfiʿites, which led him to more liberal views towards the Ashʿarites and the scholastic theologians. Many treatises against him by Ḥanbalites are mentioned by Ḥājī Khalīfa. Al-Khaṭīb, however, had been fortunate in having attained all his great hopes, namely, to read out his great *History of Baghdad* to his students in that city, and to be buried by the side of the great Sufi, Bishr al-Ḥāfī.[57]

Al-Khaṭīb compiled fifty-six books and treatises, a list of which is provided by Yāqūt.[58] The *Tārīkh Baghdad* is without question the most important of these. In this monumental work, which he read out to his students in 461/1068, he gives the topography of Baghdad, al-Ruṣāfa and al-Madā'in (Ctesiphon), and then provides biographies for 7,831 eminent men and women, mostly *ḥadīth* specialists, who were either born in the city, or came there from elsewhere and taught. He gives names, *kunyas*, death dates, and some other biographical details, together with opinions of other important Traditionists about their reliability. The book begins with the Companions, followed by those individuals who bore the auspicious name of Muḥammad, with the remaining articles being arranged alphabetically.[59] Al-Khaṭīb always tries to give the source of his information, and often adds notes in which he discusses the reliability of the traditions quoted, and of the reports received by him, attempting to discern the facts without partiality.[60] He is regarded as the greatest traditionist of his time in the East, rivalled in the West only by Ibn ʿAbd al-Barr.

Al-Khaṭīb brought his dictionary down to the year 450AH. A number of successors continued the work after him, and their contributions are also of value. Al-Samʿānī (506/1113–562/1167), al-Dubaythī (558/1163–637/1239), Ibn al-Najjār (578/1183–643/1245) and others wrote supplements (sing. *dhayl*) to his book, including the eminent men and women who had lived in the city until their own times.[61]

6.2d THE HISTORY OF DAMASCUS BY IBN ʿASĀKIR

The plan of al-Khaṭīb's work was followed by Ibn ʿAsākir in his huge biographical dictionary of the eminent persons of Damascus, in eighty volumes, which continues to earn the admiration of scholars.

Ibn ʿAsākir, whose full name was Abu'l-Qāsim ʿAlī ibn al-Ḥasan, was born to a respectable and literary family of Damascus in 499/1105. His father, and other members of his family, are all described by al-Subkī as traditionists of some eminence. Some of his predecessors seem to have taken part in the campaign against the Crusaders, and from this it appears that his title Ibn ʿAsākir ('son of soldiers') is drawn.

Having studied as a child under his father and other scholars of Damascus, Ibn ʿAsākir travelled widely and visited all the important centres of *ḥadīth* learning, a long list of which is given by al-Subkī in his *Ṭabaqāt*. He sat at the feet of more than 1,300 teachers of *ḥadīth* (of whom over eighty were women). At last he returned to settle in Damascus, where he devoted himself to the service of *ḥadīth* and related fields, compiling books, and delivering lectures in a college founded for him by the great general and jurist Nūr al-Dīn Muḥammad al-Zanjī. He died in 571/1175.

His keen intellect, sharp and retentive memory, vast knowledge of traditions, sincerity and abstemiousness, and his devotion to the science of tradition, were acknowledged by all his contemporaries. A long list of his works is given by Yāqūt;[62] many of these are still preserved in the world's libraries.

The most important of these is the *Tārīkh Dima*. Begun relatively early in his career at the urging of a friend, it languished for many years, until Nūr al-Dīn al-Zanjī encouraged the author to complete it during his old age.[63] In this book, after offering a brief history of Syria in general, and Damascus in particular, and describing the prophets who lie buried there,[64] and its famous monasteries, Ibn ʿAsākir presents the biographies of the eminent men and women of various categories (mostly *ḥadīth* experts), who lived in or visited Damascus. The biographical section commences with those whose names are Aḥmad, which are introduced by a short biography of the Prophet of Islam. In the arrangement of the remaining articles, alphabetical order is observed. Finally we are given articles on men whose names are not conventionally known according to the alphabetic order of the *kunyas*, followed by alphabetically-arranged notices on distinguished women.

No complete edition of the *History* yet exists. It is usually consulted in the abbreviated version of ʿAbd al-Qādir Badrān, *Tahdhīb Tārīkh Dimashq* (Damascus, 1329), which omits *isnāds* and repetitions.

6.2e OTHER LOCAL COLLECTIONS

Like al-Khaṭīb and Ibn ʿAsākir, many other traditionists and historians collected together biographies of men of letters who dwelt in specific towns. The best-known of these dictionaries include:

(i) *Tārīkh Wāsiṭ*, by Abu'l-Ḥasan Aslam ibn Sahl Baḥshal al-Wāsiṭī (d.288/901).[65]

(ii) *Mukhtaṣar Ṭabaqāt ʿUlamā' Ifrīqiya wa-Tūnis*, by Abu'l-ʿArab Muḥammad ibn Aḥmad al-Qayrawānī (d.333/944).[66]

(iii) *Tārīkh al-Raqqa*, by Muḥammad ibn Saʿīd al-Qushayrī (d.334/945).[67]

(iv) *Akhbār Iṣfahān*, by Abū Nuʿaym Aḥmad ibn ʿAbd Allāh al-Iṣfahānī (d.430/1039).[68]
(v) *Tārīkh Jurjān*, by Abu'l-Qāsim Ḥamza ibn Yūsuf al-Sahmī (d.427/1036).[69]

Ibn Manda (d.301/911) of Iṣfahān likewise collected material on his fellow-citizens.[70] Al-Ḥākim (321/933–405/1014) compiled a highly-regarded list of narrators of Nīsābūr.[71] Abu'l-Qāsim ʿUmar ibn Aḥmad al-ʿUqaylī, generally known as Ibn al-ʿAdīm (588/1191–660/1262) collected the biographies of eminent persons of Aleppo, in thirty volumes, which was later added to by his successors.[72] Abū Saʿīd al-Samʿānī (506/1113–561/1167) compiled a twenty-volume biographical dictionary mainly dealing with the traditionists of Merv.[73] The traditionists of Wāsiṭ, of Kūfa, of Baṣra, of Herāt, of Qazwīn, and many other towns, found able biographers in Ibn al-Dubaythī[74] (d.558/1162–637/1239), Ibn al-Najjār,[75] Ibn Shabba,[76] (173/789–263/876), Ibn al-Bazzāz,[77] and al-Rāfiʿī[78] respectively.

Provinces as well as towns were treated in this way. Ibn al-Farḍī, Ibn Bashkuwāl, al-Ḥumaydī, and others, are among the more outstanding exponents of this genre.

7

THE DISCIPLINES OF FORMAL CRITICISM

AN integral component of the *ḥadīth* literature is the genre which describes and develops the techniques of *ḥadīth* criticism. This traditionally roots itself in the Qur'ān itself, which contains clear evidence that information is not to be accepted unless its reporters are demonstrably reliable and its likelihood evident. In verse XLIX, 6, it states: 'O you who believe! If an unrighteous person comes to you with a report, ascertain it carefully!' Similarly, the accusation directed against ʿĀ'isha is denounced by the Qur'ān as an evident falsehood[1] because her character was above all suspicion. The Qur'ān similarly rejects as both unreasonable and unfounded the theory of the divine begetting of Jesus.[2]

After the Prophet's death, when people began to try and recall his words, several Companions were critical of some of the reporters, and rejected some of their reports. ʿAlī thus refused to accept a *ḥadīth* told by Maʿqil ibn Sinān.[3] ʿAmmār ibn Yāsir once reported a *ḥadīth* of the Prophet with regard to the *tayammum* ablution, in a gathering of the Companions, and ʿUmar ibn al-Khaṭṭāb spoke up and said: 'Fear God!'[4]—thereby indicating his disagreement with what ʿAmmār had reported. The *Ṣaḥīḥ* of Muslim contains a report in which Ibn ʿAbbās criticises several judgements of ʿAlī ibn Abī Ṭālib.[5] When Maḥmūd ibn al-Rabīʿ reported in an assembly of the Companions that the Prophet had said that no-one who professed that there was no god but God would be sent to hellfire, Abū Ayyūb al-Anṣārī remarked that he did not think that the Prophet had ever said such a thing.[6] Many other instances of the criticism of Companion-Narrators by their contemporaries (particularly ʿĀ'isha, ʿUmar, and Ibn ʿAbbās), may be easily discovered in works on *ḥadīth* and *asmā'*. These criticisms show that the

Companions themselves were not above criticism. In fact, according to the principles accepted by most of the Sunnī Muslim scholars, no one except a Prophet is infallible (*maʿṣūm*); and even Prophets may commit errors in matters which do not concern religion.

The Companions' practice of *ḥadīth* criticism was emulated by people such as Shuʿba ibn al-Ḥajjāj, Yaḥyā ibn Saʿīd al-Qaṭṭān, ʿAlī ibn al-Madīnī and Aḥmad ibn Ḥanbal, who laid the groundwork for the science of the principles of *ḥadīth* criticism. Thus developed two major branches of literature: *ʿilm riwāyat al-ḥadīth*, also called *muṣṭalaḥ al-ḥadīth* (the science of *ḥadīth* narration, or technical *ḥadīth* vocabulary), and *ʿilm al-jarḥ wa'l-taʿdīl* (the science of criticism of the reporters). In the present Chapter, we will deal with each of these in turn.

7.1 ʿILM RIWĀYAT AL-ḤADĪTH

The earliest written work connected with this is the *Risāla* (*Treatise*) of Imām al-Shāfiʿī (150/767–204/820), later regarded as the founder of the Shāfiʿī *madhhab*. It was followed by the works of Abū Muḥammad al-Rāmhurmuzī (d. *ca.* 350/961), al-Ḥākim (d.403/1012),[7] Abū Nuʿaym (d.430/1038), and al-Khaṭīb al-Baghdādī (463–1071), who systematised the material outlined by his predecessor in his *Kitāb al-Kifāya*.[8] He was followed by al-Qāḍī ʿIyāḍ (d.544/1149), author of *al-Ilmaʿ*.[9] After them, Ibn al-Ṣalāḥ (d.643/1245) compiled his *Kitāb ʿUlūm al-Ḥadīth*, in which he added his own observations to the material gathered by earlier authors.[10] Other scholars to have written on the field include Ibn Kathīr (d.774–1372), Zayn al-Dīn al-ʿIrāqī, and others.[11] (ʿIrāqī's thousand-line poem, *al-Alfiya*, which deals with *muṣṭalaḥ al-ḥadīth*, is often memorised today, and studied with the commentary of al-Sakhāwī, the *Fatḥ al-Mughīth*).[12] There is also Suyūṭī's *Tadrīb al-Rāwī*,[13] an exhaustive commentary on the *Taqrīb* of al-Nawawī, and the commentary of al-Zurqānī (d.1122/1710) on al-Bayqūnī's didactic poem on *ḥadīth* criticism.

Al-Shāfiʿī followed by others, defined the qualifications necessary for a transmitter of *ḥadīth* as follows:

> The transmitter must be of firm faith, and well-known for his truthfulness in what he reports. He should understand its content, and should know well how the change in expression affects the ideas expressed therein. He should report verbatim what he learnt from his teachers, and not narrate in his own words the sense of what he had learnt. He must possess a retentive memory, and should remember his book well, if he reports from it. He should

> be free of making a report on the authority of those whom he met of something he did not learn from them. His report must stand in agreement with what has been reported by those who are recognised to have memories of quality, if they also have transmitted these reports.[14]

Shāfiʿī is here articulating the view of all the main *ḥadīth* authorities, jurists as well as traditionists, to the effect that a transmitter, in order to be acceptable, must be of firm faith, mature age and proven integrity, and possess a good memory. He must be well-versed in the method of learning, preserving and transmitting the traditions. He must also be thoroughly conversant with the names, careers and characters of the earlier reporters of traditions, as well as with their various classes, and their weaknesses and special characteristics. According to most writers, traditions are to be divided into three main classes, on the basis of their reliability on account of the quality of *isnād*, the nature of the *matn*, and their acceptance or rejection by the Companions, the Followers and the Successors.

These three classes are: (i) *Ṣaḥīḥ*, or 'sound'; (ii) *Ḥasan*, or 'fair'; and (iii) *Ḍaʿīf*, or 'weak'.[15] The latter class is further subdivided according to the extent of the deficiency of its reporters, or in the texts of the reports themselves. Subcategories include: the *muʿallaq* ('suspended'), the *maqṭūʿ* ('interrupted'), the *munqaṭiʿ* ('broken'), the *mursal* ('incomplete'),[16] the *muṣaḥḥaf* (containing a mistake either in the *isnād* or the *matn*), the *shādhdh* ('rare': a tradition with a reliable *isnād* but whose *matn* is contrary to another similarly attested tradition), the *mawḍūʿ* ('forged'), and so on. These and other categories of *ḥadīth* are explained in great detail in the works on *uṣūl al-ḥadīth*. But the authorities on the subject differ from one another in their interpretation of some of these technical terms. Such differences are analysed in the above mentioned works of Sakhāwī and Suyūṭī.

The writers on *ʿulūm al-ḥadīth* also describe the methods of learning, preserving, teaching, and writing down the traditions in book form. They have also described methods of collating manuscripts with their original copies, as well as other philological and technical issues.

7.2 ʿILM AL-JARḤ WA'L-TAʿDĪL

This, the 'science of criticising the reporters of *ḥadīth*', forms an important sub-discipline of the field of *asmā'*, which has been more generally dealt with on pp.91–106 above. A short but complete description of its origins and evolution may be found in the work of al-Jazā'irī.[17]

A further categorisation of *ḥadīth*s distinguishes (i) those that have been narrated by all their transmitters verbatim, and (ii) those traditions the contents of which have been reported by their transmitters in their own words.

Another, and important, subdivision of traditions relates to the parallel authentication of *isnāds* during the first three generations. Three such types are identified: *mutawātir*, *mashhūr*, and *āḥād*.

A *Mutawātir* tradition is one which has been transmitted throughout the first three generations of Muslims by such a large number of narrators that the possibility of fabrication must be entirely discarded.[18] Opinions differ on the number of transmitters necessary for *tawātur* to be attained during each of the three generations: some authorities fix it at seven, some at forty, some at seventy,[19] and others at still higher numbers.[20] Very few of the traditions received by us belong to this category. They have been collected by several scholars, including al-Suyūṭī, in his *al-Azhār al-Mutanāthira fī'l-Akhbār al-Mutawātira*[21] and al-Zabīdī, in his *al-Durar al-Mutanāthira fī'l-Aḥādīth al-Mutawātira*.[22]

A *Mashhūr ḥadīth* is one which, although transmitted originally in the first generation by two, three or four transmitters, was later transmitted, on their authority, by a large number in the subsequent two generations.[23] To this class, sometimes also known as *al-mustafīḍ*, belong a large number of traditions which are included in all the collections of *ḥadīth*s and constitute the main foundations of Islamic law.

The *Āḥād* are traditions which were transmitted during the first three generations of Muslims by one (or two, three or four) narrators only.[24]

7.3 THE LEGAL SIGNIFICANCE OF TRADITIONS

The legal importance of these three degrees of *ḥadīth*s are abundantly discussed in the works of Islamic jurisprudence (*uṣūl al-fiqh*), The first two classes are recognised by all the important Sunnī jurists as the second source of Islamic law, after the Qur'ān. The *āḥād* (also known as *khabar al-wāḥid*) are accepted as taking precedence over *qiyās* (analogical induction) by all Sunnī schools with the exception of that of Imām Mālik, who gives priority to *qiyās*.

Acceptance of *ḥadīth* as a source of Islamic law is advocated in the Qur'ān: 'Whatever the Messenger gives you, take; and whatever he forbids, abstain from.'[25] The Prophet also emphasised the authoritative status of the *ḥadīth*,[26] and his policy of using knowledge of *ḥadīth* as a criterion when appointing government officers was followed by his immediate successors.

According to al-Dārimī, whenever any legal case came before Abū Bakr, he looked into the Qur'ān, and decided the case on its basis. If he found no applicable judgement in the Qur'ān he referred to the usage of the Prophet. If he failed to find it there, he asked the other Companions, and if they informed him of any decision of the Prophet in the matter, he thanked God and decided the case accordingly. But if the Companions were unable to cite any Prophetic precedent, he gathered the leaders of the people; and after they arrived at an agreed decision, he judged accordingly.[27]

This was also the practice of ʿUmar. Confronted with a legal case in which a woman had miscarried following an attack from another woman, he asked an assembly of the Companions to relate to him any *ḥadīth* which might furnish guidance on the subject. Al-Mughīra ibn Shuʿba was able to do this; but ʿUmar asked him to produce a witness to support his narration. Muḥammad ibn Maslama stepped forwards and concurred that the *ḥadīth* was genuine; and ʿUmar thus accepted the *ḥadīth*, and gave his judgement on the case.[28] A large number of similar cases are mentioned in the *ḥadīth* works, which relate to controversies as diverse as the fixing of the number of *takbīrs* in the *janāza* prayer, the levying of the *jizya* tax on Zoroastrians,[29] and the use of *tayammum* in cases of night pollution.[30] In all these cases, *ḥadīths* were sought and laws were established on their authority.

Cases also arose which were decided by the Companions according to their own opinion (*ra'y*), on account of the absence of any *ḥadīths* on the subject.[31] They did, of course, amend their decisions whenever a *ḥadīth* came to light. There are cases reported in which Companions such as Abu'l-Dardā' and Abū Saʿīd al-Khudrī migrated from a place because some of the people living there preferred their own opinions to the traditions which were related to them.[32]

There were, however, cases in which ʿUmar and some other Companions, on being told of a *ḥadīth* on any given subject, did not follow it, and gave their judgement against its obvious sense and according to their own views (*ra'y*). During the caliphate of ʿUmar, for instance, there arose the important problem of the right to the fifth-part of booty for the relatives of the Prophet. The Prophet's practice was in favour of this. It was discussed for several days in an assembly of the Companions, and after a long discussion ʿUmar decided against the recorded practice of the Prophet.[33] Several other cases of this type are recorded in the *ḥadīth* works. A close scrutiny, however, of all these cases shows that the *ḥadīth* of the Prophet was not rejected tout court; it was either differently interpreted in the light of circumstances and other *ḥadīths*, or the memory and understanding of those who reported it were the subject of doubt among those present.

A related issue, that of the basic nature and character of the Prophetic words and example, is also investigated by the scholars, many of whom hold that every one of his actions and words is of a religiously significant character, and must be literally followed by every Muslim. Others draw a distinction between what he said or did as a Prophet, and what he said and did as an 'ordinary mortal', the latter having, according to them, no sacred character and hence no consequent duty of obedience. The Prophet himself had said: 'I am a human being. When I command you to do anything concerning your religion, then accept it; while when I command you to do anything on account of my personal opinion, then you should know that I am also a human being;'[34] i.e., that the latter recommendation may or may not be regarded as a model. These personal actions and preferences of the Prophet are also divided into two classes: firstly, matters restricted to him alone on account of his position as a prophet (such as certain additional prayers at night); and secondly, those which are applicable to the Muslim community as a whole.

All the orthodox jurists, however, hold that every tradition of the Prophet which is proved to be reliable according to their canons, and is of a religious character, is of a legislative weight second only to the Qur'ān itself.[35] On this point there is no dispute between the traditionists and those early jurists, particularly of Iraq, who were known as *ahl al-ra'y* (the scholars who placed some reliance on independant judgement). All important jurists of the first three generations preferred traditions to *qiyās*; there were even some who refused to express their own opinion on legal matters in cases in which no tradition was known to them.[36] The practices followed by the Companions were also accepted as a legal authority by the Muslims of the following two generations because they reasonably presumed that they must have been based on the traditions and practices of the Prophet, which had informed the lives of those who were by his side. This view dictated the legal position of Imām Mālik, who accepted the practices of the Companions, and by extension the inhabitants of the Prophetic city, as a pre-eminent legal authority.

The jurists did, however, differ among themselves over the legal significance of those traditions on the reliability of which they were uncertain, particularly the *āḥād*. Imām Abū Ḥanīfa and Imām Mālik did not consider all *ḥadīth*s of this class as superior to *qiyās*. Imām Mālik preferred *qiyās* to all *āḥād* traditions which were not backed by the practices of the Companions and the Followers. Imām Abū Ḥanīfa accepted some of them, and rejected others, on the basis of his own criteria; following in this the practice of ʿUmar ibn al-Khaṭṭāb.[37] He accepted them in connection with ordinary matters, if he was satisfied about the legal acumen and instinct of the reporter; while in cases of intricate legal problems he rejected them unless they were supported by circumstantial evidence and fundamental Islamic principles. Imām al-Shāfiʿī however, preferred the *āḥād* traditions over *qiyās* in every case. He endeavours to justify this in his works by citing a large number of *ḥadīth*s in which the reports of single individuals were accepted by the Prophet himself, and, after him, by many of the Companions. It is thus evident that the difference of opinion between the various orthodox schools of Islamic law does not relate to the acceptance of *ḥadīth* in general, but to a particular class of it.[38]

7.4 TECHNIQUES OF MATN ANALYSIS AND CRITICISM

Much of the attention of the traditional *ḥadīth* scholar focuses on the chain of authorities (*isnād*) by which it is attested. He or she will also, however, pay attention to the transmitted text (*matn*) itself.[39] The mere formal soundness of an *isnād* is not considered definitive proof of the actual genuineness of the text of the traditions to which they are attached. According to the traditionists, even if the *isnād* is completely without fault, the text should still be analysed before the genuineness of its attribution can be established. According to a well-known principle: 'If you encounter a *ḥadīth* contrary to reason, or to what has been established as correctly reported, or against the accepted principles, then you should know that it is forged.'[40] Abū Bakr ibn al-Ṭayyib is reported to have remarked that it is a proof of the forged character of a tradition that it be against reason or common experience; or that it conflict with the explicit text of the Qur'ān and the *Mutawātir* tradition, or the consensus (*ijmāʿ*); or that it contains the report of an important event taking place in the presence of a large number of people (when it is related by a single individual); or that it lays down severe punishment for minor faults, or promises high rewards for insignificant good deeds.[41] Al-Ḥākim gives several examples of forged and weak *ḥadīth*s having sound *isnād*s.[42] Al-Suyūṭī remarks that such *ḥadīth*s are encountered frequently.[43] In fact, the only sure guidance in the determination of the genuineness of a tradition is, as remarked by Ibn al-Mahdī and Abū Zarʿa, a faculty that a traditionist develops through a long, continuous study of the *ḥadīth*s, and as a result of continuous discussion of them with other scholars.[44] All such research, of course, must be reconciled with a historical awareness of the circumstances (*asbāb al-wurūd*) in which a given Tradition was generated, for many *ḥadīth*s were relevant only to the early period of the Prophet's ministry, and were later abrogated by other teachings.[45]

On the basis of the above mentioned understanding, the following general principles for the criticism of the texts of the traditions have been laid down:

(a) A tradition must not be contrary to the other traditions which have already been accepted by the authorities on the subject as authentic and reliable.[46] Nor should it contradict the text of the Qur'ān,[47] a *Mutawātir ḥadīth*, the absolute consensus of the community (*ijmāʿ qaṭʿī*), or the accepted basic principles of Islam.[48]
(b) A tradition should not be against the dictates of reason, the laws of nature, or common experience.[49]
(c) Traditions establishing a disproportionately high reward for insignificant good deeds, or disproportionately severe punishments for ordinary sins, must be rejected.[50]
(d) Traditions describing the excellent properties of certain sections of the Qur'ān may not be authentic.
(e) Traditions mentioning the superior virtue of persons, tribes, and particular places should be generally rejected.[51]
(f) Traditions which contain detailed prophecies of future events, equipped with dates, should be rejected.[52]
(g) Traditions containing such remarks of the Prophet as may not be a part of his prophetic vocation, or such expressions as are clearly unsuitable for him, should be rejected.[53]
(h) A *matn* should not violate the basic rules of Arabic grammar and style.[54]

It is on account of these principles that a large number of traditions which are included in some 'sound' *ḥadīth* collections have been rejected by the compilers of the standard collections of Tradition. Much material of this type has been identified and included in special anthologies of weak or forged Traditions, like those of Ibn al-Jawzī,[55] Mullā ʿAlī al-Qārī,[56] al-Shawkānī,[57] and others.[58] Shawkānī's collection is perhaps the most judicious, drawing on the researches of earlier writers, and giving the names of the *ḥadīth* works in which the *ḥadīth*s in question are to be found. Moreover, in many cases, he has identified the narrators who were responsible for the forgeries.

Even in the standard collections of *ḥadīth*, despite the great care of their compilers, a few weak or forged traditions may still be encountered. These are discussed by the commentators on these works. Some examples of this follow:
(a) The *ḥadīth*, reported by al-Bukhārī, to the effect that Adam's height was sixty cubits, has been criticised by Ibn Ḥajar on the basis of archaeological

measurements of the homesteads of some ancient peoples, which show that their inhabitants were not of an abnormal height.[59]

(b) The *ḥadīth*, also reported by al-Bukhārī that the verse of the Qur'ān (XLIX, 9) which runs: 'And if two parties of the believers fall to fighting, then make peace between them' refers to the conflict between the sincere Companions and the followers of ʿAbd Allāh ibn Ubayy, has been criticised by Ibn Baṭṭāl, who points out that the verse refers to a quarrel between two groups of Muslims, whereas Ibn Ubayy had not accepted Islam even outwardly at the time the verse was revealed.

(c) The *ḥadīth* that if the Prophet's son Ibrāhīm had lived, he would have been a prophet, has been severely criticised by al-Nawawī, Ibn ʿAbd al-Barr and Ibn al-Athīr; while al-Shawkānī has included it on his list of forged traditions.[60]

(d) The *ḥadīth*s reported by Ibn Māja on the excellence of his home city Qazwīn have been declared forged by the traditionists.

(e) The traditions narrated by some traditionists to the effect that 'he who loves, keeps chaste, and dies, dies as a martyr', is declared by Ibn al-Qayyim as forged and baseless. He comments that even if the *isnād* of this *ḥadīth* were as bright as the sun, it would not cease to be wrong and fictitious.[61]

(f) The *ḥadīth* reported by al-Bukhārī that Abraham will pray to God on Doomsday, saying 'O Lord, Thou hast promised me that Thou wilt not humiliate me on the Day of Judgement' is criticised and rejected by al-Ismāʿīlī, whose judgement is reported by Ibn Ḥajar.[62]

(g) Most of the traditions concerning the advent of the Dajjāl and the Mahdī towards the end of time, are declared by the traditionists to be spurious, and are included in the *mawḍūʿāt* works.

*

Such, then, are the broad outlines of the Muslim science of *ḥadīth* criticism. Without question one of the most sophisticated scholarly enterprises ever undertaken, it remains today an essential underpinning for the religion of Islam, and the lives of those who try to live by it. Taught in the ancient universities of the Muslim world, such as al-Azhar in Cairo, al-Qarawiyyīn in Fez, and Deoband in India, it continues to be a lively and popular academic field. And with the arrival of the contemporary Islamic awakening, which has been accompanied by a sizeable increase in the number of texts made available, both ancient and modern, it seems likely to play a central role in the elaboration of the legal codes of the modern Islamic world, as the Muslims move away from the European legal systems bequeathed by the former colonial powers, and seek to develop a code which allows them to live in the modern world while remaining faithful to their own distinctive and sacred identity.

APPENDIX I

WOMEN SCHOLARS OF *ḤADĪTH*

HISTORY records few scholarly enterprises, at least before modern times, in which women have played an important and active role side by side with men. The science of *ḥadīth* forms an outstanding exception in this respect. Islam, a religion which (unlike Christianity) refused to attribute gender to the Godhead,[1] and never appointed a male priestly elite to serve as an intermediary between creature and Creator, started life with the assurance that while men and women are equipped by nature for complementary rather than identical roles, no spiritual superiority inheres in the masculine principle.[2] As a result, the Muslim community was happy to entrust matters of the greatest religious responsibility to women, who, as 'sisters to men', were of equal worth in God's sight. Only this can explain why, uniquely among the classical Western religions, Islam produced a large number of outstanding female scholars, on whose testimony and sound judgement much of the edifice of Islam depends.

Since Islam's earliest days, women had been taking a prominent part in the preservation and cultivation of *ḥadīth*, and this function continued down the centuries. At every period in Muslim history, there lived numerous eminent women-traditionists, treated by their brethren with reverence and respect. Biographical notices on very large numbers of them are to be found in the biographical dictionaries.

During the lifetime of the Prophet, many women had been not only the instance for the evolution of many traditions, but had also been their transmitters to their sisters and brethren in faith.[3] After the Prophet's death, many women Companions, particularly his wives, were looked upon as vital custodians of knowledge, and were approached for instruction by the other Companions, to whom they readily dispensed the rich store which they had gathered in the Prophet's company. The names of Ḥafṣa, Umm Ḥabība, Maymūna, Umm Salama, and ʿĀ'isha, are familiar to every student of *ḥadīth* as being among its earliest and most distinguished transmitters.[4] In particular, ʿĀ'isha is one of the most important figures in the whole history of *ḥadīth* literature—not only as one of the earliest reporters of the largest number of *ḥadīth*, but also as one of their most careful interpreters.

In the period of the Successors, too, women held important positions as traditionists. Ḥafṣa, the daughter of Ibn Sīrīn,[5] Umm al-Dardā' the Younger (d.81/700), and ʿAmra bint ʿAbd al-Raḥmān, are only a few of the key women traditionists of this period. Umm al-Dardā' was held by Iyās ibn Muʿāwiya, an important traditionist of the time and a judge of undisputed ability and merit, to be superior to all the other traditionists of the period, including the celebrated masters of *ḥadīth* like al-Ḥasan al-Baṣrī and Ibn Sīrīn.[6] ʿAmra was considered a great authority on traditions related by ʿĀ'isha. Among her students, Abū Bakr ibn Ḥazm, the celebrated judge of Medina, was ordered by the caliph ʿUmar ibn ʿAbd al-ʿAzīz to write down all the traditions known on her authority.[7]

After them, ʿĀbida al-Madaniyya, ʿAbda bint Bishr, Umm ʿUmar al-Thaqafiyya, Zaynab the granddaughter of ʿAlī ibn ʿAbd Allāh ibn ʿAbbās, Nafīsa bint al-Ḥasan ibn Ziyād, Khadīja Umm Muḥammad, ʿAbda bint ʿAbd al-Raḥmān, and many other members of the fair sex excelled in delivering public lectures on *ḥadīth*. These devout women came from the most diverse backgrounds, indicating that neither class nor gender were obstacles to rising through the ranks of Islamic scholarship. For example, ʿĀbida, who started life as a slave owned by Muḥammad ibn Yazīd, learnt a large number of *ḥadīth*s with the teachers in Medina. She was given by her master to Ḥabīb Daḥḥūn, the great traditionist of Spain, when he visited the holy city on his way to the Hajj. Daḥḥūn was so impressed by her learning that he freed her, married her, and brought her to Andalusia. It is said that she related ten thousand traditions on the authority of her Medinan teachers.[8]

Zaynab bint Sulaymān (d.142/759), by contrast, was a princess by birth. Her father was a cousin of al-Saffāḥ, the founder of the Abbasid dynasty, and had been a governor of Baṣra, Oman and Baḥrayn during the caliphate of al-Manṣūr.[9] Zaynab, who received a fine education, acquired a mastery of *ḥadīth*, gained a reputation as one of the most distinguished women-traditionists of the time, and counted many important men among her pupils.[10]

This partnership of women with men in the cultivation of the Prophetic Tradition continued in the period when the great anthologies of *ḥadīth* were compiled. A survey of the texts reveals that all the important compilers of traditions from the earliest period received many of them from women *shuyūkh*: every major *ḥadīth* collection gives the names of many women as the immediate authorities of the author. And when these works had been compiled, the women traditionists themselves mastered them, and delivered lectures to large classes of pupils, to whom they would issue their own *ijāzas*.

In the fourth century, we find Fāṭima bint ʿAbd al-Raḥmān (d.312/924), known as al-Ṣūfiyya on account of her great piety; Fāṭima (granddaughter of Abū Daūd of *Sunan* fame); Amat al-Waḥīd (d.377/987), the daughter of the distinguished jurist al-Muḥāmilī; Umm al-Fatḥ Amat al-Salām (d.390/999), the daughter of the judge Abū Bakr Aḥmad (d.350/961); Jumuʿa bint Aḥmad, and many other women, whose classes were always well-attended by reverential audiences.[11]

The Islamic tradition of female *ḥadīth* scholarship continued in the fifth and sixth centuries of the *hijra*. Fāṭima bint al-Ḥasan ibn ʿAlī ibn al-Daqqāq (d.480/1087), who married the famous mystic and traditionist Abu'l-Qāsim al-Qushayrī, was celebrated not only for her piety and her mastery of calligraphy, but also for her knowledge of *ḥadīth* and the quality of the *isnāds* she knew.[12] Even more distinguished was Karīma al-Marwaziyya (d.463/1070), who was considered the best authority on the *Ṣaḥīḥ* of al-Bukhārī in her time. Abū Dharr of Herāt, one of the leading scholars of the period, attached such great importance to her authority that he advised his students to study the *Ṣaḥīḥ* under no one else, because of the quality of her scholarship. She thus figures as a central point in the transmission of this seminal text of Islam.[13] 'As a matter of fact,' writes Goldziher, 'her name occurs with extraordinary frequency in the *ijāzas* for narrating the text of this book.'[14] Among her students were al-Khaṭīb al-Baghdādī[15] and al-Ḥumaydī (428/1036–488/1095).[16]

Aside from Karīma, a number of other women traditionists occupy an eminent place in the history of the transmission of the text of the *Ṣaḥīḥ*.'[17] Among these, one might mention in particular Fāṭima bint Muḥammad (d.539/1144); Shuhda 'the Writer' (d.574/1178), and Sitt al-Wuzarā' bint ʿUmar (d.716/1316).[18] Fāṭima narrated the book on the authority of the great traditionist Saʿīd al-ʿAyyār; and she received from the *ḥadīth* specialists the proud title of *Musnida Iṣfahān* (the great *ḥadīth* authority of Iṣfahān). Shuhda was a famous calligrapher and a traditionist of great repute; the biographers describe her as 'the calligrapher, the great authority on *ḥadīth*, and the pride of womanhood'. Her great-grandfather had been a dealer in needles, and thus acquired the soubriquet 'al-Ibrī'. But her father, Abū Naṣr (d.506/1112) had acquired a passion for *ḥadīth*, and managed to study it with several masters of the subject.[19] In obedience to the *sunna*, he gave his daughter a sound academic education, ensuring that she studied under many traditionists of accepted reputation.

She married ʿAlī ibn Muḥammad, an important figure with some literary interests, who later became a boon companion of the caliph al-Muqtafī, and founded a college and a Sufi lodge, which he endowed most generously. His wife, however, was better-known: she gained her reputation in the field of *ḥadīth* scholarship, and was noted for the quality of her *isnāds*.[20] Her lectures on *Ṣaḥīḥ al-Bukhārī* and other *ḥadīth* collections were attended by large crowds of students; and on account of her great reputation, some people even falsely claimed to have been her disciples.[21]

Also known as an authority on Bukhārī was Sitt al-Wuzarā', who, besides her acclaimed mastery of Islamic law, was known as 'the *musnida* of her time', and delivered lectures on the *Ṣaḥīḥ* and other works in Damascus and Egypt.[22] Classes on the *Ṣaḥīḥ* were likewise given by Umm al-Khayr Amat al-Khāliq (811/1408–911/1505), who is regarded as the last great *ḥadīth* scholar of the Ḥijāz.[23] Still another authority on Bukhārī was ʿĀ'isha bint ʿAbd al-Hādī.[24]

Apart from these women, who seem to have specialised in the great *Ṣaḥīḥ* of Imām al-Bukhārī, there were others, whose expertise was centred on other texts. Umm al-Khayr Fāṭima bint ʿAlī (d.532/1137), and Fāṭima al-Shahrazūriyya, delivered lectures on the *Ṣaḥīḥ* of Muslim.[25] Fāṭima al-Jawzdāniyya (d.524/1129) narrated to her students the three *Muʿjams* of al-Ṭabarānī.[26] Zaynab of Ḥarrān (d.688/1289), whose lectures attracted a large crowd of students, taught them the *Musnad* of Aḥmad ibn Ḥanbal, the largest known collection of *ḥadīth*s.[27] Juwayriya bint ʿUmar (d.783/1381), and Zaynab bint Aḥmad ibn ʿUmar (d.722/1322), who had travelled widely in pursuit of *ḥadīth* and delivered lectures in Egypt as well as Medina, narrated to her students the collections of al-Dārimī and ʿAbd ibn Ḥumayd; and we are told that students travelled from far and wide to attend her discourses.[28] Zaynab bint Aḥmad (d.740/1339), usually known as Bint al-Kamāl, acquired 'a camel-load' of diplomas; she delivered lectures on the *Musnad* of Abū Ḥanīfa, the *Shamā'il* of al-Tirmidhī, and the *Sharḥ Maʿānī al-Āthār* of al-Ṭaḥāwī, the last of which she had read with another woman traditionist, ʿAjība bint Abī Bakr (d.740/1339).[29] 'On her authority is based,' says Goldziher, 'the authenticity of the Gotha codex...in the same *isnād* a large number of learned women are cited who had occupied themselves with this work.'[30] With her, and various other women, the great traveller Ibn Baṭṭūṭa studied traditions during his stay at Damascus.[31] The famous historian of Damascus, Ibn ʿAsākir, who tells us that he had studied under more than 1,200 men and 80 women, obtained the *ijāza* of Zaynab bint ʿAbd al-Raḥmān for the *Muwaṭṭā'* of Imām Mālik.[32] Jalāl al-Dīn al-Suyūṭī studied the *Risāla* of Imām al-Shāfiʿī with Hājar bint Muḥammad.[33] ʿAfīf al-Dīn Junayd, a traditionist of the ninth century AH, read the *Sunan* of al-Dārimī with Fāṭima bint Aḥmad ibn Qāsim.[34]

Other important traditionists included Zaynab bint al-Shaʿrī (524–615/1129–1218). She studied *ḥadīth* under several important traditionists, and in turn lectured to many students—some of who gained great repute—including Ibn Khallikān, author of the well-known biographical dictionary *Wafayāt al-Aʿyān*.[35] Another was Karīma the Syrian (d.641/1218), described by the biographers as the greatest authority on *ḥadīth* in Syria of her day. She delivered lectures on many works of *ḥadīth* on the authority of numerous teachers.[36]

In his work *al-Durar al-Kāmina*,[37] Ibn Ḥajar gives short biographical notices of about 170 prominent women of the eighth century, most of whom are traditionists, and under many of whom the author himself had studied.[38] Some of these women were acknowledged as the best traditionists of the period. For instance, Juwayriya bint Aḥmad, to whom we have already referred, studied a range of works on traditions, under scholars both male and female, who taught at the great colleges of the time, and then proceeded to give famous lectures on the Islamic disciplines. 'Some of my own teachers,' says Ibn Ḥajar, 'and many of my contemporaries, attended her discourses.'[39] ʿĀ'isha bint ʿAbd al-Hādī (723–816), also mentioned above, who for a considerable time was one of Ibn Ḥajar's teachers, was considered to be the finest traditionist of her time, and many students undertook long journeys in order to sit at her feet and study the truths of religion.[40] Sitt al-ʿArab (d.760/1358) had been the teacher of the well-known traditionist al-ʿIrāqī (d.742/1341), and of many others who derived a good proportion of their knowledge from her.[41] Daqīqa bint Murshid (d.746/1345), another celebrated woman traditionist, received instruction from a whole range of other women.

Information on women traditionists of the ninth century is given in a work by Muḥammad ibn ʿAbd al-Raḥmān al-Sakhāwī (830–897/1427–1429), called *al-Ḍaw' al-Lāmiʿ*, which is a biographical dictionary of eminent persons of the ninth century.[42] A further source is the *Muʿjam al-Shuyūkh* of ʿAbd al-ʿAzīz ibn ʿUmar ibn Fahd (812–871/1409–1466), compiled in 861AH and devoted to the biographical notices of more than 1,100 of the author's teachers, including over 130 women scholars under whom he had studied.[43] Some of these women were acclaimed as among the most precise and scholarly traditionists of their time, and trained many of the great scholars of the following generation. Umm Hānī Maryam (778–871/1376–1466), for instance, learnt the Qur'ān by heart when still a child, acquired all the Islamic sciences then being taught, including theology, law, history, and grammar, and then travelled to pursue *ḥadīth* with the best traditionists of her time in Cairo and Mecca. She was also celebrated for her mastery of calligraphy, her command of the Arabic language, and her natural aptitude for poetry, as also her strict observance of the duties of religion (she performed the *ḥajj* no fewer than thirteen times). Her son, who became a noted scholar of the tenth century, showed the greatest veneration for her, and constantly waited on her towards the end of her life. She pursued an intensive programme of lecturing in the great colleges of Cairo, giving *ijāzas* to many scholars. Ibn Fahd himself studied several technical works on *ḥadīth* under her.[44]

Her Syrian contemporary, Bā'ī Khātūn (d.864/1459), having studied traditions with Abū Bakr al-Mizzī and numerous other traditionists, and having secured the *ijāzas* of a large number of masters of *ḥadīth*, both men and women, delivered lectures on the subject in Syria and Cairo. We are told that she took especial delight in teaching.[45] ʿĀ'isha bint Ibrāhīm (760/1358–842/1438), known in academic circles as Ibnat al-Sharā'iḥī, also studied traditions in Damascus and Cairo (and elsewhere), and delivered lectures which the eminent scholars of the day spared no efforts to attend.[46] Umm al-Khayr Saʿīda of Mecca (d.850/1446) received instruction in *ḥadīth* from numerous traditionists in different cities, gaining an equally enviable reputation as a scholar.[47]

So far as may be gathered from the sources, the involvement of women in *ḥadīth* scholarship, and in the Islamic disciplines generally, seems to have declined considerably from the tenth century of the *hijra*. Books such as *al-Nūr al-Sāfir* of al-ʿAydarūs, the *Khulāṣat al-Akhbār* of al-Muḥibbī, and the *al-Suḥub al-Wābila* of Muḥammad ibn ʿAbd Allāh (which are biographical dictionaries of eminent persons of the tenth, eleventh and twelfth centuries of the *hijra* respectively) contain the names of barely a dozen eminent-women traditionists. But it would be wrong to conclude from this that after the tenth century, women lost interest in the subject. Some women traditionists, who gained good reputations in the ninth century, lived well into the tenth, and continued their services to the *sunna*. Asmā' bint Kamāl al-Dīn (d.904/1498) wielded great influence with the sultans and their officials, to whom she often made recommendations—which, we are told, they always accepted. She lectured on *ḥadīth*, and trained women in various Islamic sciences.[48] ʿĀ'isha bint Muḥammad (d.906/1500), who married the famous judge Muṣliḥ al-Dīn, taught traditions to many students, and was appointed professor at the Ṣāliḥiyya College in Damascus.[49] Fāṭima bint Yūsuf of Aleppo (870/1465–925/1519), was known as one of the excellent scholars of her time.[50] Umm al-Khayr granted an *ijāza* to a pilgrim at Mecca in the year 938/1531.[51]

The last woman traditionist of the first rank who is known to us was

Fāṭima al-Fuḍayliya, also known as al-Shaykha al-Fuḍayliya. She was born before the end of the twelfth Islamic century, and soon excelled in the art of calligraphy and the various Islamic sciences. She had a special interest in *ḥadīth*, read a good deal on the subject, received the diplomas of a good many scholars, and acquired a reputation as an important traditionist in her own right. Towards the end of her life, she settled at Mecca, where she founded a rich public library. In the Holy City she was attended by many eminent traditionists, who attended her lectures and received certificates from her. Among them, one could mention in particular Shaykh ʿUmar al-Ḥanafī and Shaykh Muḥammad Ṣāliḥ. She died in 1247/1831.[52]

Throughout the history of feminine scholarship in Islam it is clear that the women involved did not confine their study to a personal interest in traditions, or to the private coaching of a few individuals, but took their seats as students as well as teachers in public educational institutions, side by side with their brothers in faith. The colophons of many manuscripts show them both as students attending large general classes, and also as teachers, delivering regular courses of lectures. For instance, the certificate on folios 238–40 of the *al-Mashīkhat maʿ al-Takhrīj* of Ibn al-Bukhārī, shows that numerous women attended a regular course of eleven lectures which was delivered before a class consisting of more than five hundred students in the ʿUmar Mosque at Damascus in the year 687/1288. Another certificate, on folio 40 of the same manuscript, shows that many female students, whose names are specified, attended another course of six lectures on the book, which was delivered by Ibn al-Ṣayrafī to a class of more than two hundred students at Aleppo in the year 736/1336. And on folio 250, we discover that a famous woman traditionist, Umm ʿAbd Allāh, delivered a course of five lectures on the book to a mixed class of more than fifty students, at Damascus in the year 837/1433.[53]

Various notes on the manuscript of the *Kitāb al-Kifāya* of al-Khaṭīb al-Baghdādī, and of a collection of various treatises on *ḥadīth*, show Niʿma bint ʿAlī, Umm Aḥmad Zaynab bint al-Makkī, and other women traditionists delivering lectures on these two books, sometimes independently, and sometimes jointly with male traditionists, in major colleges such as the ʿAzīziyya Madrasa, and the Ḍiyāʾiyya Madrasa, to regular classes of students. Some of these lectures were attended by Aḥmad, son of the famous general Ṣalāḥ al-Dīn.[54]

APPENDIX II

THE *ḤADĪTHS* AND ORIENTALISM

WESTERN scholars have taken an interest in the *ḥadīth* material for almost two centuries, making a welcome contribution by editing and sometimes translating many of the original Arabic works, and by the diligent preparation of concordances and indices.[1] But while some have accepted the traditional canons of *ḥadīth* criticism as developed by the Muslim scholars themselves, others have offered alternative accounts of the subject.[2] Orientalists of this school have raised some fundamental issues with regard to the literature, and attempted to address them according to modern Western canons of literary and historical criticism.

The first scholar to make this attempt was Aloys Sprenger (according to his own claim), who summarised the results of his research into *ḥadīth* in the introduction to his *Das Leben und die Lehre des Muhammad* (1869CE). Another nineteenth-century scholar, William Muir, also touched on the subject in his rather hostile and now outclassed biography of the Prophet.

IGNAZ GOLDZIHER

But such attempts were far surpassed in their treatment and criticism by Ignaz Goldziher, an Orientalist who was secretary at the Hebrew Congregation in the Hungarian city of Pecs. Goldziher, a brilliant but often choleric man, who studied under the Ottomanist scholar and convert to Islam Arminius Vambéry (1832–1913), spent the year of 1873 travelling in the Middle East, where, sitting with the polite and literate Muslim elite, he seems to have experienced something of a love affair with the Muslim faith. Thanks to 'this year full of honours, full of lustre, full of light',[3] as he later wrote in his diary,

> I truly entered into the spirit of Islam to such an extent that

> ultimately I became inwardly convinced that I myself was a Muslim, and judiciously discovered that this was the only religion which, even in its doctrinal and official formulation, can satisfy philosophical minds. My ideal was to elevate Judaism to a similar rational level.[4]

Goldziher had seen enough of Islam to be convinced of its truth. Yet so total was his conceit, so absolute his academic obsession, that he refused to follow his teacher Vambéry into an honest and open declaration of faith; opting instead for this private agenda of reforming the religion which he had inherited. It is perhaps a symptom of the inner pain he experienced from living this kind of reverse hypocrisy, whereby he privately acknowledged the superiority of Islam and yet remained in public a busy synagogue official, that he should have embarked on a policy of attempted demolition of the literary sources of Islam, by borrowing those techniques of academic 'higher criticism' which had already undermined belief in the textual integrity of the Hebrew scriptures. His thesis, that the *ḥadīth*s are to a large degree the fraudulent propaganda of rival legal theorists of the early second century, was in many ways a characteristic product of his troubled and instinctively polemical mind.[5]

But despite the attractiveness of this thesis, which, to nineteenth century Europeans, seemed to offer a way of pulling the carpet from beneath Islam,[6] it soon became evident that his theories were at best conjectural, and were lacking in systematic textual evidence. No serious attempt was made to adduce the missing body of proof until the time of Joseph Schacht, half a century later.

Goldziher's main claims, as expounded in the second volume of his *Muslim Studies*, may be summarised as follows:

1. The *ḥadīth* literature is largely based on mere oral transmission, which lasted for more than a century; and the extant *ḥadīth* collections do not refer to any records of *ḥadīth*s which may have been made at an earlier period.
2. The number of *ḥadīth*s in the later collections is far larger than the number of those contained in the earlier anthologies or the early works on Islamic law. This, it is said, shows that many of the *ḥadīth*s are of questionable authenticity.
3. The *ḥadīth*s reported by the younger Companions are far more numerous than those related by the older Companions.
4. The *isnād* system was applied, arbitrarily, to *ḥadīth* not earlier than the close of the first Islamic century, and does not furnish a proof of the genuineness of the tradition to which it is attached.

5. Many of the *ḥadīths* contradict each other.
6. Definite evidence exists of the large-scale forgery of the *isnād* as well as of the texts of *ḥadīths*.
7. The Muslim critics confined their criticism of the literature to the *isnād* alone, and never criticised the texts transmitted.

Many of these controversies have been discussed in detail in Chapters 1, 6 and 7 of this book. Here, however, it may be useful to provide a summary point-by-point response:

1. Goldziher has himself recognised that more than a dozen *ṣaḥīfas* containing Prophetic *ḥadīths* were compiled by the Companions and their Successors. As for the lack of reference to them in the later *ḥadīth* collections, Sprenger has explained that this is due to the fact that the early traditionists referred to the authors of the books from whom they received them through their own teachers, instead of referring to the books themselves, which were liable to suffer interpolation and forgery.[7] He has demonstrated this with reference to the practice followed by Wāqidī and Ibn Saʿd, and has also collected a good deal of material on the writing down of *Ḥadīths*, and the existence of Arabic books during the pre-Islamic and early Islamic periods.[8] The more recent publication of one such early document, the *ṣaḥīfa* of Hammām ibn Munabbih by Dr. Hamidullah, and the identification of its contents with those of part of the *Musnad* of Ibn Ḥanbal, with very slight variations, strongly supports the theory of Sprenger. Similarly, Abbott, basing herself on early papyrus documents unknown to Goldziher, surveys the very considerable evidence for extensive written records in the first century, and concludes that 'oral and written transmission went hand in hand almost from the start.'[9]

2. The increase in the number of *ḥadīths* included in the later collections (i.e. of the third century CE) is easily fathomed by anyone conversant with the history of the collection of *ḥadīth*. The early compilers did not know as many Traditions as were known to their successors. For, simultaneously with the expansion of the Islamic empire, the custodians of the *ḥadīths* travelled widely and settled throughout the new dominions, narrating the *ḥadīths* known to them to create a provincial corpus. It was only after students of *ḥadīth* had travelled through all these countries and collected together the traditions known to the specialists living there, and narrated them to their own disciples, that larger and more complete collections of *ḥadīths* could be compiled.[10]

3. Some European scholars have envisaged a natural course of events in which those who associated with the Prophet for a long period would have reported more traditions about him than those who only knew him for a short while. This, however, was not the case. The younger generations of Companions reported a far larger number of traditions than their older brethren. From this, certain Orientalists have concluded, many *isnāds* of the younger Companions were forged. This question, however, has already been raised by the classical *ḥadīth* scholars themselves, who point out that since the older Companions passed away not long after the death of the Prophet, they had less time to pass on all the traditions known to them, whereas the younger Companions, such as ʿĀ'isha, Ibn ʿAbbās and Abū Hurayra, lived for a far longer period, and were able to disseminate the *ḥadīth*s known to them much more extensively. J. Fück has pointed out that this in fact supports the veracity of the traditionists; for if all the *isnāds* had been forged by them, they would have tried to produce *isnāds* from the older Companions in larger numbers.[11]

4. As the *isnād*, its origin, development and importance, have been discussed in Chapter 5 of this book, and Robson and Abbott have thoroughly dealt with the pertinent views of Muslim and non-Muslim scholars,[12] readers are referred to the observations contained in those sources.

5. There is no doubt that a large number of *ḥadīth*s contradict one another. But to conclude from this that most are therefore forged is not a logical inference. For it is a natural thing for the leader of a fast-developing movement to change the instructions he issues to his followers, in order to respond to a changing situation. Hence we find that the Prophet at times issued advice or instructions which superceded those which he had given earlier. An instance of this is furnished by the presence of contradictory *ḥadīth*s concerning the admissibility of recording *ḥadīth*s in writing: the earlier *ḥadīth*s prohibit it, while later *ḥadīth*s regard it as permissible. In some cases of evident contradiction, the clashes can be resolved by pointing out the different circumstances under which the contradictory instructions were given. In various other cases, contradictions have been explained by isolating ideas common to them which were expressed in various ways at different times. This is not to say, of course, that no *ḥadīth*s were forged, and that forged *ḥadīth*s did not conflict with sound ones; in fact, the Muslim scholars have already recognised and analysed this point.[13] But one cannot

but be surprised to find that some European scholars have cited *ḥadīths* as evidence of contradictions in the literature, when Muslim scholars have for a thousand years dismissed those very *ḥadīths* as spurious, or as cases of abrogation.

6. The large-scale forgery of *isnāds* as well as the texts of traditions is a historical fact accepted by all the Muslim scholars, and has been described at length in Chapter 3 of this book. The development of an extensive and sophisticated literature on the *mawḍūʿāt* (forged narrations discarded by the traditionists) is sure and sufficient proof of this. Here again, one is surprised to find some European scholars citing these *ḥadīths* not only to illustrate the vagaries of the sectarian mind in various periods—a wholly legitimate deduction—but also to prove that the literature as a whole is of questionable reliability.

On other occasions, they have cited *ḥadīths* traditionally considered authentic as forged. For instance:

6a. Goldziher[14] and (following him) Guillaume[15] cite the following *ḥadīth* from Tirmidhī:

> Ibn ʿUmar related that Muḥammad ordered all dogs to be killed save sheep-dogs and hounds. Abū Hurayra added the words *au zarʿin* (or field dogs). Whereupon Ibn ʿUmar makes the remark that Abū Hurayra owned cultivated land. A better illustration of the underlying motive of some *ḥadīth* can hardly be found.[16]

Having produced this *ḥadīth*, Goldziher says that the remark of Ibn ʿUmar proves that even the earliest transmitters were not free from selfish and dishonest motives. The Muslim traditionists, however, have explained Ibn ʿUmar's remark as meaning that Abū Hurayra, being possessed of personal experience of the subject-matter of this *ḥadīth*, was in a better position to know exactly what its wording was.[17]

6b. Goldziher[18] and (following him) Guillaume[19] assert that the *ḥadīth* reported by Bukhārī: 'Make journey (for pilgrimage) only to three (mosques)—the Inviolable Mosque, the Mosque of the Prophet, and the Mosque of Jerusalem', was forged by Ibn Shihāb al-Zuhrī in order to help ʿAbd al-Malik against his rival ʿAbd Allāh ibn al-Zubayr. J. Fück, however, points out that this assertion is chronologically unsound. Ibn al-Zubayr was killed in 73 AH, while al-Zuhrī was born in 51, or even later. He therefore would have been too young at the time of Ibn al-Zubayr's death to have become a widely-accepted authority on tradition; had the caliph really wished to find a *ḥadīth* propagandist, he would probably have chosen someone more venerable and established. Goldziher's theory is further weakened by the fact that al-Zuhrī's authority for this *ḥadīth* (the famous Saʿīd ibn al-Musayyib, who died in 94AH) was still alive, which would have made it hard to misuse his name: a propagandist would have chosen someone safely defunct. Again, al-Zuhrī is not the only traditionist who reported this *ḥadīth* from Saʿīd.[20]

6c. One further example should suffice to demonstrate the purely speculative nature of many of Goldziher's assertions. He states that once the fabrication of *ḥadīth* had become a common and established practice among the traditionists, they attempted to stop it by forging a *ḥadīth* which prohibited the practice. The well-known *ḥadīth* (in which the Prophet is reported to have said that whoever falsely attributed anything to him would be preparing an abode in Hell), together with a set of similar traditions, was, according to Goldziher, fabricated in order to stop the fabrication process.[21] The *ḥadīth*, however, is *mutawātir*, having been reported by more than seventy Companions and numerous independant chains of authorities. It is found in different forms in all the important *ḥadīth* collections, and has been accepted by all the traditionists as one of the most reliable and extensively-attested of all traditions. It is hard to conceive how it could have been concocted verbatim and at the same time by a large number of scholars distributed over several provinces.

Fabrications were made in the name of the prophets who came before Muḥammad, of which he was aware, and to which reference is made in the Qur'ān; similarly, forged traditions were attributed to Muḥammad himself during his lifetime. Under such circumstances, it is hardly surprising that the great leader should have warned his followers against this practice. Goldziher was surely well-acquainted with these facts; yet he persisted in asserting that these *ḥadīth*s were forged—without offering any proof. And Guillaume has followed him almost verbatim.[22]

7. It is true that all the *muṣannaf* collections of *ḥadīth* are arranged into books and chapters according to subject-matter, and contain a short description of the *isnād* in technical language, without much analysis being presented of the character of the text. Yet in the very extensive exegetic literature, the commentators do of course subject the texts to a close critique, following the principles which we have given in the last Chapter of our book. It appears, however, that the function of the collection and

formal *isnād* criticism of the *ḥadīth*s was reserved for the collectors, while the function of their material criticism was left for the jurists and the commentators on the various anthologies.

According to the Muslim critics, the *isnād* provides good evidence, but not an absolute guarantee of the soundness of a *ḥadīth* text. If such a text is contrary to reason and common experience, or to the explicit text of the Qur'ān, or to the text of a *mutawātir* tradition, or the *ijmā*ᶜ, it is considered to have been forged. Goldziher appears to be unaware of the extensive literature on *matn* criticism.[23]

For more on Goldziher's understanding of *ḥadīth*, reference should be made to the studies of al-Sibāᶜī[24] and al-Khaṭīb;[25] the more recent criticisms directed at Schacht are also relevant.

ALFRED GUILLAUME

The Traditions of Islam, published in 1924 by Alfred Guillaume, formerly professor of Arabic at London University, gained some currency for a while as the only English-language critique of traditional Muslim *ḥadīth* scholarship. It represents, however, little more than a reiteration of Goldziher's work; indeed, accusations of plagiarism dogged the latter years of this author's career.

JOSEPH SCHACHT

Our comments on Goldziher serve also to interpret much of the later work of Joseph Schacht. Schacht's conviction, in some ways even more radical than his predecessor's, was that for the Prophet, 'law as such fell outside the sphere of religion', and that 'the technical aspects of law were a matter of indifference to the [early] Muslims'.[26] The *ḥadīth* literature which elaborates it, then, despite the efforts of the Muslim scholars to ensure its authenticity, can be dismissed as a monumental fraud.

Partly because of Schacht's habit of making 'all too readily formulated and at the same time sweeping theories,'[27] many subsequent Western scholars have expressed grave doubts about his work. Quite apart from the fact that its 'supercilious' approach 'makes heavy reading, and its style seems to rub many readers, Western and Muslim, up the wrong way,' its central thesis, that the Prophet, despite the Qur'ān's concern with law, and the example of the Hebraic prophetic tradition in which the Qur'ān places him, was not interested in legislation, has seemed improbable. Fifteen years after Schacht's *Origins* was published, Samuel Goitein was writing that for the Prophet, 'even strictly legal matters were not irrelevant to religion, but were part and parcel of the divine revelation,'[28] and that 'the idea of the *Sharīʿa* was not the result of post-Quranic developments, but was formulated by Muḥammad himself.'[29] Similar objections to Schacht's opinions are aired by N. J. Coulson, who finds them 'too rigid', and 'not wholly convincing';[30] while J. Robson[31] and N. Abbott[32] are even more critical. However, the most rigorous articulation of this scepticism comes from M. M. Azami, whose *Studies in Early Ḥadīth Literature*, and, more recently, *On Schacht's Origins of Muhammadan Jurisprudence*, can be considered the definitive rebuttal of Schacht's thesis. Readers interested in pursuing the debate further are referred to these texts.

NABIA ABBOTT

This American scholar has given us what is in many ways the most well-written and coherent account of the literature. It has the advantage of being rooted in a series of very early texts whose authenticity is beyond question, taking the form of collections of Arabic papyrus documents, some little more than fragments, acquired by Chicago's Oriental Institute between 1929 and 1947. Abbott set herself the laborious task of identifying, transcribing and translating these; a work which bore fruit first in a brief preliminary article,[33] and then in her monumental *Studies in Arabic Literary Papyri*. Volume I of this, published in 1957, dealt with historical texts; Volume II (1967) concerned Qur'ānic commentary and Tradition; while Volume III (1972) included documents on language and literature. Academic recognition for this achievement culminated in an invitation to contribute the key article on *ḥadīth* for the *Cambridge History of Arabic Literature*.[34]

In Volume II of her *Studies*, Abbott presents thirteen very early *ḥadīth* papyri, and discovers that when set beside the matter included in the canonical collections, they 'contain very little, beyond some rather minor textual variants, that was not already available to us in the rich heritage of *tafsīr* and *ḥadīth* literature'.[35] A study of the *isnāds*, moreover, reveals a distinction between the often poor *isnāds* attached to material concerning Companions and Successors, which was, according to orthodoxy, of less legal and doctrinal significance, and the good *isnāds* used for the Prophetic *ḥadīth*. This confirms the verdict that 'the special attention to and extra care with Muhammad's *ḥadīth* and *sunnah* were stressed from the very beginning of the caliphate.'[36]

Although she rarely mentions Schacht or Goldziher, Abbott is clearly targeting their theories when she emphasizes the importance attached to religious law from the earliest days of Islam: the Companions were enthusiastic emulators of the Prophet's example,[37] while even relatively profane Umayyad rulers like ʿAbd al-Malik, who, according to Schacht, had set little or no store by the *ḥadīth* of the Prophet, actually took the trouble to memorise a number of *ḥadīth*.[38] She similarly adduces detailed evidence for the view, held by Sprenger and Robson as well as the Muslim authorities, that the importance attached to the prophetic *ḥadīth* was so great that ʿUmar II appointed a commission to record it, and ensure its authenticity.[39] As we have seen on p.24 above, Abbott also presents reasons to believe that the early written records of *ḥadīth* were very substantial. And again, she is clearly targeting Goldziher when she concludes that

> Oral and written transmission went hand in hand almost from the start; the traditions of Muhammad as transmitted by his Companions and their Successors were, as a rule, scrupulously scrutinized at each step of the transmission, and that the so-called phenomenal growth of tradition in the second and third centuries of Islam was not primarily growth of content, so far as the *ḥadīth* of Muhammad and the *ḥadīth* of the Companions are concerned, but represents largely the progressive increase of parallel and multiple chains of transmission.[40]

JAMES ROBSON

This Scottish clergyman, who became Professor of Arabic at Manchester University, dedicated the later years of his career to an extensive programme of reading in the *ḥadīth* literature, which culminated most visibly in his translation of al-Tabrīzī's *Mishkāt al-Maṣābiḥ*, a work which can be considered the most competent English rendition of a large *ḥadīth* collection.[41] Robson also gave us the first and so far the only translation of a classical manual on *ḥadīth* criticism: the *Madkhal* of al-Ḥākim al-Nīsābūrī.[42]

In the introduction to his *Mishkāt*, and also in a series of articles,[43] Robson voices a growing dissatisfaction with the Schachtian thesis, which by the early 1960's had become a kind of Orientalist orthodoxy. Analysing some of Schacht's more sweeping judgements, he became convinced that the traditional Muslim account of *ḥadīth* genesis had much to commend it, and had in some ways been misrepresented—or at least misunderstood—by Goldziher and Schacht.[44]

G.H.A. JUYNBOLL

This author, in his article 'On the Origins of Arabic Prose',[45] and especially in his recent monograph *Muslim Tradition: Studies in Chronology, Provenance, and Authorship of Early Ḥadīth*,[46] expresses regret that Schacht's work has passed almost unnoticed by Muslims, and condescendingly decides that this is perhaps because of its difficult and objectionable language. Juynboll, who announces quite explicitly that he is 'writing for Muslims',[47] articulates his disquiet that the traditional view of *ḥadīth* should still be maintained among Muslims, and his hopes that his book will serve to call this view into question. None the less, while accepting the main thrust of some of Schacht's theories, he adopts a somewhat more moderate position, in holding that 'a judiciously and cautiously formulated overall view of what all those early reports [...] collectively point to, may in all likelihood be taken to be not very far from the truth of "what really happened".'[48]

A noticeable fault in Juynboll's work is his explicit and frequent reliance on his own 'intuition'. At times, readers equipped with the kind of Muslim background which Juynboll lacks find this damagingly misguided. An example of this is his dismissal of Abbott's proof of the rapid growth of *ḥadīths*, a proof which cites reports of—in Juynboll's description—'mass meetings during which certain famous *muḥaddithūn* were alleged to have transmitted traditions to crowds totalling 10,000!' He goes on to remark, 'Visualising sessions such as this with many dozens of *mustamlīs* moving about, shouting the traditions down to the last rows of eager *ḥadīth* students may lift the reader into the realm of 1,001-night fantasies, but in whatever way you look at it, it is difficult to take accounts like that seriously.'[49] The exotic stereotyping here merely serves to confirm the Muslim reader's suspicion of an impairing cultural distance. *Ḥadīth* classes involving comparable numbers of students are regular events even today in the Muslim world. In 1405/1984, the Meccan *muḥaddith* Muḥammad Yāsīn al-Fādānī (d.1411/1991) visited Indonesia, where he gave open-air classes to crowds well outnumbering the ten thousand which arouses Juynboll's incredulity.[50] It is only in the West that Islamic studies are a small, almost imperceptible activity.

Students of the book likewise complain of apparent contradictions. For instance, Juynboll tells us that before the time of ʿUmar II, 'the Umayyad rulers may have only been vaguely interested in the political possibilities present in the *faḍā'il/mathālib* genres.'[51] Only a few pages on, however, the reader discovers that 'it is most probable that another important genre of *ḥadīth*s originated in those early days immediately following the prophet's demise: the *faḍā'il* genre,'[52] and is presented with an early text to support this: 'Muʿāwiya wrote one and the same letter to his tax collectors after the year of the Jamāʿa in which he said: 'Let the conquered people refrain from mentioning any merit of Abū Turāb [ʿAlī] or his kinsmen [...] Make a search for those you can find who were partisans of ʿUthman and those who supported his rule and those who uphold his merits and qualities. Seek their company, gain access to them and honour them. Write down for me everything which every one of them relates[...]'. In exchange, Muʿāwiya sent them presents.'[53] The resultant picture of Umayyad policy towards *ḥadīth*, which is pivotal to any discussion on the subject, is thus acutely confused.

Another area of the debate, that of the reliability of the *asmā' al-rijāl* literature, is explored in a separate chapter of Juynboll's work.[54] Here, too, the Muslim student of *ḥadīth* confesses to a certain puzzlement. Juynboll focusses on Ibn Ḥajar's biographical dictionary, the *Tahdhīb al-Tahdhīb*, and offers some general and dismissive comments about it, but without exploring or even showing an awareness of Ibn Ḥajar's sources. As the title of his book indicates, the *Tahdhīb al-Tahdhīb*—'that splendid work', as Arberry describes it[55]—represents one of several condensed versions of the *Tahdhīb al-Kamāl* of Jamāl al-Dīn al-Mizzī (d.742/1341), a well-known biographical dictionary which is now in the process of publication.[56] Unaware of the work's origin and hence its nature, Juynboll merely remarks that 'Ibn Ḥajar must have had sources from which he worked,'[57] thereby leaving the reader with the impression that Ibn Ḥajar's material comes from unknown and hence dubious sources.

Finally, acceptance of the book has been handicapped by his uneven prose style, which at times renders the meaning difficult to unravel. Many undergraduates have wrestled unsuccessfully with solecisms such as: 'Now, it must be conceded, first of all that, in my opinion, the common-link theory is a brilliant one.'[58] Similar offenses against the rules of grammar, style and logic are scattered thickly throughout the book.

*

One final remark. The above notes on the most outspoken Western commentators on the *ḥadīth* literature can also, and rewardingly, be read as a commentary on evolving Western instincts towards Islam in general.

We do not need Foucault to remind us that academic discourse is a product of power relationships: Goldziher's diary gives us very adequate proof that scholarly theories, especially those which involve the assessment of one culture by a historic rival, can easily be deconstructed into their psychological, historical and political constituents. The point is often noted, too, that American scholars, whose government has had no direct colonial involvement in Muslim countries, have in the past been somewhat more sympathetic to Islamic culture and its scholarship than their European colleagues[59] (the cases of Abbott and Powers are suggestive in this regard), and it will be interesting to see whether this transatlantic disparity endures. But it is, in any case, not unreasonable to hope that traditional *engagé* scholarship, newly self-conscious following the efforts of Edward Said and others to lay bare its inner metabolism, will, and despite the West's continuing fear of the Islamic world-community, slowly wither away.

APPENDIX III

THE LEIDEN EDITION OF IBN SAᶜD

IBN ḤAYAWAYH'S recension of the *Ṭabaqāt* of Ibn Saᶜd was the object of intense study by a host of students of the *asmā'* for more than three centuries, as is demonstrated by the *ijāza* and *isnād* annotations found in the various manuscripts which have come down to us. But from the end of the eighth century AH, on account of its great bulk and the appearance of many handier books on the various branches of *asmā'*, interest in it began to decline, and copies became increasingly scarce. No complete manuscript of the book is now known to exist.[1]

Among Western orientalists, Sprenger and Wüstenfeld were the first to realise the great importance of Ibn Saᶜd's work. They published articles describing its manuscripts, and drawing the orientalists' attention to its value as a source for early Islamic history, also using it as an important source for their own work. Other Orientalists such as Muir and Nöldeke also made extensive use of it. But a thorough and minute study of Ibn Saᶜd had to wait for another German scholar, Otto Loth, who in 1869CE published his treatise *Das Classenbuch des Ibn Sa'd*,[2] together with an article on the origin and meaning of *Ṭabaqāt*,[3] describing the Gotha and Berlin manuscripts of the book, the nature of their contents, the origins and history of the *Ṭabaqāt* type of biographical dictionaries, and the place of Ibn Saᶜd's work among them. It was Loth who paved the way for the edition of the book.

Its great size, however, stood in the way of its publication. For eighteen years after the publication of Loth's works, no-one appears to have considered seriously the possibility of preparing a critical edition. It was only in June 1887 that the Prussian Academy of Sciences resolved to publish the book, placing E. Sachau in charge of the undertaking. Within a year, Sachau had discovered five more manuscripts of the book which had escaped Loth's attention. All were collected together with the help of scholars, librarians, and government officials, and in 1898 their collation and editing were begun. In 1904 the eighth and third volumes were published; the others followed, and the text was completed in 1918 with the publication of Volume VII. Three indices followed.[4]

This edition was reprinted in Beirut in 1376–77/1957–58.

NOTES

NOTES TO CHAPTER ONE

1 al-Bukhārī, *al-Jāmiʿ al-Ṣaḥīḥ* (Cairo, 1309), I.20.

2 al-Dārimī, *al-Sunan* (Kanpur, 1292–3), 46.

3 al-Dhahabī, *Tadhkirat al-Ḥuffāẓ* (Hyderabad, 1330), I, 6–7.

4 al-Qasṭallānī, *al-Mawāhib al-Ladunniyya*, with commentary of al-Zurqānī (Cairo, 1291), V, 454.

5 *al-Mufaḍḍaliyyāt*, ed. Lyall, C.J., (Oxford, 1918–21CE), LXVI.5; CXXIII.16. Cf. Kamali, M. H. *Principles of Islamic Jurisprudence* (Cambridge, 1991CE), 44–5; Azami, M. M. *On Schacht's Origins of Muhammadan Jurisprudence* (Riyadh, New York and Chichester, 1985CE), 29–30.

6 Azami, *Schacht's Origins*, 30.

7 al-Khaṭīb, Muḥammad, *Al-Sunna qabl al-Tadwīn* (Cairo, 1383), 14–22; Azami, *Schacht's Origins*, 29–54. Azami (*op. cit.*, 23), quotes a statement of the second Caliph, ʿUmar, to demonstrate that although the term *sunna* was not restricted to the Prophet in early Islam, his *sunna* had priority: 'Whose *sunna* deserves more to be observed by you, the *sunna* of the Prophet or the *sunna* of ʿUmar?' For an extensive summary of the concept of *Sunna*, see Kamali, *Principles*, 44–85.

8 Goldziher, I. *Muslim Studies*, tr. S. Stern (London, 1967CE), II. 24–5; Kamali, *Principles*, 47.

9 Biographies of the Prophet include: Lings, M., *Muhammad: His Life based on the Earliest Sources* (Cambridge, 1991CE); Montgomery Watt, *Muḥammad at Mecca* (Oxford, 1953CE), and *Muḥammad at Medina* (Oxford, 1956CE).

10 Ibn Saʿd, *al-Ṭabaqāt al-Kabīr*, ed. Sachau, E., *et. al.* (Leiden, 1322–59/1904–40), I/i, 145.

11 Ibid., I/i, 136.

12 Ibid., I/i, 136.

13 Very numerous examples of this are given in Khaṭīb, *Sunna*, 29–74; Azami, *Schacht's Origins*, 10–18.

14 Bukhārī, *Ṣaḥīḥ*, Iʿtiṣām, bāb al-iqtiḍā' bi-afʿāl al-Nabī (IV, 166).

15 Ibid., Tahajjud, bāb ṣalāt al-layl (I, 136).

16 Ibid.

17 Ibid., Iʿtiṣām, bāb al-taʿammuq (IV, 166).

18 Muslim, *al-Ṣaḥīḥ* (Delhi, 1309), Birr, bāb tafsīr al-birr (II, 314).

19 Abū Daūd, *al-Sunan*, ed. ʿAbd al-Aḥad (Delhi, 1346), Istighfār (I, 119).

20 Ibid., Takhfīf al-ukhrayayn (I, 124).

21 For the various definitions and classes of *tābiʿūn* see Khaṭīb, *Sunna*, 124–26.

22 Khaṭīb, *Sunna*, 155, 176–84; al-Khaṭīb al-Baghdādī, *al-Riḥla fī Ṭalab al-Ḥadīth*, ed. Nūr al-Dīn ʿIṭr (Damascus, 1395); cf. above, 40–2.

23 Bukhārī, *Ṣaḥīḥ*, IV. 62.

24 Ibn Saʿd, VII, 234.

25 Ibid., VIII, 73.

26 Ibid., IV/ii, 56.

27 Dārimī, *Sunan*, 45.

28 Ibn Saʿd, II/ii, 125.

29 Ibid., IV/ii, 80.

30 Bukhārī, ʿIlm, bāb al-tanāwub (I, 19).

31 *ZDMG*, X, 2.

32 Ibid.

33 al-Tabrīzī, *Mishkāt al-Maṣābiḥ* (Lucknow, 1326),ʿIlm (32).

34 Ibid., 35.

35 Hammām ibn Munabbih, *Ṣaḥīfa*, ed. Hamidullah, M. (Paris, 1380), 9.

36 Ibid.

37 Ibn Saʿd, II/ii, 107. Cf. Kamali, *Principles*, 45.

38 Von Kremer, *The Orient under the Caliphs* (Calcutta, 1920CE), 260.

39 For the dissemination of *ḥadīth*, see Azami, *Schacht's Origins*, 109–11.

40 Khaṭīb, *Sunna*, 164–76.

41 A Companion known as al-Munaydhir is said to have visited Spain. See al-Maqqarī, *Nafḥ al-Ṭīb* (Cairo, 1302), I, 130.

42 See M. Ishaque, *India's Contribution to the Study of Hadith Literature* (Dacca, 1955CE), chap. 1.

43 For the letters of the Prophet, see Serjeant, R.B., in *Cambridge History of Arabic Literature*, I (Cambridge, 1983CE), 139–42; for his treaties, see ibid., 134–39.

44 ʿAbd al-Khāliq, *al-Imām al-Bukhārī wa-Ṣaḥīḥuh* (Jedda, 1405), 45–52.

45 Ibn Saʿd, III/i, 206; N. Abbott, 'Hadith Literature–II: Collection and Transmission of *Hadith*', (in *Cambridge History of Arabic Literature*, I, 289–98), 289; ʿAbd al-Khāliq, 90–1; Khaṭīb, *Sunna*, 99–105; Abbott, *Studies in Arabic Literary Papyri* Vol. I, Historical Texts (Chicago, 1957CE); Vol. II, Qur'ānic Commentary and Tradition (Chicago, 1967CE); Vol. III, Language and Literature (Chicago, 1972CE), 1, 7, 10. ʿUmar did, none the less, effectively disseminate *ḥadīth* in other ways.

46 See Sezgin, F. *Geschichte des arabischen Schrifttums*, I (Leiden, 1967CE), 56–7; Abdul-Rauf, M. '*Ḥadīth* Literature–I: The Development of the Science of *Ḥadīth*', (*Cambridge History of Arabic Literature*, I, 271–88), 272; Abbott, '*Hadith* Literature', 293–94; Goldziher, *Muslim Studies*, II, 43.

47 Maqqarī, *Nafḥ*, 1, 130.

48 Ibn Saʿd, II/ii, 134; Bukhārī, ʿIlm, bāb al-kitāba. For the involvement of women in *ḥadīth* scholarship see Appendix I.

49 Ibn ʿAbd al-Barr, *Jāmiʿ Bayān al-ʿIlm wa-Faḍlih* (Cairo, n.d.), I, 76.

50 al-Sakhāwī, *Fatḥ al-Mughīth* (Lucknow, n.d.), 239.

51 As cited in Ibn Ḥajar al-ʿAsqalānī, *Fatḥ al-Bārī* (Cairo, 1320), I, 174.

52 Dhahabī, Tadhkira, I, 82.

53 Ibid., I, 95.

54 Ibn al-Nadīm, *al-Fihrist* (Leipzig, 1871–72CE), 225–27.

55 Ibn Saʿd,II/ii, 136.

56 *Fihrist*, 225–27.

57 For the *Muwaṭṭa'* see above, 7.

58 *Fihrist*, 225.

59 Goldziher, *Muslim Studies*, II, 197–04. The *Muwaṭṭa'* has recently been translated into English by the American Muslim scholar Aisha Bewley: *Al-Muwaṭṭa' of Imām Mālik ibn Anas: the first Formulation of Islamic law* (London, 1989CE). For the background to the *Muwaṭṭa'*, see Abdul Rauf, 272–73; Azami, *Schacht's Origins*, 79–85.

60 Goldziher, *Muslim Studies*, II, 202. *Ijmāʿ* is a term denoting the authoritative consensus of scholars.

61 For the primacy of Medina, see Abbott, *Studies*, II, 81–2.

62 Ibid., II, 202. For these terms see above, 109.

63 Dihlawī, *Bustān al-Muḥaddithīn* (Delhi, 1898CE), 25.

64 Namely, Yaḥyā al-Tamīmī, Abū Ḥudhayfa and Suwayd ibn Saʿīd.

65 Zurqānī, *Sharḥ Muwaṭṭa' Mālik* (Cairo, 1310), I, 8.

66 Ibn Saʿd, III/i, 164.

67 Bukhārī, *Ṣaḥīḥ*, Jihād, bāb man ḥaddatha bi-mashāhidihi (II, 97).

68 Ibn ʿAbd al-Barr, *Jāmiʿ*, II, 27.

69 Ḥājī Khalīfa, *Kashf al-ẓunūn* (Leipzig, 1835-42CE), I,174–75.

70 Ibid., IV, 254ff.

71 Ibid., II, 68.

72 Ibid., VI, 167. This number is based on my own calculation.

73 Abdul Rauf, '*Ḥadīth* Literature', 271–72.

74 Goldziher, Muslim *Studies*, II, 22–4.

75 *Ṣaḥīfa Hammām ibn Munabbih*; see Bibliography.

76 Ibn Saʿd, IV/i, 262; Sezgin, I, 84; Goldziher, *Muslim Studies*, II, 23.

77 Abbott, *Studies*, II, 58.

78 Ibid., I, 22; cf. also II, 58–9.

79 Dihlawī, *Risāla dar Fann-i Uṣūl-i Ḥadīth* (Delhi, 1255), 22.

80 Ibid., 19–20, 22–3.

81 Abdul Rauf, 272–73.

82 For the debate over the definition of the term see al-Jazā'irī, *Tawjīh al-Naẓar ilā Uṣūl al-Athar* (Cairo, 1328), 66.

83 For a list of *Musnad* works see Ḥājī Khalīfa, *Kashf*, V, 532–43.

84 Goldziher, *Muslim Studies*, II, 210.

85 Dihlawī, Risāla, 21.

86 Dihlawī, *Bustān*, 37.

87 Ḥājī Khalīfa, *Kashf*, V, 534.

88 Goldziher, *Muslim Studies*, II, 212.

89 al-Subkī, *Ṭabaqāt al-Shāfiʿiyya al-Kubrā* (Cairo, 1324), I, 202.

90 Ḥājī Khalīfa, *Kashf*, V, 534.

91 Similar texts arranged in chronological order are termed *mashīkha*. See *Catalogue of the*

Arabic and Persian Manuscripts in the Oriental Public Library at Bankiport (Patna, 1925), V/ii, 41n.

92 Dihlawī, *Bustān*, 56, 95.

93 Ṭabarānī's *al-Muʿjam al-Kabīr* has been edited by Ḥamdī al-Salafī (2nd. ed., Baghdad, 1984–90CE).

94 For the structure and function of this important work, see Maḥmūd al-Ṭaḥḥān, *Uṣūl al-Takhrīj wa-Dirāsat al-Asānīd* (Cairo, n.d.), 214–15; Abdul Rauf, 279.

95 Several English translations exist of this, for instance Izzedine Ibrahim and Denys (Abdul Wadud) Johnson-Davies, *An-Nawawis Forty Hadith: an anthology of the sayings of the Prophet Muhammad*, 14th ed. (Beirut, 1409). The whole genre is discussed in al-Qāḍī ʿIyāḍ, *al-Ilmāʿ fī Maʿrifat Uṣūl al-Riwāya wa-Taqyīd al-Samāʿ*, ed. al-Sayyid Aḥmad Ṣaqr, 2nd ed. (Cairo, 1398), 22; Abdülkader Karahan, 'Aperçu général sur les "Quarante ḥadīths" dans la littérature islamique', *SI*, IV (1955CE), 39–55; L. Pouzet, *Une Herméneutique de la tradition islamique* (Beirut, 1982CE).

96 Goldziher, Muslim Studies, II, 214–16.

NOTES TO CHAPTER TWO

1 Khaṭīb, *Sunna*, 387–94.

2 For the role of the Companions in *ḥadīth* transmission see Azami, *Studies in Early Ḥadīth Literature* (Beirut, 1968CE), 35–59; and the material collected in Khaṭīb, *Sunna*, 57–65.

3 al-Nawawī, *Tahdhīb al-Asmā' wa'l-Lughāt* (Göttingen, 1842–7CE), 18; Sakhāwī, *Fatḥ*, 367–73; Ibn al-Ṣalāḥ, *Muqaddima* (Cairo, 1326), 118–19.

4 Ibn al-Ṣalāḥ, *Muqaddima*, 121.

5 Ibn Ḥajar al-ʿAsqalānī, *al-Iṣāba fī Tamyīz al-Ṣaḥāba* (Calcutta, 1856–58CE), I, 3.

6 Ḥājī Khalīfa, *Kashf*, V, 534.

7 Ibn al-Jawzī, *Talqīḥ Fuhūm Ahl al-Āthār* (Delhi, n.d.), 184–97.

8 Ibn ʿAbd al-Barr, *al-Istīʿāb fī Maʿrifat al-Aṣḥāb* (Hyderabad, 1318), I, no.1109.

9 Ibn Ḥajar al-ʿAsqalānī, *Tahdhīb al-Tahdhīb* (Hyderabad, 1326), IV, no.573.

10 Ibid., no.425.

11 Ibid., XII, no.1124.

12 Ibn ʿAbd al-Barr, *Istīʿāb*, II.

13 Ibn Ḥajar, *Tahdhīb al-Tahdhīb*, V, no.653.

14 Ibn ʿAbd al-Barr, *Istīʿāb*, II, no.2806.

15 Ibn Ḥajar, *Tahdhīb al-Tahdhīb*, VII, no.340.

16 Ibid., III, no.254.

17 Ibn ʿAbd al-Barr, *Istīʿāb*, I, no.1095.

18 Ibid., II, no.1896.

19 Ibn Ḥajar, *Tahdhīb al-Tahdhīb*, III, no. 267.

20 Ibid., no.592.

21 Ibn ʿAbd al-Barr, *Istīʿāb*, II, no.2850.

22 Ibn Ḥajar, *Tahdhīb al-Tahdhīb*, II, no.775.

23 Ibid., IV, no.428.

24 Ibn ʿAbd al-Barr, *Istīʿāb*, I, no.1081.

25 Ibn Ḥajar, *Tahdhīb al-Tahdhīb*, VI, no.74.

26 Ibnʿ Abd al-Barr, *Istīʿāb*, I, no. 1081.

27 Ibn Ḥajar, *Tahdhīb al-Tahdhīb*, VI, no.74.

28 Ibn ʿAbd al-Barr, *Istīʿāb*, II, no.2844.

29 Ibn Ḥajar, *Tahdhīb al-Tahdhīb*, VIII, no. 788.

30 Ibid., II, no.115.

31 Ibn ʿAbd al-Barr, *Istīʿāb*, II, no.2434.

32 Ibn Ḥajar, *Tahdhīb al-Tahdhīb*, I, no.797.

33 Ibid., VIII, no.219.

34 Ibn ʿAbd al-Barr, *Istīʿāb*, II, no.2799.

35 Ibn al-Jawzī, *Talqīḥ*, 184–86.

36 Zurqānī, *Sharḥ Muwaṭṭa' Mālik*, I, 8.

37 Subkī, *Ṭabaqāt*, I, 202.

38 Ibn al-Jawzī, *Talqīḥ*, 197–205.

39 Sakhāwī, *Fatḥ*, 379; Nawawī, *Tahdhīb*, 352.

40 Ibn Saʿd, IV/ii, 54ff; Khaṭīb, *Sunna*, 411–68.

41 F. Wüstenfeld, *Genealogische Tabellen der Arabischen Stämme und Familien* (Göttingen, 1852–53CE), no.10.

42 Ibn Saʿd, IV/ii, 54.

43 Azami, *Schacht's* Origins, 110.

44 Ibn Saʿd, 60; Khaṭīb, *Sunna*, 415.

45 Ibid., 56.

46 Ibid., 58.

47 *Ṣaḥīfa Hammām ibn Munabbih*, 38–9.

48 *Ṣaḥīfa Hammām ibn Munabbih*, 36–40.

49 Khaṭīb, *Sunna*, 446–54.

50 Ibn Saʿd, IV/ii, 105–137; Azami, *Early Ḥadīth Literature*, 45–6.

51 Ibid., IV/i, 106–25.

52 Ibid., IV/i, 124.

53 Nawawī, *Tahdhīb*, 166; Khaṭīb, *Sunna*, 472–74; Abbott, '*Ḥadīth Literature*', 290; Azami, *Early Ḥadīth Literature*, 49.
54 Dhahabī, *Tadhkira*, I, 38.
55 Dhahabī, *Tadhkira*, I, 38.
56 Nawawī, *Tahdhīb*, 167.
57 Dhahabī, *Tadhkira*, I, 24.
58 Khaṭīb, *Sunna*, 474–76.
59 Dhahabī, *Tadhkira*, I, 24.
60 See for instance above, 19.
61 Bukhārī, Maghāzī, Badr (III, 5). Numerous other instances of ʿĀ'isha's careful criticism of *ḥadīth* have been collected by the Indian scholar Sayyid Sulaymān Nadwī in his book *Sīrat-i ʿĀ'isha* (Lucknow, 1330).
62 Ibn Ḥajar, *Tahdhīb al-Tahdhīb*, XII, no.2841.
63 Ibn al-Athīr, *Usd al-Ghāba fī Maʿrifat al-Ṣaḥāba* (Cairo, 1280), III, 193.
64 Ibid, III, 195; Khaṭīb, *Sunna*, 476–78; Nawawī, *Tahdhīb*, 351–54.
65 Ibn Ḥajar, *Tahdhīb al-Tahdhīb*, V, no.474.
66 Ibn Saʿd, II/ii, 121; cf. Ibn ʿAbd al-Barr, *Jāmiʿ*, I, 85–6.
67 Abbott, *Studies*, II, 4.
68 Nawawī, *Tahdhīb*, 351–54; *EI²*, I. 41–1 (L. Veccia Vaglieri).
69 Dhahabī, *Tadhkira*, I, 37.
70 Nawawī, *Tahdhīb*, 185.
71 Sezgin, I, 85; Khaṭīb, *Sunna*, 478–80; Nawawī, *Tahdhīb*, 184–86.
72 Ibn Ḥajar, *Tahdhīb al-Tahdhīb*, II, no.67.
73 Nawawī, *Tahdhīb*, 723; Khaṭīb, *Sunna*, 480–1.
74 Ibn ʿAbd al-Barr, *Istīʿāb*, II, 308–16.
75 Ibn al-Athīr, *Usd*, III, 233–35.
76 Ibid., cf. above, 10.
77 Sakhāwī, *Fatḥ*, 379.
78 Khaṭīb, *Sunna*, 92–9.
79 Abū Daūd, *Sunan*, Farā'iḍ, bāb al-jadda (II, 45).
80 Dhahabī, *Tadhkira*, I, 3.
81 Abū Daūd, *Sunan*, Diyat al-janīn (II, 280).
82 Bukhārī, *Ṣaḥīḥ*, IV, 58.
83 Ṭayālisī, no.1364.
84 Ibn Saʿd, IV/i, 13–4.
85 Dhahabī, *Tadhkira*, I, 7. For ʿUmar's policy see Khaṭīb, *Sunna*, 99–111.
86 Ibn Saʿd, III/i, 39.
87 Abū Daūd, *Sunan*, I, 220.
88 Ibn Saʿd, III/i, 102.
89 Ibid., 210.
90 Ibid., 110.
91 Ibid., 102.
92 Ibn ʿAbd al-Barr, *Jāmiʿ*, I, 78–9.
93 Dārimī, *Sunan*, 46.
94 Ibid.
95 Ibn Māja, *al-Sunan* (Delhi, 1333), 4.
96 Ibn Saʿd, III/i, 161; Bukhārī, *Ṣaḥīḥ*, II, 97.
97 Information on this extensive controversy may be found in ʿIyāḍ, *Ilmāʿ*, 146–61; Khaṭīb, *Sunna*, 45–114, 295–328; Azami, *Early Ḥadīth Literature*, 22–7.
98 Ibn Saʿd, IV/ii, 9.
99 See above, 10.
100 Ibn Ḥajar, *Tahdhīb al-Tahdhīb*, VIII, no.80; Khaṭīb, *Sunna*, 348–52.
101 Bukhārī, *Ṣaḥīḥ*, ʿIlm, bāb kitābat al-ʿilm (I, 21); Azami, *Early Ḥadīth Literature*, 47.
102 al-Tirmidhī, *al-Jāmiʿ* (Delhi, 1315), al-Yamīn maʿ al-shāhid, I, 160.
103 Khaṭīb, *Sunna*, 352; Goldziher, *Muslim Studies*, II, 15.
104 Ibid.
105 Ibid.; Azami, *Early Ḥadīth Literature*, 42–3.
106 Dhahabī, *Tadhkira*, I, 5; Azami, *Early Ḥadīth Literature*, 34–5.
107 Ibn Saʿd, II/ii, 123; Azami, *Early Ḥadīth Literature*, 40–1.
108 Tirmidhī, 238.
109 Ibn Saʿd, V, 216; Abbott, *Studies*, I, 23.
110 Qasṭallānī, *Mawāhib*.
111 Ibn Ḥajar, *Fatḥ*, I, 148.
112 Ibn ʿAbd al-Barr, *Jāmiʿ*, I, 74.
113 *Ṣaḥīfa Hammām ibn Munabbih*; cf. *Sunna*, 355–62.
114 Tirmidhī, *Sunan*, II, 91.
115 Sprenger, A. 'On the Origin and Progress of Writing Down Historical Facts among the Musalmans' (*JASB* XXV, 303–29, 375–81), 315.
116 Bukhārī, *Ṣaḥīḥ*, ʿIlm, bāb al-kitāba; Azami, *Early Ḥadīth Literature*, 40.
117 Ibid., 52.
118 al-Dāraquṭnī, *al-Sunan* (Delhi, n.d.), 204, 209, 485.
119 Ibn Saʿd, I/ii, 19.
120 Abū Daūd, *Sunan*, Zakāt al-sā'ima (I, 226). For other such documents see above, 6.
121 Azami, *Early Ḥadīth Literature*, 20–7.
122 Ibn Ḥanbal, *al-Musnad* (Cairo, 1313), II, 403; III, 13; V, 183; Dārimī, *Sunan*, 64ff; Mus-

lim, *Ṣaḥīḥ*, Zuhd, bāb ḥukm kitāba... (II, 414); Azami, *Early Ḥadīth Literature*, 22–3, 39.
123 Ibn ʿAbd al-Barr, *Jāmiʿ*, I, 63–8; Sprenger, 'On the Origins', 304–17.
124 Dārimi, *Sunan*, 64; Sprenger, 'On the Origins', 306.
125 Ibn Qutayba, *Ta'wīl Mukhtalif al-Ḥadīth*. Beirut, n.d.
126 Ibn Ḥajar, *Fatḥ*, 471.
127 These are: Abū ʿAbs, Ubayy ibn Kaʿb, ʿAbd Allāh ibn Rawāḥa, Aws ibn Khawlī, al-Mundhir ibn ʿAmr, Usayd and his father al-Ḥuḍayr, Saʿd ibn ʿUbāda, and Rāfiʿibn Malik.
128 Ibn Saʿd, III/ii, 91.
129 al-Iṣfahānī, *Kitāb al-Aghānī* (Cairo, 1323), XVI, 121. 'The Bedouin,' says Goldziher, 'despises reading and writing even today.' (Goldziher, *Muslim Studies*, I, 1.)
130 Ibn al-Athīr, *Usd*, sv. "ʿAbd Allāh ibn Saʿīd ibn al-ʿĀṣī'.
131 IbnʿAbd al-Barr, *Jāmiʿ*, 472.
132 Ibn Saʿd, II/ii, 14.
133 Ibid.
134 Ibn Ḥanbal, *Musnad*, V, 315.
135 Goldziher, *Muslim Studies*, II, 22.

NOTES TO CHAPTER THREE

1 Tirmidhī, *Jāmiʿ*, II, 90; cf. ʿIyāḍ, *Ilmāʿ*, 13; Azami, *Schacht's Origins*, 109.
2 Dhahabī, *Tadhkira*, I, 22.
3 Ibn Ḥanbal, *Musnad*, V, 328.
4 Ibn Saʿd, III/ii, 23.
5 Ibid.
6 Ibid.V, 213.
7 Ibn ʿAbd al-Barr, *Jāmiʿ*, I, 45.
8 Sakhāwī, *Fatḥ*, 396–97.
9 Ibid.
10 Ibn Saʿd, V, 140.
11 Ibn Khallikān, *Wafayāt al-Aʿyān* (Göttingen, 1835CE) no.574.
12 Ibn ʿAbd al-Barr, *Jāmiʿ*, I, 97.
13 Yāqūt, *Muʿjam al-Udabā'* (London, 1923–25CE), I, 17.
14 Nawawī, *Tahdhīb*, 629–30.
15 Dhahabī, *Tadhkira*, I, 290.
16 Nawawī, *Tahdhīb*, 174.
17 Dhahabī, *Tadhkira*, I, 355.
18 Yāqūt, *Muʿjam al-Udabā'*, I, 17.
19 Ibid.
20 Dhahabī, *Tadhkira*, I, 172.
21 Ibid., II, 147.
22 Ibn ʿAbd al-Barr, *Jāmiʿ*, I, 98.
23 Ibn Ḥajar al-ʿAsqalānī, *Muqaddima Fatḥ al-Bārī* (Delhi, 1302), 566.
24 Ibn ʿAbd al-Barr, *Jāmiʿ*, I, 97–8.
25 Suyūṭī, *Tadrīb al-Rāwī* (Cairo, 1307), 279.
26 Nawawī, *Tahdhīb*, 719.
27 Ibid., 534.
28 Dhahabī, Tadhkira, I, 290.
29 al-Khaṭīb al-Baghdādī, *Tārīkh Baghdād*, IX, 33.
30 Dhahabī, *Tadhkira*, I, 291.
31 Suyūṭī, *Ṭabaqāt al-Ḥuffāẓ* (Göttingen, 1833CE), IX, 100; al-Khaṭīb al-Baghdādī, *Tārīkh Baghdād* (Cairo, 1349), VI, 122. It should be observed here that the vast majority of these students may have been irregular students. Regular students, particularly those entered in a formal institution, were far fewer. For instance, the number (one thousand) of students who attended the *ḥadīth* college founded by Abū ʿAlī al-Ḥusaynī (d.393/1003) at Nīsābūr is remarkably high for an organised institution. See J. Pedersen/G. Makdisi, 'Madrasa' in *EI²* V, 1126.
32 Azami, *Early Ḥadīth Literature*, 188–94; cf. above, 86.
33 Suyūṭī, *Ṭabaqāt*, IX, 100; al-Khaṭīb al-Baghdādī, *Tārīkh Baghdād*, VI, 122.
34 Nawawī, *Tahdhīb*, 532.
35 Kamali, *Principles*, 65–8; Azami, *Schacht's Origins*, 2.
36 Muir, W. *Life of Mahomet* (Edinburgh, 1912CE), xxxvi. Cf. Kamali, *Principles*, 65.
37 Ibn Ḥazm, *al-Iḥkām fī* Uṣūl *al-Aḥkām* (Cairo, 1345–47), II, 2–3, 83–4.
38 Kamali, *Principles*, 65.
39 See also below, Chapter 7.
40 For details on the process of falsification, see Khaṭīb, *Sunna*, 185–292; Kamali, *Principles*, 65–8.
41 Khaṭīb, *Sunna*, 206–8; Kamali, *Principles*, 66–7; al-Ḥākim al-Nīsābūrī, translated by J. Robson, *An Introduction to the Science of Tradition* (London, 1953CE), 27.
42 Suyūṭī, *Tadrīb*, 103.
43 Ibid.
44 Yāqūt, *Muʿjam al-Udabā'*, I, 286.

45 Ḥākim (Robson), *Madkhal*, 27–8. For Shīʿī *ḥadīth* invention, see Khaṭīb, *Sunna*, 195–203; for the Khawārij, ibid., 204–6.
46 Goldziher, *Muslim Studies*, II, 52; cf. Ibn Khallikān, no.764.
47 Yāqūt, *Muʿjam al-Udabā'*, VI, 94.
48 Ibn Ḥajar al-ʿAsqalānī, *Lisān al-Mīzān* (Hyderabad, 1329–31), V, no.1136.
49 Suyūṭī, *Tadrīb*, 103.
50 Ibn Ḥajar, *Lisān*, IV, no.1296.
51 Guillaume, *Traditions*, 73.
52 Ibn Ḥajar, *Lisān*, V, 431.
53 Cf. for instance Ibn al-Jawzī, *Mawḍūʿāt*, ed. ʿAbd al-Raḥmān ʿUthmān (Medina, 1386–89), passim; Khaṭīb, *Sunna*, 208–10; Kamali, *Principles*, 67.
54 For their influence on the generation of *ḥadīth*, see Khaṭīb, *Sunna*, 210–12; Kamali, *Principles*, 67. For background to their activities, and a translation of some typical Quṣṣāṣ tales, see M. L. Swartz's edition and translation of Ibn al-Jawzī's *Kitāb al-Quṣṣāṣ wa'l-Mudhakkirīn* (Beirut, 1971CE), especially the editor's introduction, pp 39–80.
55 Considered by al-Ḍāmirī to have been the first storyteller in Islam. Goldziher, *Muslim Studies*, II, 152.
56 According to Ibn Saʿd, he, rather than al-Dārī, was Islam's first 'storyteller'. Ibn Saʿd, V, 34.
57 al-Kindi, *al-Wulāt wa'l-Quḍāt* (Leiden, 1912CE), 303–4 fn; cf. Goldziher, *Muslim Studies*, II, 151.
58 Goldziher, *Muslim Studies*, II, 151.
59 Ibid., II, 151–52; Iṣfahānī, *Aghanī*, XII, 5.
60 Ibid.
61 al-Thaʿālibī, *Yatīmat al-Dahr* (Cairo, 1352), III, 179.
62 Goldziher, *Muslim Studies*, II, 158.
63 al-Ṭabarī, *Tārīkh al-Rusul wa'l-Mulūk* (Leiden, 1888CE), III, 2131.
64 Ḥākim (Robson), *Madkhal*, 28–9; Khaṭīb, *Sunna*, 213–15.
65 al-Dhahabī, *Mīzān al-Iʿtidāl fī Naqd al-Rijāl* (Cairo, 1325), III, 245; Suyūṭī, *Tadrīb*, 102; cf. Kamali, *Principles*, 68.
66 Dhahabī, *Mīzān*, I, 7–8; cf. Kamali, *Principles*, 68.
67 Dhahabī, *Mīzān*, 67.
68 Ibn Ḥajar, *Lisān*, I, 419.
69 Ibid., VI, no.819.
70 Ibid., no.480; Suyūṭī, *Tadrīb*, 102.
71 Dhahabī, *Mīzān*, I, no.321.
72 Ibid., II, 13.
73 Ibid., 23.
74 Ibid., III, 257.
75 Goldziher, *Muslim Studies*, II, 55.
76 Suyūṭī, *Tadrīb*, 102.
77 Ibid., 100.
78 Dhahabī, *Mīzān*, I, no.22.
79 Ibid., no. 562.
80 Ibid., no.564.
81 Ibid., no.403.
82 Ibid., no. 2918.
83 Ibid., no.3641.
84 Ibid., no. 3950.
85 Ibn ʿAbd al-Barr, *Jāmiʿ*, II, 129.
86 Khaṭīb, *Sunna*, 219–49; see above, p. 30.
87 Ibn Abd al-Barr, *Jāmiʿ*, II, 132.
88 Ibid., I, 80.
89 Muslim, *Ṣaḥiḥ*, I, 11.
90 Dārimī, *Sunan*, 61.
91 Muslim, *Ṣaḥīḥ*, I, 4.
92 Suyūṭī, *Tadrīb*, 183. For some instances of the very early use of *isnād*, see Khaṭīb, *Sunna*, 220–26.
93 Muslim, *Ṣaḥīḥ*, I, 12.
94 Dārimī, *Sunan*, 61. Criticism of narrators by the first two generations is described in Khaṭīb, *Sunna*, 232–39.
95 Nawawī, *Tahdhīb*, 531–32.
96 Ibn Abd al-Barr, *Jāmiʿ*, II, 48; Ibn ʿAsākir, *Tārīkh Dimashq* (Damascus, 1332), IV, 172.
97 al-Shāfiʿī, *al-Risāla* (Cairo, 1312), 57ff.
98 Subkī, *Ṭabaqāt*, I, 10.
99 Nawawī, *Tahdhīb*, 629; Suyūṭī, *Ṭabaqāt*, VIII, 17.
100 Dhahabī, *Mīzān*, I, 18; Suyūṭī, *Ṭabaqāt*, VIII, 110.
101 Subkī, *Ṭabaqāt*, I, 202–3.
102 Abbott, *Studies*, II, 83.
103 See above, 132; also Loth, 'Ursprung und Bedeutung der Ṭabaqāt,' *ZDMG* XXIII, 593; Goldziher, *Muslim Studies*, II, 56.
104 Muslim, *Ṣaḥīḥ*, I, 15.
105 Ibid., I, 6.
106 Ibid., I, 13.
107 Nawawī, *Tahdhīb*, 316.
108 Suyūṭī, *Tadrīb*, 262.
109 These traditionists included al-Aʿmash, Shuʿba, Mālik, Maʿmar, Hishām al-Dastuwā'ī, al-Awzāʿī, al-Thawrī, Ibn al-Mājishūn, Ḥammād ibn Salama, al-Layth ibn Saʿd, and, somewhat later, Hushaym, Ibn al-Mubārak, Abū

Isḥāq al-Fazārī, al-Muʿāfā ibn ʿImrān, Bishr ibn al-Mufaḍḍal, Ibn ʿUyayna, Ibn ʿUlayya, Ibn Wahb and Wakīʿ ibn al-Jarrāḥ. (Cited by al-Jazā'irī, *Tawjīh*, 114).

110 Ibn Saʿd, IV/ii, 111.
111 Ibn al-Athīr, *Usd*, III, 194.
112 Ibid., 234.
113 Ibn Saʿd, IV/i, 161.
114 Ibid., III/ii, 20.
115 Ibid., V, 90ff.
116 Ibid., VII/i, 82.
117 Ibid., 103.
118 Ibid., VII/i, 119.
119 Ibid., VI, 52.
120 Ibid., V, 90, 93, 95–6.
121 Dhahabī, *Tadhkira*, I, 115.
122 al-Mubarrad, *al-Kāmil* (Leipzig, 1864CE), I, 284.
123 Ibn Khallikān, no.560.
124 Nawawī, *Tahdhīb*, 287.
125 Ibn Khallikān, no.304.
126 Ibid., no.270.
127 Ibid., nos.251, 278.
128 Ibid., no.155.
129 Dhahabī, *Tadhkira*, I, 162–64.
130 Ibn Khallikān, no.775.
131 Dhahabī, *Tadhkira*, I, 183ff.
132 Subkī, *Ṭabaqāt*, I, 203–16.
133 Dhahabī, *Tadhkira*, I, 6ff.
134 Ibid., 161ff.
135 Suyūṭī, *Ṭabaqāt*, VII, 62.
136 Ibn ʿAbd al-Barr, *Jāmiʿ*, I, 163–86.
137 Ibid., I, 93–4.
138 Ibid., I, 35.
139 Ibid.
140 For the *riḥla* phenomenon, see al-Khaṭīb al-Baghdādī, *al-Riḥla fī Ṭalab al-Ḥadīth*, ed. Nūr al-Dīn ʿItr (Damascus, 1395); Khaṭīb, *Sunna*, 176–84; Abbott, *Studies*, II, 40–3.
141 Dhahabī, *Tadhkira*, I, 95.
142 Ibn Ḥajar, *Tahdhīb al-Tahdhīb*, IV, no.145.
143 Dhahabī, *Tadhkira*, I, 71.
144 Ibn ʿAbd al-Barr, *Jāmiʿ*, I, 95.
145 Dhahabī, *Tadhkira*, I, 46ff.
146 Goldziher, *Muslim Studies*, II, 166.
147 Nawawī, *Tahdhīb*, 646.
148 Dhahabī, *Tadhkira*, I, 255.
149 Nawawī, *Tahdhīb*, 353.
150 Suyūṭī, *Ṭabaqāt*, VII, 69.
151 Ibid., V, 45.
152 Yāqūt, *Muʿjam al-Udabā'*, V, 140.
153 Ibn Saʿd, II/ii, 131.
154 Nawawī, *Tahdhīb*, 218.
155 Ibid., 210.
156 Dhahabī, *Tadhkira*, I, 153.
157 Dhahabī, *Tadhkira*, I, 153.
158 Ibid, I, 111.

NOTES TO CHAPTER FOUR

1 Cf. pp.9–10 above. A list of some of the earliest legal texts is given in Azami, *Schacht's Origins*, 24–5.

2 For some insights into the change in consciousness, both positive and negative, brought about by mass literacy, see A. K. Coomaraswamy, *The Bugbear of Literacy* (London, 1948CE).

3 Cf. F. Sezgin, *Geschichte des arabischen Schrifttums* (Leiden, 1967CE).

4 Ibn al-Nadīm, *Fihrist*, 89.

5 R. Nicholson, *Literary History of the Arabs* (Cambridge, 1930CE), 13. It is surprising that Margoliouth does not even mention the name of this author in his Lectures *on Arabic Historians* (Calcutta, 1930CE).

6 Ibn al-Nadīm, *Fihrist*, 90.

7 Ibid. For other Arabic medical works of this period, see my *Studies in Arabic and Persian Medical Literature* (Calcutta, 1959CE).

8 J. Horovitz, 'The Earliest Biographies of the Prophet and their Authors' (i), *IC*, I (1927), 535–59, 536–39.

9 Ibid.

10 Ibn Saʿd, V, 133.

11 Ḥājī Khalīfa, V, 535–6.

12 Ibid, 540–41.

13 A. Harley, 'The Musnad of ʿUmar b. ʿAbdi'l-ʿAzīz', *JASB*, XX, 391–488.

14 Ṭayālisī, *Musnad*, titlepage.

15 Ḥājī Khalīfa, V, 533.

16 *COPL*, v/i, 157–62.

17 Ibn Ḥajar, *Tahdhīb al-Tahdhīb*, IV, no. 316; Dhahabī, *Tadhkira*, I, 322; ʿIyāḍ, *Ilmāʿ*, 61.

18 The printed text, as well as the Patna MS, appear to be incomplete. The traditions related by al-ʿAbbās ibn al-Muṭṭalib, al-Faḍl ibn ʿAbbās, ʿAbd Allāh ibn Jaʿfar, Kaʿb ibn Mālik,

Salama ibn al-Akwaʿ, Sahl ibn Saʿd, Muʿāwiya, and ʿAmr ibn al-ʿĀṣ, whose *ḥadīths* are referred to on other pages, are entirely missing from the body of this version. Some of the traditions narrated by ʿUmar are likewise misplaced. Cf. Ṭayālisī, *Musnad*, 20–1.

19 Students of Ṭayālisī are greatly assisted by the concordance of al-Sāʿātī, *Minḥat al-Maʿbūd fī tartīb Musnad al-Ṭayālisī Abū Daūd* (Cairo, 1372).

20 Ḥājī Khalīfa, V, 533; cf. Sakhāwī, *Fatḥ*, 34.

21 All sections of the book are transmitted on his common authority.

22 Robson, J., 'Standards Applied by Muslim Traditionists,' (*Bulletin of the John Rylands Library* XLIII (1961CE), 459–79), 461.

23 Ṭayālisī, *Musnad*, nos.77, 241, 263, 387, 484, 1060, 1158, 2179, etc.

24 Ibid., nos.1021, etc.

25 Ibid., nos.393, 644, 837, 886, 892, 917, 938, etc.

26 For instance, ibid., no.381.

27 For instance, ibid., nos.456, 718, 2254.

28 For instance, ibid., nos.519, 1539.

29 For instance, ibid., no.794.

30 *COPL*, V/i, 157–62.

31 Two later editions of the *Musnad* have been published in Egypt: one by al-Bannā, and the other by Shākir. The latter (Cairo, vols. 1–16, 1373/1954) is extremely scholarly, and includes a precise and illuminating introduction to the author and his work. Shākir numbers each *ḥadīth*, and adds to each volume several useful indices. Unfortunately, the editor passed away before completing the work; a serious loss to the world of scholarship. The former was reprinted in 1389 in Beirut by al-Maktab al-Islāmī and Dār Ṣādir, together with a useful index of companions.

32 Ibn Ḥazm, *Jamharat Ansāb al-ʿArab* (MS in library of M. Z. Siddiqi), 230.

33 Ibid.

34 Ibid., 321; Ṭabarī, *Tārīkh*, II, 1358.

35 al-Dīnawarī, *al-Akhbār al-Ṭiwāl* (Leiden, 1888CE), 335.

36 Patton, W. M., *Aḥmad ibn Ḥanbal and the Miḥna* (Leiden, 1897), 10.

37 Ibn Ḥajar, *Tahdhīb al-Tahdhīb*, I, no.126; Wüstenfeld, F. *Der Imām el-Schāfiʿi: seine Schüler und Anhänger bis zum J. 300 d.H.* (Göttingen, 1890CE), no.13.

38 Ibid.

39 Ibid.

40 Subkī, *Ṭabaqāt*, I, 203; Patton, 108, 112, 145.

41 Patton, 142.

42 Subkī, *Ṭabaqāt*, I, 203–4; Patton, 172.

43 Patton, 14, 141, 147.

44 Ibid., 150.

45 Ibid., 144.

46 Patton, 152.

47 Ibn Ḥajar, *Tahdhīb al-Tahdhīb*, I, no.1261; Nawawī, *Tahdhīb*, 142–45.

48 Patton, 194.

49 Ibn al-Nadīm, *Fihrist*, 229.

50 Subkī, *Ṭabaqāt*, I, 202.

51 Ibid. 203.

52 Ibn Ḥanbal, *Musnad*, I, 308; IV, 269.

53 Ibn al-Nadīm, *Fihrist*, 229.

54 Subkī, *Ṭabaqāt*, I, 202; Goldziher, 'Neue Materialen zur Litteratur des Überlieferungswesens bei den Muhammedaner,' (*ZDMG* L (1896CE), 465–506), 472fn.

55 Dihlawī, *Bustān*, 31.

56 Goldziher, 'Neue Materialen', 485–86.

57 Cf. Khoury, R. G., 'L'importance d'Ibn Lahīʿa et de son papyrus conservé à Heidelberg dans la tradition musulmane du deuxième siécle de l'hégire,' *Arabica*, XXII (1975), 6–14; Azami *Early Ḥadīth Literature*, 29.

58 Ibn Ḥanbal, *Musnad*, II, 252–53.

59 Ibid., III, 202.

60 Ibid., VI, 101.

61 Ibid., III, 201. For some other instances of his exactitude, see ibid., I, 308; III, 33; V, 352, 385.

62 Ibid., II, 184; VI, 420.

63 In connection with some traditions, he states, for instance, that he read them with his father (Ibn Ḥanbal, *Musnad*, II, 157). Others, he says, he found in his father's manuscript (III, 310). Still others he found in the manuscript and had heard from his father, but had not made a note of them (IV, 96).

64 Ibid., III, 182; IV, 96; V, 26.

65 Ibid., I, 252; II, 449; III, 3; IV, 225; V, 382; VI, 73.

66 Ibid., V, 358.

67 Ibid., 336; V, 326; VI, 326.

68 Ibid., IV, 91. ʿAbd Allāh's editing has, however, been criticised by an eminent Indian traditionist of the last century, who claims that he committed many mistakes in the actual arrangement of the work, by including, for instance, the

narrations of the Madinans in the *musnad* of the Syrians, and vice versa. Dihlawī, *Bustān*, 31.

69 Goldziher, 'Neue Materialen', 466.

70 Ḥājī Khalīfa, V, 534–35.

71 Yāqūt, *Muʿjam al-Udabāʾ*, VII, 29.

72 Ibn al-Athīr, *Usd*, I, 9–11.

73 Suyūṭī, *Ṭabaqāt*, XXIV, no.12.

74 Ḥājī Khalīfa, V, 535.

75 Ibid., V, 534–35.

76 Goldziher, 'Neue Materialen', 470.

77 Dihlawī, *Bustān*, 31–2.

78 *EI*, 'Aḥmad ibn Muḥammad ibn Ḥanbal'.

79 Goldziher, 'Neue Materialen', 467.

80 Published at Hyderabad, 1362. Sezgin, I, 174.

81 Published at Bombay, 1386–90. Sezgin, I, 108–9.

82 Schacht, J., 'Ibn Rāhawayh,' *EI*² III, 902; Abbott, *Studies*, II, 69.

83 Sezgin, I, 101–2; Ṭaḥḥān, *Takhrīj*, 41–2.

84 Sezgin, I, 170–1; ed. A. al-Aʿāmī, Beirut, 1300.

85 Ḥājī Khalīfa, V, 532–43.

86 For this genre see Ṭaḥḥān, *Takhrīj*, 134–35; Abdul Rauf, '*Ḥadīth* Literature', 272–73.

87 Ibn Ḥanbal, *Musnad*, I, 308.

88 Beirut, 1390–92; in 11 volumes. Cf. Ibn Ḥajar, *Muqaddima Fatḥ al-Bārī* (Delhi, 1302), 489; Sezgin, I, 99.

89 Ibn Khallikān, no.409.

90 Ibn al-Nadīm, *Fihrist*, 228.

91 Hājī Khalīfa, III, 629.

92 Dihlawī, *Bustān*, 51.

93 al-Samʿānī, *al-Ansāb* (Leiden, 1912CE) 355b.

94 Bombay, 1386–90. Cf. Sezgin, I, 108–9.

95 The best-known study of his life and *Ṣaḥīḥ* is *al-Imām al-Bukhārī wa-Ṣaḥīḥuh* by the late ʿAbd al-Ghanī ʿAbd al-Khāliq, known as Abu'l-Kamāl, formerly Imām of the Sayyida Nafīsa mosque complex in Cairo. This book was originally an introduction to ʿAbd al-Khāliq's edition of the *Ṣaḥīḥ*, published in Mecca by the Maktabat al-Nahḍa in 1376, and was later republished as a separate work, both in Jedda and the United States. Here we are using the Jedda edition of 1405.

96 For detailed accounts of the life and *Ṣaḥīḥ* of Bukhārī, see, in addition to the work of ʿAbd al-Khāliq: Sezgin, I, 115–34; Ṭaḥḥān, *Takhrīj*, 110–4; Abdul Rauf, '*Ḥadīth* Literature,' 274–75.

97 Qasṭallānī, *Irshād*, I, 36.

98 Arberry, A., 'The Teachers of Al-Bukhārī,' *IQ* XXXI (1967), 34–49; Sezgin, M. F, *Buhârî'nin Kaynaklari hakkinda araştirmalar* (Istanbul, 1956).

99 Ibn Ḥajar, *Muqaddima*, 564.

100 Qasṭallānī, *Irshād*, I, 44f.

101 Ibn Ḥajar, *Muqaddima*, 566.

102 Subkī, *Ṭabaqāt*, II, 4.

103 Nawawī, *Tahdhīb*, 90.

104 Subkī, *Ṭabaqāt*, II, 6.

105 For these see Abbott, *Studies*, II, 52–3.

106 Qasṭallānī, *Irshād*, I, 36ff; Ibn Ḥajar, *Muqaddima*, 568ff; Nawawī, *Tahdhīb*, 87–91.

107 Subkī, *Ṭabaqāt*, II, 5.

108 ʿAbd al-Khāliq, 147–54; cf. Ibn al-Nadīm, *Fihrist*, 230; Ibn Ḥajar, *Muqaddima*, 493; Qasṭallānī, *Irshād*, 35. Bukhārī's best-known works, apart from the *Ṣaḥīḥ*, are: *al-Tārīkh al-Kabīr*, Hyderabad, 1361, in 8 vols., cf., above 100; *al-Tārīkh al-Ṣaghīr*, Allāhabad, 1325; and *Rafʿ al-yadayn*, Delhi, 1299.

109 Qasṭallānī, *Irshād*, I, 33ff., 46.

110 Guillaume, A. *The Traditions of Islam* (Oxford, 1924CE), 93.

111 Nawawī, *Tahdhīb*, 95; Suyūṭī, *Tadrīb*, 24. For a listing and assessment of the various printed editions, see ʿAbd al-Khāliq, 245–56.

112 Or 300,000, according to another account. Of these, he had 100,000 by heart. Abbott, *Studies*, II, 69.

113 For a detailed analysis of Bukhārī's understanding of the term 'sound' (*Ṣaḥīḥ*), see Qasṭallānī, *Irshād*, I, 22ff; ʿAbd al-Khāliq, 200–1.

114 Qasṭallānī, *Irshād*, I, 22ff.

115 Ibid.

116 Suyūṭī, *Tadrīb*, 30.

117 Ibn Ḥajar, *Muqaddima*, 13; Qasṭallānī, *Irshād*, I, 11–2.

118 Ibn Ḥajar, *Muqaddima*, 12f; Qasṭallānī, *Irshād*, I, 22f.

119 ʿAbd al-Khāliq, 230–39. Twenty-eight shorter glosses are also listed in this source (pp.239–42), sixteen epitomes (pp.242–43), and sixteen works on matters relating to its indexing, biographical information, and so forth (pp.243–45). Other lists of commentaries may be consulted in Qasṭallānī, *Irshād*, I, 39–42, and Ḥājī Khalīfa, II, 521–39.

120 Ḥājī Khalīfa, II, 545.

121 Jazāʾirī, *Tawjīh*, 96–113.

122 Nawawī, *al-Minhāj fī Sharḥ Ṣaḥīḥ Muslim ibn al-Ḥajjāj* (Cairo, 1347), 8.
123 A. Mingana has published a note on a MS. of some old fragments of the *Ṣaḥīḥ* of al-Bukhārī as 'An Important MS. of Bukhārī's *Ṣaḥīḥ*', *JRAS* (1936), pp.287–92. He describes the special features of the manuscript, and promises to publish a complete set of facsimile reproductions of it (this was apparently never achieved). His suggestion, however, that the book was not composed by al-Bukhārī, but by a student of the book one or two generations after the great traditionist, on the grounds that the word *akhbaranā* is used for him, and *ḥaddathanā* for the later narrators, is mistaken. For the strict use of these terms was far from being definitely fixed at the time of al-Bukhārī. In the *Risāla Taqyīd al-ʿIlm* of al-Khaṭīb al-Baghdādī, the author is introduced by the term *akhbaranā*, and other narrators by *ḥaddathanā*.
124 'al-Bukhārī', *EI*, I, 783.
125 For his life and work see Sezgin, I, 136ff; Abdul Rauf, '*Ḥadīth* Literature', 275.
126 Ibn Ḥajar, *Iṣāba*, I, 752.
127 Ibn Ḥazm, *Jamhara*, fol.288.
128 Ibid.
129 Ibid.
130 Ibn Ḥajar, *Tahdhīb al-Tahdhīb*, X, no.226.
131 Ibn Khallikān, no.727.
132 Dihlawī, *Bustān*, 117.
133 Ibn al-Nadīm, *Fihrist*, 231. Perhaps Muslim's best known work, other than the *Ṣaḥīḥ*, is his *Kitāb al-Tamyīz*, ed. M. M. al-Aʿẓamī, Riyadh, 1395/1975.
134 Ḥājī Khalīfa, II, 541ff; cf. Nawawī, *Minhāj*, I, 4.
135 Nawawī, *Minhāj*, I, 5.
136 Qasṭallānī, *Irshād*, 8–9.
137 Nawawī, *Minhāj*, 5.
138 Muslim, *Ṣaḥīḥ*, muqaddima, 3ff.
139 The distinction is explained in greater detail in ʿIyāḍ, *Ilmāʿ*, 122–34.
140 Nawawī, *Minhāj*, 5.
141 Dihlawī, *Bustān*, 117.
142 Nawawī, *Minhāj*, 8.
143 Twenty-seven commentaries on the work are listed by Sezgin, I, 136–40.
144 Edited by M. M. Aʿẓamī, Beirut, 1391–97 in four volumes. Cf. Ṭaḥḥān, *Takhrīj*, 213.
145 Ibn Ḥibbān's *ḥadīth*s are most usually consulted in the work of al-Haythamī (d.807/1405), *Mawārid al-Zam'ān ilā zawā'id Ibn Ḥibbān.* This includes such of Ibn Ḥibbān's *ḥadīth*s as are not also recorded by Bukhārī and Muslim, numbering 2,647.
146 Tirmidhī's work is more properly a *Jāmiʿ* collection, including material on all the various topics; but as it has conventionally acquired the title *Sunan*, it has been included in this Chapter for ease of reference.
147 Nawawī, *Tahdhīb*, 709. Wüstenfeld, *Schāfiʿi*, 91, doubts the accuracy of the statement that Abū Daūd had been engaged on his book for this period.
148 Samʿānī, *Ansāb*, 293; Nawawī, *Tahdhīb*, 709.
149 Ibn Khallikān, no.271.
150 Yāqūt, *Muʿjam al-Buldān*, III, 44.
151 Samʿānī, *Ansāb*, 293.
152 Subkī, *Ṭabaqāt*, II, 48.
153 Yāqūt, *Muʿjam al-Buldān*, III, 44.
154 Nawawī, *Tabdhīb*, 710.
155 An account of many of these teachers may be found in the works on *asmā' al-rijāl.*
156 Subkī, *Ṭabaqāt*, II, 49.
157 Nawawī, *Tahdhīb*, 710.
158 For the *Sunan*, see Sezgin, I, 149–52; Abdul Rauf, '*Ḥadīth* Literature', 276.
159 Goldziher, *Muslim Studies*, II, 230.
160 See Abū Daūd's *Risāla ilā ahl Makka* (Beirut, n.d.).
161 Abū Daūd, *Sunan*, I, 4.
162 Ibid., I, 26.
163 Ibid., 32–3.
164 Ibid., 133–34.
165 Ibid., 138.
166 Ibid., 162.
167 Ibid., 221.
168 Nawawī, *Tahdhīb*, 711–12.
169 For this work see Sezgin, I, 154–59; Abdul Rauf, '*Ḥadīth* Literature', 276.
170 It is interesting to record that his tomb, vandalised by the Soviets, was restored by the Uzbek authorities in 1410/1990, and is now once again an important centre for pious visits.
171 Dihlawī, *Bustān*, 121.
172 Tirmidhī, *Jāmiʿ*, I, 5.
173 Ibid., I, 13.
174 Ibid., II, 16.
175 Other terms, which need not detain us here, are occasionally encountered in his work.
176 Ibn al-Ṣalāḥ, *Muqaddima*, 14–5.
177 Ibid., 14ff; Suyūṭī, *Tadrīb*, 53–4.

178 Subkī, *Ṭabaqāt*, II, 83–4; Ibn Khallikān, no.28.
179 Wüstenfeld, *Schāfiʿi*, 70.
180 Dhahabī, *Tadhkira*, II, 268.
181 For the *Sunan* see Sezgin, 167–69; Abdul Rauf, '*Ḥadīth* Literature', 276.
182 Subkī, *Ṭabaqāt*, II, 84. The original *Sunan* was published in a six-volume facsimile edition in Beirut in 1411/1991.
183 Goldziher, *Muslim Studies*, II, 232.
184 Dhahabī, *Tadhkira*, II, 268.
185 Ḥājī Khalīfa, III, 626–27.
186 Cf. Sezgin, I, 114–15; Abdul Rauf, '*Ḥadīth* Literature', 277. An ancient manuscript copy was brought from Mecca, and lithographed and published in India at the instance of Nawwab Siddiq Hasan Khan of Bhopal, one of the nineteenth century's great patrons of *ḥadīth* learning.
187 al-Diyārbakrī, *Tārīkh al-Khamīs* (Cairo, 1309 [?]), II, 341.
188 Dārimī, *Sunan*, editor's introduction, 6.
189 Samʿānī, *Ansāb*, 218b; Dhahabī, *Tadhkira*, II, 115–17.
190 Ibn al-Ṣalāḥ, *Muqaddima*, 15.
191 Dārimī, *Sunan*, editor's introduction, 7; Dihlawī, *Bustān*, 48.
192 Ibn al-Ṣalāḥ, *Muqaddima*, 15.
193 Dihlawī, *Muqaddima*, introduction.
194 Ḥājī Khalīfa, V, 540.
195 For the work see Sezgin, I, 147–48; Abdul Rauf, '*Ḥadīth* Literature', 276–77.
196 Dhahabī, *Tadhkira*, II, 209ff.
197 Dihlawī, *Muqaddima*, introduction. One might also note the verdict of Ibn al-Jawzī to the effect that *ḥadīth*s on the merits of individuals, tribes or towns are usually fraudulent. Ibn al-Jawzī's work, however (the *Mawḍūʿāt*), is generally regarded as exaggerated in its approach; cf. al-Zurqānī, *Sharḥ ʿalā al-Manẓūma al-Bayqūnīya fi'l-Muṣṭalaḥ*, ed. Nabīl al-Sharīf (Beirut, 1405/1985), 94–5.
198 al-Khaṭīb al-Baghdādī, *Tārīkh Baghdad*, XII, 34–40.
199 See above, 91.
200 Ibn Khallikān, no.32.
201 Ibid., no.626.
202 Ibid., p.38.
203 Ibid.
204 Ibid., nos. 132, 445.
205 For a list of these, see Wüstenfeld, *Schāfiʿi*, no.235.
206 For the *Sunan*, see Sezgin, I, 206–9.
207 al-Baghawī, *Maṣābīḥ al-Sunna* (Cairo, n.d.), 2.
208 Dihlawī, *Bustān*, 48.
209 Subkī, *Ṭabaqāt*, III, 4.
210 Ḥājī Khalīfa, III, 627; Abdul Rauf, '*Ḥadīth* Literature', 281–82. His best-known work, *al-Sunan al-Kubrā*, was published in a ten volume edition in Hyderabad, 1344.
211 Subkī, *Ṭabaqāt*, III, 3–5.
212 Sezgin, I, 104.
213 Dhahabī, *Tadhkira*, II, 5.
214 Ibn Ḥajar, *Tahdhīb al-Tahdhīb*, III, no.148.
215 Dhahabī, *Tadhkira*, II, 5; Dihlawī, *Bustān*, 51.
216 Samʿānī, *Ansāb*, sub. nom.
217 See below, 31.
218 al-Khaṭīb al-Baghdādī, *Tārīkh Baghdad*, VI, 122.
219 Dhahabī, *Tadhkira*, III, 129.
220 Dhahabī, *Tadhkira*, III, 129.
221 Ḥājī Khalīfa, V, 629; Ṭaḥḥān, *Takhrīj*, 45.
222 Ṭaḥḥān, *Takhrīj*, 45–6.
223 Ṭabarānī, *al-Muʿjam al-Ṣaghīr* (Cairo, 1388); for which see Ṭaḥḥān, *Takhrīj*, 36. Towards the end of the book, however, two or three traditions with the same *isnād* are sometimes given. *Ḥadīths* included in these three *Muʿjams*, and in the *Musnads* of al-Bazzār and Abū Yaʿlā al-Mawṣilī, but not found in the Sound Six collections, are gathered in the *Majmaʿ al-Zawā'id wa-Manbaʿ al-Fawā'id* of al-Haythamī, published in ten volumes in Cairo in 1352. Cf. Ṭaḥḥān, *Takhrīj*, 120.
224 Ḥājī Khalīfa, V, 623–30. The best known are the *Muʿjam al-Ṣaḥāba* of Aḥmad ibn ʿAlī ibn Lāl (d.398/1008), the *Muʿjam al-Ṣaḥāba* of Abū Yaʿlā al-Mawṣilī (d.307/919), cf. Ṭaḥḥān, *Takhrīj*, 46; and the *Muʿjam al-Ṣaḥāba* of Ibn Qāniʿ (d.351/962); cf. Sezgin, I, 189.
225 Shāh Walī Allāh al-Dihlawī, *Ḥujjat Allāh al-Bāligha* (Cairo, 1352), I, 132–4.
226 Ibid.
227 Ibn al-Ṣalāḥ, *Muqaddima*, 8.
228 Sakhāwī, *Fatḥ*, 16.
229 Goldziher, *Muslim Studies*, II, 240–41.
230 Distinguished *ḥadīth* expert who died in 353/964 in Egypt, and whose *Muṣannaf* was recognised a century after his death by Ibn Ḥazm as one of the finest collections of *ḥadīth*.
231 Suyūṭī, *Tadrīb*, 29.
232 Ibid., 32.
233 Ibid., 56.

234 Cf. Goldziher, *Muslim Studies*, II, 240–41.
235 Goldziher, *Muslim Studies*, II, 243.
236 Such as, for instance, Dihlawī, *Ḥujja*, I, 134–35.

NOTES TO CHAPTER FIVE

1 For the *isnād* system, see ʿIyāḍ, *Ilmāʿ*, 194–98; Azami, *Early Ḥadīth Literature*, 212–47; idem, *Schacht's Origins*, 154–212; J. Robson, 'The Isnād in Muslim Tradition', reprinted from *Transactions of the Glasgow University Oriental Society*, XV (1965CE), pp.15–26.

2 Leone Caetani, *Annali dell' Islam* (Milan 1905–18; Rome, 1926CE), I, 30.

3 J. Horovitz, 'Alter und Ursprung des Isnād', *Der Islam*, VIII (1917CE), 39–47. Cf. Azami, *Schacht's Origins*, 167.

4 Their conclusions are summarised in A. H. Harley, 'The *Musnad* of ʿUmar ibn ʿAbd al-ʿAziz', (*JASB*, New Series, XX (1924CE), 391–488), 404–5.

5 The falsity of this presupposition has been shown by Abbott, *Studies*, II, 64, and passim.

6 *Lectures on Arabic Historians*, 20.

7 Horovitz, 'Alter'. Whether the *isnād* system really goes back a long distance towards the Mosaic period is, however, open to doubt; Horovitz has not proved that these '*isnāds*' are not later interpolations.

8 Ibn Ḥazm, *al-Fiṣal fi'l-Milal wa'l-Ahwā' wa'l-niḥal* (Cairo, 1347), II, 67–70.

9 As far as I am aware, no serious notice of this fact has yet been taken. It was pointed out to me for the first time by my late friend Dr. Prabodhchandra Bagchi, the Vice-Chancellor of Visva-Bharati University (India).

10 *Mahabharata*, Book 1, canto I; cf. Winternitz, *History of Indian Literature* (Calcutta, 1927CE), I, 323.

11 Translated by A. B. Keith, *The Sānkhāyana Āraṇyaka, with an appendix on the Mahāvrata* (London, 1908CE), 71–2.

12 *Sacred Books of the East*, XV, 224–27.

13 Winternitz, *A History of Indian Literature*, II, 34, fn.3.

14 P. Cordier, *Catalogue du fond Tibetain de la Bibliothèque Nationale* (Paris, 1915CE), III, 163.

15 Caetani, *Annali*, I, 31.

16 Horovitz, 'Alter', 43–4.

17 Who, according to Caetani, never used the *isnād* method.

18 J. Horovitz, 'The Earliest Biographies of the Prophet and their Authors', (*IC* I (1927CE), 535–59), 550–51.

19 Schacht, Joseph. *The Origins of Muhammadan Jurisprudence* (Oxford, 1959CE), 37, 163.

20 Ibid., 36.

21 For this account, see Khaṭīb, *Sunna*, 220; Nawawī, *Minhāj*, I, 84.

22 Robson, 'Standards,' 460; cf. Khaṭīb, *Sunna*, 220.

23 Robson, 164, fn.1.

24 Abbott, *Studies*, II, 2; cf. II, 5–32.

25 Qasṭallānī, *Mawāhib*, V, 454.

26 Khaṭīb, *Sunna*, 221.

27 Azami, *Schacht's Origins*, 155.

28 Horovitz, 'Alter', 47.

29 Suyūṭī, *Tadrīb*, 20–1.

30 Sakhāwī, *Fatḥ*, 8–10. This *isnād* has been criticised by Schacht (*Origins*, 170, 176), on the grounds that Mālik was too young at the time of Nāfiʿ's death, and therefore could not have heard from the latter. This argument, however, assumes that the reader will not check the facts for himself, for Mālik was almost 23 years of age when Nāfiʿ died, and was hence in a perfectly good position to study under him. Cf. Azami, *Schacht's Origins*, 171. Coulson, despite his reservations about certain aspects of Schacht's theory, here repeats Schacht's sweeping assertion without comment (*Cambridge History of Arabic Literature*, I, 319).

31 Nawawī, *Tahdhīb*, 507.

32 Suyūṭī, *Tadrīb*, 22–3. Another exercise occasionally indulged in was locating the 'weakest *isnād*'. Some thought that this was the *isnād* Marwān-al-Kalbī-Abū Ṣāliḥ-Ibn ʿAbbās. Cf. Goldziher, *Muslim Studies*, II, 247 fn.2.

33 There are *ḥadīth* scholars even today who can recite their *ḥadīth*s complete with *isnāds* stretching back from themselves to the Prophet without interruption. Such a chain typically contains between twenty and thirty narrators, and is termed *al-ḥadīth al-musalsal*.

34 al-Munajjid, 'Ijāzat al-Samāʿ fī al-Makhṭūṭāt al-Qadīma', in *Journal of the In-*

stitute of Arabic Manuscripts, I/ii (Cairo, 1375/1955), 232ff.

35 Ateş, *Corum ve Yozgat kütüphanelerinden bazı mühim Arapça yazmalar* (Istanbul, 1959CE), 3–4.

36 C. H. Becker, *Papyri Schott-Reinhardt I* (Heidelberg, 1906CE). I am indebted to Professor Otto Spies for a copy of page 8 of Becker's work. For additional information see J. Horovitz, 'Wahb ibn Munabbih', *EI*, IV, 1084–85.

37 Ibn al-Ṣalāḥ, *Muqaddima*, 81f; Suyūṭī, *Tadrīb*, 158; Sakhāwī, *Fatḥ*, 265.

38 *COPL*, V/i, no.241.

39 Ibid., no.254.

40 Ibid., ii, no.322.

41 Ibid., no.483.

42 Ibid., XII, no.800.

43 W. Ahlwardt, *Die Handschriften-Verzeichnisse der Königlichen Bibliothek zu Berlin* (Berlin, 1895CE), II, no.246.

44 Ibn al-Ṣalāḥ, *Muqaddima*, 82.

45 A number of Arabic MSS on subjects other than tradition and provided with notes of this type are described by G. Vajda in his *Les certificats de lecture et de transmission dans les manuscrits arabes de la Bibliothèque nationale de Paris* (Paris, 1956CE). See in particular pp.37ff.

46 Margoliouth, *Lectures on Arabic Historians*, 19.

47 al-Khaṭīb al-Baghdādī, *al-Kifāya fī ʿilm al-Rīwāya* (Hyderabad, 1368/1949), 171–203.

48 Ibid.

49 Ibn al-Ṣalāḥ, *Muqaddima*, 49; ʿIyāḍ, *Ilmāʿ*, 201.

50 Suyūṭī, *Tadrīb*, 164.

51 Yāqūt, *Muʿjam al-Udabā'*, I, 17, 26.

52 Suyūṭī, *Tadrīb*, 164.

53 Yāqūt, *Muʿjam al-Udabā'*, IV, 135.

54 ʿIyāḍ, *Ilmāʿ*, 48.

55 Ibid., 69–70; Sezgin, 58–9; Robson, 'Standards', 470.

56 ʿIyāḍ, *Ilmāʿ*, 70–9; Sezgin, 59; Robson, 'Standards', 470.

57 ʿIyāḍ, *Ilmāʿ*, 88–107; Khaṭīb, *Sunna*, 311–26; Sezgin, 59; Robson, 'Standards', 470.

58 ʿIyāḍ, *Ilmāʿ*, 79–83; Khaṭīb, *Sunna*, 330–34; Sezgin, 59; Robson, 'Standards', 472–73; Abbott, Studies, I, 25.

59 ʿIyāḍ, *Ilmāʿ*, 83–7; Khaṭīb, *Sunna*, 334; Sezgin, 59; Robson, 'Standards', 473–74.

60 ʿIyāḍ, *Ilmāʿ*, 107–15; Sezgin, 59.

61 ʿIyāḍ, *Ilmāʿ*, 115–16; Khaṭīb, *Sunna*, 352–53; Sezgin, 59; Robson, 'Standards', 474.

62 ʿIyāḍ, *Ilmāʿ*, 116–17; Sezgin, 59–60; Robson, 'Standards', 474; Abbott, *Studies*, II, 45–6. For more on these eight categories, see also Ibn al-Ṣalāḥ, *Muqaddima*, 50–69; Suyūṭī, *Tadrīb*, 129–50; Sakhāwī, *Fatḥ*, 170–236.

63 Suyūṭī, *Tadrīb*, 4–8.

64 Suyūṭī, *Tadrīb*, 159–70.

65 For all these points, see Ibn al-Ṣalāḥ, *Muqaddima*, 70–82; Sakhāwī, *Fatḥ*, 236–68; Suyūṭī, *Tadrīb*, 151–59; Khaṭīb, *Sunna*, 237–41.

66 Goldziher, *Muslim Studies*, II, 41.

67 Ibn ʿAbd al-Barr, *Jāmiʿ*, I, 163–86.

68 Ibid.

69 Goldziher, *Muslim Studies*, II, 46–7.

70 Horovitz, J, 'The Earliest Biographers of the Prophet and their Authors' (ii) (*IC* II (1928CE), 22–50), 48.

71 Ibid., 41–2.

72 See above, 47–49.

73 See above, 54.

NOTES TO CHAPTER SIX

1 Suyūṭī, *Tadrīb*, 9.

2 Ibid., 256.

3 Ibid.

4 Cf. Wellhausen, J. *Reste arabischen Heidentums* (Berlin, 1897CE), 94–101.

5 Ibn al-Ṣalāḥ, *Muqaddima*, 154.

6 Suyūṭī, *Tadrīb*, 254.

7 Horovitz, 'The Earliest Biographies', 550, 558; Ibn Saʿd, V, 133.

8 Ibn ʿAdī, *al-Kāmil fī Ḍuʿafā' al-Rijāl* (Beirut, 1402). This text has been quoted by Jazā'irī, *Tawjīh*, 114.

9 Loth, O. 'Ursprung und Bedeutung der Tabaḳāt', (*ZDMG* XXIII, 593–614), 600.

10 Ibn al-Nadīm, *Fihrist*, 228, 199.

11 Der Islam, VIII, 47.

12 Khaṭīb, *Sunna*, 265.

13 Ibn al-Nadīm, *Fihrist*, 99f.

14 Cf. Ibn al-Khayyāṭ, *Tārīkh*, and his *Ṭabaqāt* (Sezgin, 110-11; Khaṭīb, *Sunna*, 265).

15 Ibn al-Nadīm, *Fihrist*, 992.

16 Ibid., 230, 231, 233; Ḥājī Khalīfa, II, 141. Best-known amongst these are Bukhārī, *al-Tārīkh al-Kabīr* (Hyderabad, 1381; cf. Sezgin, I, 132–3) and his *al-Tārīkh al-Ṣaghīr* (Allahabad, 1324; cf. Sezgin, I, 133); Muslim, *Kitāb al-Tamyīz* (Sezgin, I, 143); Nasā'ī, *al-Ḍuʿafā' al-Ṣaghīr* (Hyderabad, 1325); cf. also Ibn Ḥanbal, *al-ʿIlal wa-Maʿrifat al-Rijāl* (ed. Talat Kocyigit, Ankara, 1963CE).

17 Ibn Ḥajar, *Iṣāba*, I, editor's introduction, I.

18 Margoliouth, *Lectures*, 7f.

19 Khaṭīb, *Sunna*, 274–5.

20 The best known of which is al-Dawlāhī, *al-Kunā wa'l-asmā'* (Hyderabad, 13 22; cf. Sezgin, I, 172). For others see Khaṭīb, *Sunna*, 276–9.

21 Leiden, 1912CE; cf. Khaṭīb, *Sunna*, 280. For more in this class see ibid., 279–80.

22 See above, 103–5.

23 Beirut, 1402.

24 Ed. Būrān al-Ḍannāwī and Kamāl al-Ḥūt. Beirut, 1405/1985.

25 For some more, see Khaṭīb, *Sunna*, 281–87; Ṭaḥḥān, *Takhrīj*, 200ff.

26 See above, 136.

27 Ibn Saʿd, III/i, editor's introduction.

28 al-Khaṭīb al-Baghdādī, *Tārīkh Baghdād*, V, 312f.

29 Ibn al-Nadīm, *Fihrist*, 171.

30 Nawawī, *Tahdhīb*, 7; Ibn Khallikān, no.656.

31 al-Khaṭīb al-Baghdādī, *Tārīkh Baghdād*, VIII, 92ff.

32 Ibid., V, 160.

33 Ibid., III, 121.

34 For the history of the Sachau edition of the *Ṭabaqāt*, see Appendix III.

35 For some important lacunae in this volume see the references given in J. Fück, 'Ibn Saʿd', *EI²*, III, 923.

36 Ibn Saʿd, III/i, editor's introduction, xxx *et seq.*

37 Loth, 'Ursprung', 604–5; Ibn Saʿd, III/i, xxxvii–xxxviii.

38 Hitti, P. *The Origins of the Islamic State* (Columbia, 1924CE), I, 9.

39 Ṭabārī, *Tārīkh*, I, 1113–16. Cf. Ibn Saʿd, *Fatḥ*, 28, 29.

40 Nawawī, *Tahdhīb*, 7.

41 Ibn Ḥajar, *Iṣāba*, I, 2.

42 Cf. Khaṭīb, *Sunna*, 265–66; Abdul Rauf, '*Ḥadīth* Literature,' 278–79; Ṭaḥḥān, *Takhrīj*, 175–77.

43 Ṭaḥḥān, *Takhrīj*, 177–78.

44 Ibn Ḥajar, *Iṣāba*, I, 1.

45 al-Khaṭīb al-Baghdādī, *Tārīkh Baghdād*, X, 111–17.

46 Ṭaḥḥan, *Takhrīj*, 171.

47 Suyūṭī, *Ṭabaqāt*, XIII, 62.

48 Ibn Khallikān, no.847. Ibn ʿAbd al-Barr's book, *al-Istīʿāb*, contained the biographies of only three hundred Companions; a supplement was appended by Ibn Fatḥūn, which contained notices of an approximately equal number. Cf. Ḥajī Khalīfa, I, 277; Ṭaḥḥān, *Takhrīj*, 170.

49 Ṭaḥḥān, *Takhrīj*, 170–71.

50 Suyūṭī, *Tadrīb*, 32; Ḥajī Khalīfa, I, 278F.

51 Ṭaḥḥān, *Takhrīj*, 171–73.

52 Ibid., 32n.

53 Ibid., 172.

54 Ibid., 205–6.

55 For the importance of 'theological local historiography' note the following passage, attributed to Ṣāliḥ ibn Aḥmad, author of *Ṭabaqāt al-Hamadhāniyyīn*: 'When religious scholarship has been cultivated in a place and scholars lived there in ancient and modern times, the students of traditions there and all those interested in traditions should begin with a thorough study of the *ḥadīth*s of their own home town. Once the student knows what is sound and what is unsound in their traditions, and is completely acquainted with the *ḥadīth* scholars of his city and their conditions, he may occupy himself with the traditions of other places, and with travelling in search of traditions.' (Al-Khaṭīb al-Baghdādī, *Tārīkh Baghdād*, I, 214, cited in F. Rosenthal, *History of Muslim Historiography* (Leiden, 1952CE), 144. See also Ibn al-Ṣalāḥ, 100ff.)

56 Khaṭīb, *Sunna*, 267. The only previous history of the city, by Ṭayfūr Aḥmad ibn Abī Ṭāhir (204–280/819–883), of which only the sixth volume is known (lithographed and translated into German by H. Keller (Leipzig, 1980CE)), deals only with the history of the Caliphs.

57 al-Khaṭīb al-Baghdādī, *Kifāya*, appendix, p.5.

58 Yāqūt, *Muʿjam al-Udabā'*, I, 248–49.

59 Access to the *ḥadīth* content of the book is facilitated by the separate index of Aḥmad al-Ghummārī: *Miftāḥ al-Tartīb li-Aḥādīth Tārīkh*

al-Khaṭīb (Cairo, 1372). Cf. Ṭaḥḥān, *Takhrīj*, 81–3 for the method of using this index.

60 al-Khaṭīb al-Baghdādī, *Tarīkh Baghdād*, I, 224; II, 521; IV, 176; VI, 101.

61 Ḥājī Khalīfa, II, 119f.

62 Yāqūt, *Muʿjam al-Udabā'*, V, 140–44. Apart from the *History*, his best-known work is his *Tabyīn Kādhib al-Muftarī*, in which he defends the doctrines of Ashʿarī orthodoxy against the anthropomorphism of the neo-Ḥanbalites.

63 Ibn ʿAsākir, *Tārīkh Dimashq*, I, 10f.

64 'Syria' (*al-Shām*) at this time included present-day Palestine.

65 Ed. Girgis ʿAwaḍ, Baghdad, 1967CE.

66 Ed. ʿAlī al-Shabbī and Naʿīm Ḥasan al-Yāfī, Tunis, 1968CE.

67 Ed. Ṭāhir al-Naʿsānī, Ḥamā, n.d.

68 Leiden, 1931CE.

69 Ed. ʿAbd al-Raḥmān al-Muʿallimī, Hyderabad, 1369.

70 Ibn Khallikān, nos, 32, 631.

71 Ibid., no.626.

72 Ḥājī Khalīfa, II, 125f.

73 Ibn Khallikān, no.406.

74 Ibid., no.672.

75 Yāqūt, *Muʿjam al-Udabā'*, I, 410; Ḥājī Khalīfa, II, 143.

76 Ibn Khallikān, no.502.

77 Ḥājī Khalīfa, II, 157.

78 Ibid., II, 140f.

NOTES TO CHAPTER SEVEN

1 Qur'ān, XXIV, 12.

2 Qur'ān, IX, 30.

3 Mullā Jiwān, *Nūr al-Anwār* (Calcutta, 1359), 180; al-Mubārakfūrī, *Tuḥfat al-Aḥwadhī* (Delhi, 1346–53), II, 197.

4 Muslim, *Ṣaḥīḥ*, bāb al-tayammum (I, 61).

5 Ibid., I, 10.

6 Bukhārī, *Ṣaḥīḥ*, I, 141.

7 Al-Ḥākim's work, *al-Madkhal ilā Maʿrifat al-Iklīl*, is the only book of this type with an English translation: J. Robson, *An Introduction to the Science of Tradition* (London, 1953CE).

8 Published Hyderabad, 1357.

9 Published Cairo, 1398.

10 Published Cairo, 1326, another edition 1974CE.

11 For a list see Suyūṭī, *Tadrīb*, 9.

12 Published Lucknow, n.d.

13 Published Cairo, 1307; new edition 1379.

14 Shāfiʿī, *Risāla*, 99.

15 For more on this division, see Zurqānī, *Sharḥ*, 22ff, 59; Kamali, *Principles*, 81–2.

16 'A *ḥadīth* which a Successor (*tābiʿī*) has directly attributed to the Prophet without mentioning the last link, namely the Companion who might have narrated it from the Prophet' (Kamali, *Principles*, 79).

17 Jazā'irī, *Tawjīh*, 113–18; cf. Ṭaḥḥān, *Takhrīj*;, 156–66.

18 Kamali, *Principles*, 68–70; ʿAbd al-Khāliq, 63–4.

19 Jiwān, *Nūr*, 176.

20 Nawawī, *Taqrīb*, 190.

21 Ibid., 191.

22 Beirut, 1405.

23 Kamali, *Principles*, 70–1.

24 Ibid., 71–8; Khaṭīb, *Sunna*, 18–20, 25.

25 Qur'ān, LIX, 7; cf. Azami, *Schacht's Origins*, 7–15.

26 Dārimī, *Sunan*, 26.

27 Ibid., 32–3.

28 Bukhārī, *Ṣaḥīḥ*, II, 124.

29 Ibid., 137; Shāfiʿī, *Risāla*, 114.

30 Ibn Saʿd, I, 52.

31 For *ra'y* see Kamali, *Principles*, 251–52.

32 Shāfiʿī, *Risāla*, 118–20.

33 See ʿAsqalānī's commentary on Bukhārī, *Ṣaḥīḥ*, kitāb farḍ al-khumus, bāb qismat al-imām.

34 Muslim, *Ṣaḥīḥ*, II, 264; Dihlawī, *Ḥujjat Allāh al-Bāligha* (Lahore edition, 1351AH), I, 249–50.

35 Kamali, *Principles*, 48; Khaṭīb, *Sunna*, 23–7.

36 Dārimī, *Sunan*, 26ff; Shāfiʿī, *Risāla*, 117–119; Ibn ʿAbd al-Barr, *Jāmiʿ*, II, 31–3.

37 Shiblī Nuʿmānī, *al-Fārūq*, II, 196.

38 Khaṭīb, *Sunna*, 8–12. For more on the legal force of *ḥadīth*, see Kamali, *Principles*, 48–50.

39 As Abbott notes (*Studies*, II, 75–6), Orientalist scholarship has generally ignored the phenomenon of *matn* criticism. Even so late a writer as Coulson ('European Criticism', 317) believes of the *ḥadīth* scholars that 'their test for authenticity was confined to an investigation of the chain of transmitters (*isnād*). There could, by the

terms of the religious faith itself, be no questioning of the content of the report; for this was the substance of divine revelation and therefore not susceptible to any form of legal or historical criticism.' A brief inspection of works such as Ibn al-Jawzī's *Mawḍūʿāt*, together with the contents of the present section, readily corrects this assumption.

40 Suyūṭī, *Tadrīb*, 100.

41 Ibid., 99.

42 al-Hākim, *Maʿrifa ʿUlūm al-Ḥadīth* (Cairo, 1937CE), 58ff.

43 Suyūṭī, *Tadrīb*, 48.

44 Ibid., 89.

45 Khaṭīb, *Sunna*, 243.

46 Azami, *Schacht's Origins*, 114; Kamali, *Principles*, 59.

47 Khaṭīb, *Sunna*, 244–45. For the techniques of reconciling *ḥadīth* see Kamali, *Principles*, 356–65.

48 Khaṭīb, *Sunna*, 242; Azami, *Schacht's Origins*, 114.

49 Ibid., 247.

50 Khaṭīb, *Sunna*, 208–20; Kamali, *Principles*, 66–7.

51 Khaṭīb, *Sunna*, 244.

52 Ibid., 243.

53 Ibid., 242.

54 *al-Mawḍūʿāt* (Medina, 1386–89).

55 *al-La'ālī al-Maṣnūʿa fi'l-Aḥādīth al-Mawḍūʿa* (Beirut, 1408).

56 *al-Fawā'id al-Majmūʿa fī bayān al-Aḥādīth al-Mawḍūʿa* (Lahore, 1223 [1323?]).

57 Ṭaḥḥān, *Takhrīj* 64–71, 148–49; Khaṭīb, *Sunna*, 282–91.

58 Bukhārī, *Ṣaḥīḥ*, bāb khalq Ādam; Ibn Ḥajar, *Fatḥ al-Bārī*, VI, 230.

59 Bukhārī, *Ṣaḥīḥ*, Kitāb al-Ṣulḥ, bāb 1; cf. Ibn Ḥajar, *Fatḥ*, ad. loc.

60 [Cf. Ibrāhīm in] Ibn ʿAbd al-Barr, *Istiʿāb;* Ibn al-Athīr, *Usd al-Ghāba*; Shawkānī, *Fawā'id*, 144.

61 Ibn al-Qayyim, *Zād al-Maʿād* (Kanpur, 1298), 97. Cf. Bell, *Love Theory in Early Hanbalite Islam*, 26.

62 Ibn Ḥajar, *Fatḥ al-Bārī*, VIII, 354.

NOTES TO APPENDIX I

1 Maura O'Neill, *Women Speaking, Women Listening* (Maryknoll, 1990CE), 31: 'Muslims do not use a masculine God as either a conscious or unconscious tool in the construction of gender roles.'

2 For a general overview of the question of women's status in Islam, see M. Boisard, *L'Humanisme de l'Islam* (3rd. ed., Paris, 1985CE), 104–10.

3 al-Khaṭīb, *Sunna*, 53–4, 69–70.

4 See above, 18, 21.

5 Ibn Saʿd, VIII, 355.

6 Suyūṭī, *Tadrīb*, 215.

7 Ibn Saʿd, VIII, 353.

8 Maqqarī, *Nafḥ*, II, 96.

9 Wüstenfeld, *Genealogische Tabellen*, 430.

10 al-Khaṭīb al-Baghdādī, *Tārīkh Baghdād*, XIV, 434f.

11 Ibid., XIV, 441–44.

12 Ibn al-ʿImād, *Shadharāt al-Dhahab fī Akhbār man Dhahab* (Cairo, 1351), V, 48; Ibn Khallikān, no.413.

13 Maqqarī, *Nafḥ*, I, 876; cited in Goldziher, *Muslim Studies*, II, 366.

14 Goldziher, *Muslim Studies*, II, 366. 'It is in fact very common in the *ijāza* of the transmission of the Bukhārī text to find as middle member of the long chain the name of Karīma al-Marwaziyya', (ibid.).

15 Yāqūt, *Muʿjam al-Udabā'*, I, 247.

16 *COPL*, V/i, 98f.

17 Goldziher, *Muslim Studies*, II, 366.

18 Ibn al-ʿImād, IV, 123, 248. Sitt al-Wuzarā' was also an eminent jurist. She was once invited to Cairo to give her *fatwā* on a subject that had perplexed the jurists there.

19 Ibn al-Athīr, *al-Kāmil* (Cairo, 1301), X, 346.

20 Ibn Khallikān, no.295.

21 Goldziher, *Muslim Studies*, II, 367.

22 Ibn al-ʿImād, VI, 40.

23 Ibid., VIII, 14.

24 Ibn Sālim, *al-Imdād* (Hyderabad, 1327), 36.

25 Ibn al-ʿImād, IV, 100.

26 Ibn Sālim, 16.

27 Ibid., 28f.

28 Ibn al-ʿImād, VI, 56.

29 Ibid., 126; Ibn Sālim, 14, 18; al-ʿUmarī, *Qiṭf al-Thamar* (Hyderabad, 1328), 73.

30 Goldziher, *Muslim Studies*, II, 407.

31 Ibn Baṭṭūṭa, *Riḥla*, 253.

32 Yāqūt, *Muʿjam al-Buldān*, V, 140f.

33 Yāqūt, *Muʿjam al-Udabā'*, 17f.

34 *COPL*, V/i, 175f.

35 Ibn Khallikān, no.250.

36 Ibn al-ʿImād, V, 212, 404.

37 Various manuscripts of this work have been preserved in libraries, and it has been published in Hyderabad in 1348–50. Volume VI of Ibn al-ʿImād's *Shadharāt al-Dhahab*, a large biographical dictionary of prominent Muslim scholars from the first to the tenth centuries of the *hijra*, is largely based on this work.

38 Goldziher, accustomed to the exclusively male environment of nineteenth-century European universities, was taken aback by the scene depicted by Ibn Ḥajar. Cf. Goldziher, *Muslim Studies*, II, 367: 'When reading the great biographical work of Ibn Ḥajar al-ʿAsqalānī on the scholars of the eighth century, we may marvel at the number of women to whom the author has to dedicate articles'.

39 Ibn Ḥajar, *al-Durar al-Kāmina fī Aʿyān al-Mi'a al-Thāmina* (Hyderabad, 1348–50), I, no.1472.

40 Ibn al-ʿImād, VII, 120f.

41 Ibid., VI, 208. We are told that al-ʿIrāqī (the best-known authority on the *ḥadīth*s of Ghazālī's *Iḥyā' ʿUlūm al-Dīn*) ensured that his son also studied under her.

42 A summary by ʿAbd al-Salām and ʿUmar ibn al-Shammāʿ exists (C. Brockelmann, *Geschichte der arabischen Litteratur*, second ed. (Leiden, 1943–49CE), II, 34), and a defective manuscript of the work of the latter is preserved in the O.P. Library at Patna (*COPL*, XII, no.727).

43 Ibid.

44 Sakhāwī, *al-Ḍaw' al-Lāmiʿ li-Ahl al-Qarn al-Tāsiʿ* (*Cairo*, 1353–55), XII, no.980.

45 Ibid., no.58.

46 Ibid., no.450.

47 Ibid., no.901.

48 al-ʿAydarūs, *al-Nūr al-Sāfir* (Baghdad, 1353), 49.

49 Ibn Abī Ṭāhir, see *COPL*, XII, no.665ff.

50 Ibid.

51 Goldziher, *Muslim Studies*, II, 407.

52 *al-Suḥub al-Wābila*, see *COPL*, XII, no.785.

53 *COPL*, V/ii, 54.

54 Ibid., V/ii, 155–9, 180–208. For some particularly instructive annotated manuscripts preserved at the Ẓāhiriya Library at Damascus, see the article of ʿAbd al-ʿAzīz al-Maymanī in *al-Mabāḥith al-ʿIlmiyya* (Hyderabad: Dā'irat al-Māʿarif, 1358), 1–14.

NOTES TO APPENDIX II

1 Pre-eminent among such undertakings was the preparation of the *Concordance and Indices of Muslim Tradition* (Leiden, 1936–88CE), which utilises the six canonical collections, together with the *Sunan* of al-Dārimī, the *Muwaṭṭa'* of Imām Mālik and the *Musnad* of Aḥmad ibn Ḥanbal. Originally planned by Wensinck, Horovitz and certain other orientalists, it was patronised by the Royal Academy of Amsterdam, and assisted by more than a dozen academies of research in Holland and elsewhere. The work was continued by de Haas, and assisted by Muḥammad Fu'ād ʿAbd al-Bāqī and others. Preparation began in 1916, and the first volume was published in 1936, the eighth and final volume (pertaining to proper names) appearing in 1988. The work lists all the important expressions occurring in the works mentioned above, in alphabetical order, the personal and place names being listed in the last volume. But although this monumental work is of considerable value, and has underpinned much recent research, it contains an unacceptably large proportion of errors (cf. Ṭaḥḥān, *Takhrīj*, 92–105). For this reason, a number of institutions such as al-Azhar in Cairo are now preparing computer-based substitutes, cross-checked by some of the world's greatest specialists in this field.

2 The best-known Orientalist names in this area are: A. Sprenger, E. E. Salisbury, O. V. Houdas, L. Krehl, I. Goldziher, T. W. Juynboll, J. Horowitz, A. J. Wensinck, and, more recently, J. Schacht, J. Robson, N. Abbott, W. M. Watt, and G. H. A. Juynboll. The British scholar

J. Robson and the American N. Abbott provide examples of Orientalists who are inclined to accept the traditional picture of *ḥadīth* genesis, while Goldziher and Schacht represent a more sceptical approach. For an account of the early development of *ḥadīth* scholarship in the West, see D. G. Pfannmüller, *Handbuch der Islam Literatur* (Berlin and Leipzig, 1923CE); for more recent works see von Denffer, Ahmad, *Literature on Ḥadīth in European Languages* (Leicester, 1981CE).

3 Cited in R. Patai, *Ignaz Goldziher and his Oriental Diary* (Detroit, 1987CE), 29. This book represents the first English publication of Goldziher's travel diary, and offers a fascinating insight into the psychological makeup of a certain type of Orientalist scholar.

4 Cited in Patai, 20.

5 Reading his bilious and xenophobic diaries gives one a clue to understanding why this dismissive and contemptuous theory should have appealed to his brain. He decides, for instance, that Wallachia can be dismissed as 'the primal home of all physical and moral dirt, of all bodily and psychic imperfection' (cited in Patai, 87). Istanbul is 'the great Jew-town of the Muslims' (Patai, 96; he appears to have intended this as an insult); while the American missionary efforts in Syria were 'an insolence of which only Christianity, the most abominable of all religions, is capable' (Patai, 21).

6 Among the most enthusiastic proponents of Goldziher's theories were Protestant missionaries like Samuel Zwemer and Temple Gairdner.

7 Sprenger, 'Notes on Alfred von Kremer's edition of Wakidi's Campaigns,' (*JASB* XXV, 53–74), 62. Proof of this contention has been supplied more recently by Abbott, *Studies*, I, 24.

8 Sprenger, 'On the Origins,' 303–29 and 375–81.

9 Abbott, *Studies*, II, 2.

10 Ibid; Azami, *Early Ḥadīth Literature*, 301–5.

11 J. Fück, 'Die Rolle des Traditionismus im Islam', (*ZDMG* XCIII (1939), 1–32), 17; cf. Robson, *The Isnād in Muslim Tradition* (reprinted from *Transactions of the Glasgow University Oriental Society* XV(1965), 15–26), 26.

12 Ibid.; Abbott, *Studies*, II, 5–32.

13 Cf. for instance, the famous *Ta'wīl Mukhtalif al-Ḥadīth* (*Interpretation of Variant Ḥadīths*) by Ibn Qutayba (d.276/889). (Beirut, n.d.)

14 Goldziher, *Muslim Studies*, II, 56.

15 Guillaume, *Traditions*, 78.

16 Tirmidhī, *Jāmiʿ*, I, 281.

17 Tirmidhī, *Jāmiʿ* (with *Tuḥfa*), II, 350.

18 Goldziher, *Muslim Studies*, II, 44.

19 Guillaume, *Traditions*, 47–8.

20 Fück, 'Rolle', 23f. Cf. Khaṭīb, *Sunna*, 502–16, for some aspects of Goldziher's position here.

21 Goldziher, *Muslim Studies*, II. 127.

22 Guillaume, *Traditions*, 78f.

23 See above, 113–5.

24 Sibāʿī, *al-Sunna wa-Makānatuhā*, 365–420.

25 al-Khaṭīb, *Sunna*, 249–54.

26 Schacht, *Introduction*, 19.

27 Juynboll, 3–4.

28 S. D. Goitein, *Studies in Islamic History and Institutions* (Leiden, 1965CE), 129–30.

29 Ibid., 133. For all this, see Azami, *On Schacht's Origins*, 15–18.

30 Coulson, 'European Criticism', 319; see also his *History of Islamic Law* (Edinburgh, 1964CE), 64–5.

31 Robson, 'Standards Applied by Muslim Traditionists,' 460; cf. also above, 132.

32 See in particular her objections to Schacht's views on 'family *isnāds*': *Studies*, II, 36–9.

33 'An Arabic Papyrus in the Oriental Institute: Stories of the Prophets,' *Journal of Near Eastern Studies* V (1946CE), 169–80.

34 'Ḥadīth Literature—II: Collection and Transmission of *Ḥadīth*'. *Cambridge History of Arabic Literature* I (Cambridge, 1983CE), 289–98.

35 Abbott, *Studies*, II, 1.

36 Ibid., II, 77–8.

37 Ibid., I, 6–7; I, 26.

38 Ibid., I, 16.

39 Ibid., I, 18, 19; II, 22–32.

40 Ibid., II, 2; cf. II, 64.

41 Lahore: 1960–5.

42 *An Introduction to the Science of Tradition, being Al-Madkhal ilā maʿrifat al-Iklīl by Al-Ḥākim Abū ʿAbdallāh Muḥammad b. ʿAbdallāh al-Naisābūrī* (London, 1953CE).

43 'Ibn Ishaq's Use of Isnād', *Bulletin of the John Rylands Library*, XXXVIII:2 (March 1965), 449–65; 'Muslim Traditions—the Question of Authenticity,' *Memoirs and Proceedings*,

Manchester Literary and Philosophical Society, XCIII (1951), no.7; 'The Isnād in Muslim Tradition,' *Transactions of the Glasgow University Oriental Society*, XV (1965), pp.15–26; 'Standards Applied by Muslim Traditionists,' *Bulletin of the John Rylands Library* XLIII:2 (1961), 459–79.

44 Cf. for instance, 'Standards Applied', 460.

45 In G. H. A. Juynboll (ed.), *Papers on Islamic History. Studies on the first century of Islamic society* (Carbondale, 1982CE), 161–75.

46 Cambridge, 1983CE.

47 Juynboll, 8.

48 Ibid., 7.

49 Ibid., 6; cf. Abbott, II, 69. This scepticism is not shared by G. Makdisi in his updated and enlarged version of J. Pedersen's *EI* article 'Madrasa': he accepts the existence of classes of this size without comment (*EI*², V, 1133).

50 Some of Shaykh Fādānī's public *samāʿ* sessions, delivered complete with *musalsal isnād*, were recorded on videotape. Copies of this are in the possession of many of his students in Mecca.

51 Ibid., 5. *Faḍā'il* and *mathālib* are literary accounts describing respectively the virtues or vices of a given individual, tribe or place.

52 Ibid., 12.

53 Ibid., 13.

54 Chapter Four.

55 Arberry, 'The Teachers of Al-Bukhārī,'35.

56 The *Tahdhīb al-Kamāl* is itself an epitome of an enormous book called *al-Kamāl fī Asmā' al-Rijāl* by ʿAbd al-Ghanī ibn ʿAbd al-Wāḥid al-Maqdisī (d.600/1204), whose sources are meticulously specified; Ibn Ḥajar, after noting this relationship, also mentions his indebtedness to the *Ikmāl Tahdhīb al-Kamāl* of ʿAlā' al-Dīn Mughlaṭai (d.762/1360), who had augmented Mizzī's work with material from his own sources (*Tahdhīb al-Tahdhīb*, I, 8). For the relationship between these and other works deriving from the *Kamāl*, with a detailed description of al-Mizzī's book, see Ṭaḥḥān, *Takhrīj* 181–98. Clearly, it is not Ibn Ḥajar's abbreviation which is 'the most complete list of *ḥadīth* transmitters' (Juynboll, 135), but the earlier work of al-Maqdisī. Cf. also Khaṭīb, *Sunna*, 270–1, 272–73.

57 Ibid., 135.

58 Ibid., 207.

59 The School of Oriental and African Studies, a faculty of London University, still displays the Baconian motto 'Knowledge is Power' on its publications—a faded imperial conceit which until recently would have seemed out of place at Princeton or Chicago.

NOTES TO APPENDIX III

1 Loth, 'Ursprung,' 611.

2 Leipzig, 1869CE.

3 Loth, 'Ursprung,' 593–614.

4 See above, 99.

WORKS CITED

(All dates conform to the Islamic calendar, unless otherwise stated)

Abbott, Nabia. *Studies in Arabic Literary Papyri*. Vol. I, Historical Texts (Chicago, 1957CE); Vol.II, Qur'ānic Commentary and Tradition (Chicago, 1967CE); Vol. III, Language and Literature (Chicago, 1972CE).

——'Ḥadīth Literature—II: Collection and Transmission of *Ḥadīth*'. *Cambridge History of Arabic Literature*, I (Cambridge, 1983CE), 289–98.

——'An Arabic Papyrus in the Oriental Institute: Stories of the Prophets.' *Journal of Near Eastern Studies*, V (1946CE), 169–80.

ʿAbd al-Khāliq, ʿAbd al-Ghanī. *al-Imām al-Bukhārī wa-Ṣaḥīḥuh*. Jedda, 1405.

ʿAbd al-Razzāq al-Ṣanʿānī. *al-Muṣannaf*. Ed. Ḥabīb al-Raḥmān al-Aʿẓamī. Beirut, 1390–92.

Abdul Rauf, M. '*Ḥadīth* Literature—I: The Development of the Science of *Ḥadīth*'. *Cambridge History of Arabic Literature*, I, 271–88.

Abū Daūd al-Sijistānī. *al-Sunan*. Ed. ʿAbd al-Aḥad. Delhi, 1346.

——*Risāla ilā Ahl Makka*. Beirut, n.d.

Ahlwardt, W. *Die Handschriften-Verzeichnisse der Königlichen Bibliothek zu Berlin*. Berlin, 1895CE.

Ansari, Zafar Ishaq. 'The Significance of Shāfiʿī's Criticism of the Medinese School of Law.' *IS*, XXX, 485–99.

Arberry, A. J. 'The Teachers of Al-Bukhārī,' *IQ*, XXXI (1967CE), 34–49.

Ates, A. *Corum ve Yozgat kütüphanelerinden bazı mühim Arapça yazmalar*. Istanbul, 1959CE.

ʿAydarūs, Muḥyi'l-Dīn ʿAbd al-Qādir, al-. *al-Nūr al-Sāfir ʿan Akhbār al-Qarn al-ʿĀshir*. Baghdad, 1353.

Al-Azami, M.M. *On Schacht's Origins of Muhammadan Jurisprudence*. Islamic Texts Society, Cambridge, UK, 1993.

——*Studies in Early Hadith Literature*, Beirut, 1968, reprinted Indianapolis, 1978CE.

Baghawī, Ḥusayn ibn Masʿūd, al-. *Maṣābīḥ al-Sunna*. Cairo, n.d.

Bayhaqī, Aḥmad ibn al-Ḥusayn, al-. *al-Sunan al-Kubrā*. Hyderabad, 1344.

Becker, C.H. *Papyri Schott-Reinhardt* I. Heidelberg, 1906CE.
Bell, R. *Love Theory in Early Hanbalite Islam*. Albany, 1978CE.
Brockelmann, C. *Geschichte der arabischen Litteratur*. Second edition. Leiden, 1943–49CE.
Boisard, M. *L'Humanisme de l'Islam*. 3rd. ed. Paris, 1985CE.
Bukhārī, Abū ʿAbd Allāh Muḥammad ibn Ismāʿīl, al-. *al-Jāmiʿ al-Ṣaḥīḥ*. Ed. Muḥammad al-Zuhrī. Cairo, 1309.
——*al-Tārīkh al-Kabīr*. Hyderabad, 1361–62.
——*al-Tārīkh al-Ṣaghīr*. Allāhabad, 1325.
——*Rafʿ al-Yadayn*. Delhi, 1299.
Caetani, Leone. *Annali dell'Islam*. Milan, 1905–18; Rome, 1926CE.
Catalogue of the Arabic and Persian Manuscripts in the Oriental Public Library at Bankipore. Patna, 1920CE (vol I/I); 1925 (V/II); 1927 (XII).
Coomaraswamy, A.K. *The Bugbear of Literacy*. London, 1948CE.
Cordier, P. *Catalogue du fonds Tibetain de la Bibliothèque Nationale*. Vol. III. Paris, 1915CE.
Coulson, N. J. *A History of Islamic Law* Edinburgh, 1964CE.
——'European Criticism of *Hadith* Literature'. *Cambridge History of Arabic Literature*, I, 317–21.
Dāraquṭnī, ʿAlī ibn ʿUmar, al-. *al-Sunan*. Ed. Shams al-Ḥaqq ʿAẓīmābādī. Delhi,n.d.
Dārimī, Abū Muḥammad, al-. *al-Sunan*. Ed. ʿAbd al-Rashīd al-Kashmīrī. Kanpur, 1292–93.
Dawlābī, al-. *al-Kunā wa'l-asmā'*. Hyderabad, 1322.
al-Dhahabī, Shams al-Dīn Muḥammad ibn Aḥmad, *Tadhkirat al-Ḥuffāẓ*. Hyderabad, 1330.
——*Mīzān al-Iʿtidāl fī Naqd al-Rijāl*. Cairo, 1325.
Dihlawī, Shāh ʿAbd al-ʿAzīz. *Bustān al-Muḥaddithīn*. Delhi, 1898CE.
Dihlawī, Shāh Walī Allāh. *Ḥujjat Allāh al-Bāligha*. Cairo, 1352.
Dīnawarī, Abū Ḥanīfa, al-. *al-Akhbār al-Ṭiwāl*. Leiden, 1888CE.
——*Risāla dar Fann-i Uṣūl-i Ḥadīth* (*ʿUjūla-yi Nāfiʿa*). Delhi, 1255.
Diyārbakrī, al-Ḥusayn ibn Muḥammad, al-. *Tārīkh al-Khamīs*. Cairo, 1309 [?].
Djaït, H. *Europe and Islam: Cultures and Modernity*. Berkeley, 1985CE.
Ebeid, R. Y. and Young, M. J. L. 'New Light on the Origin of the Term "Baccalaureate".' *IQ*, XVIII (1974CE), 3–7.
Fück, J. 'Die Rolle des Traditionalismus im Islam', *ZDMG*, XCIII (1939CE), 1–32.
Ghummārī, Muḥammad, al-. *Miftāḥ al-Tartīb bi-Aḥādīth Tārīkh al-Khaṭīb*. Cairo, 1372.

Goitein, S. D. *Studies in Islamic History and Institutions*. Leiden, 1965CE.
Goldziher, Ignaz. *Muslim Studies*. Translated from the German by Samuel Stern. London, 1967CE.
——'Neue Materialen zur Litteratur des Überlieferungswesens bei den Muhammedaner.' *ZDMG*, L (1896CE), 465–506.
Guillaume, A. *The Traditions of Islam*, Oxford, 1924CE.
Ḥājī Khalīfa. *Kashf al-ẓunūn ʿan asāmī al-kutub wa'l-funūn*. Ed. G. Flügel. Leipzig, 1835–42CE.
Ḥākim al-Nīsābūrī, al-. *al-Mustadrak ʿalā al-Ṣaḥīḥayn*. Hyderabad, 1334–42.
——*Maʿrifa ʿUlūm al-Ḥadīth*. Cairo, 1937CE.
Harley, A. H. 'The Musnad of ʿUmar b. ʿAbdi'l-ʿAzīz'. *JASB*, New Series, XX (1924CE), 391–488.
Haythamī, ʿAlī ibn Abī Bakr, al-. *Mawārid al-ẓam'ān ilā zawā'id Ibn Ḥibbān*. Cairo, 1340.
——*Majmaʿ al-Zawā'id wa-Manbaʿ al-Fawā'id*. Cairo, 1352.
Hitti, P. *The Origins of the Islamic State*. Translation of a section from al-Balādhurī's *Futūḥ al-Buldān*. Columbia, 1924CE.
Horovitz, J. 'Alter und Ursprung des Isnad.' *Der Islam*, VIII (1917CE), 39–47.
——'The Earliest Biographies of the Prophet and their Authors' (i). *IC*, I (1927CE), 535–59.
——'The Earliest Biographies of the Prophet and their Authors' (ii). *IC*, II (1928CE), 22–50.
Ibn ʿAbd al-Barr, Abū ʿUmar Yūsuf. *Jāmiʿ Bayān al ʿIlm wa-Faḍlih*. Cairo, n.d.
——*al-Istīʿāb fī Maʿrifāt al-Aṣḥāb*. Hyderabad, 1318.
Ibn Abī Shayba, *al-Muṣannaf*. Bombay, 1386–90.
Ibn Abī Ṭāhir, Ṭayfūr Aḥmad. *Tārīkh Baghdād*. Vol. VI. Translated into German by H. Keller. Leipzig, 1908CE.
Ibn ʿAdī, *al-Kāmil fī Ḍuʿafā' al-Rijāl*. Beirut, 1404.
Ibn ʿAsākir, Abu'l-Qāsim ʿAlī ibn al-Ḥasan. *Tārīkh Dimashq* (*al-Tārīkh al-Kabīr*). Ed. ʿAbd al-Qādir Badrān. Damascus, 1332.
——*Tabyīn Kadhib al-Muftarī*. Ed. M. al-Kawtharī. Cairo, 1355.
Ibn al-Athīr, ʿIzz al-Dīn. *Usd al-Ghāba fī Maʿrifat al-Ṣaḥāba*. Cairo, 1280.
——*Tārīkh al-Kāmil*. Cairo, 1301.
Ibn Baṭṭūṭa, *al-Riḥla*. Ed. C. Defremery et. al., as *Voyages d'Ibn Batoutah*. Paris, 1843CE.
Ibn Ḥajar al-ʿAsqalānī, *Fatḥ al-Bārī*. Cairo, 1319.

——*al-Iṣāba fī Tamyīz al-Ṣaḥāba*. Ed. Muḥammad Wajīh, A. Sprenger, *et al.* Calcutta, 1856–58CE.

——*Tahdhīb al-Tahdhīb*. Hyderabad, 1326.

——*Muqaddima Fatḥ al-Bārī*. Delhi, 1302.

——*Lisān al-Mīzān*. Hyderabad, 1329–31.

——*al-Durar al-Kāmina fī Aᶜyān al-Mi'a al-Thāmina*. Hyderabad, 1348–50.

Ibn Ḥanbal, Aḥmad ibn Muḥammad. *al-Musnad*. Ed. Muḥammad Ghamrāwī. Cairo, 1313.

——*al-Musnad*. Ed. Aḥmad Muḥammad Shākir. Cairo, 1949–55CE.

——*K. al-ᶜIlal wa-maᶜrifat al-rijāl*. Ed. Talat Kocyigit. Ankara, 1963 CE.

Ibn Ḥazm, Abū Muḥammad ᶜAlī ibn Aḥmad. *Jamharat Ansāb al-ᶜArab*. MS in library of M. Z. Siddiqi.

——*al-Iḥkām fī Uṣūl al-Aḥkām*. Cairo, 1345–47.

——*al-Fiṣal fi'l-Milal wa'l-Ahwā' wa'l-Niḥal* Cairo, 1347.

Ibn al-ᶜImād, Abu'l-Fidā' ᶜAbd al-Ḥayy. *Shadharāt al-Dhahab fī Akhbār man Dhahab*. Cairo, 1351.

Ibn al-Jawzī, ᶜAbd al-Raḥmān. *al-Mawḍūᶜāt*. Ed. ᶜAbd al-Raḥmān ᶜUthmān. Medina, 1386–89.

——*Talqīḥ Fuhūm Ahl al-Āthār*. Ed. Muḥammad Yūsuf Barelvī Delhi, n.d.

——*Kitāb al-Quṣṣāṣ wa'l-Mudhakkirīn*. Ed. and translated by M. L. Swartz. Beirut, 1971CE.

Ibn Khallikān. *Wafayāt al-Aᶜyān wa-Anbā' Abnā' al-Zamān*. Ed. F. Wüstenfeld. Göttingen, 1835CE.

Ibn al-Khayyāṭ, Khalīfa. *al-Tārīkh*. Ed. S. Zakkār. Damascus, 1968CE.

——*al-Ṭabaqāt*. Ed. S. Zakkār. Damascus, 1967CE.

Ibn Khuzayma, Muḥammad ibn Isḥāq. *al-Ṣaḥīḥ*. Ed. M.M. Aᶜẓamī, Beirut, 1391–97.

Ibn Mājah al-Qazwīnī. *al-Sunan*. Delhi, 1333.

Ibn Munabbih, Hammām. *al-Ṣaḥīfa*. Ed. M. Hamidullah. 5th edition. Paris, 1380.

Ibn al-Nadīm. *al-Fihrist*. Ed. G. Flügel. Leipzig, 1871–72CE.

Ibn Qayyim al-Jawziyya. *Zād al-Maᶜād*. Kanpur, 1298.

Ibn Qutayba al-Dīnawarī. *Ta'wīl Mukhtalif al-Ḥadīth*. Beirut, n.d.

Ibn Saᶜd, Muḥammad. *Kitāb al-Ṭabaqāt al-Kabīr*, Ed. E. Sachau *et. al.* Leiden, 1904–18CE.

Ibn al-Ṣalāḥ, ᶜUthmān ibn ᶜAbd al-Raḥmān, al-. *Muqaddima* (*ᶜUlūm al-Ḥadīth*). Cairo, 1316.

Ibn Salīm, Jamāl al-Dīn ᶜAbd Allāh. *Kitāb al-Imdād*. Hyderabad, 1327.

Iṣfahānī, Abu'l-Faraj, al-. *Kitāb al-Aghānī*. Ed. Aḥmad al-Shinqīṭī. Cairo, 1323.

Ishaque, M. *India's Contribution to the Study of Hadith Literature*. Dacca, 1955CE.

ʿIyāḍ, al-Qāḍī. *al-Ilmāʿ fī maʿrifat uṣūl al-riwāya wa-taqyīd al-samāʿ*. Ed. al-Sayyid Aḥmad Ṣaqr. 2nd ed. Cairo, 1398.

Jazā'irī, Ṭāhir ibn Ṣalīḥ, al-. *Tawjīh al-Naẓar ilā Uṣūl al-Āthār*. Cairo, 1318.

Jīwān, Mullā. *Nūr al-Anwār*. Calcutta, 1359.

Johnson-Davies, Denys (Abdul Wadud), and Ibrahim, Izzedine. *An-Nawawi's Forty Hadith: an anthology of the sayings of the Prophet Muhammad*, 14th ed. Beirut, 1409.

Juynboll, G. H. A. *Muslim Tradition. Studies in chronology, provenance and authorship of early hadith*. Cambridge, 1983CE.

——'On the Origins of Arabic Prose'. In G. H. A. Juynboll (ed.), *Papers on Islamic History. Studies on the first century of Islamic society* (Carbondale, 1982CE), 161–75.

Kamali, Mohammad Hashim. *Principles of Islamic Jurisprudence*. Revised ed. Cambridge (U.K.), 1991CE.

Karahan, Abdülkader. 'Aperçu général sur les "Quarante hadiths" dans la littérature Islamique,' *SI*, IV (1955CE), 39–55.

Keith, A. B., *The Sānkhāyana Āraṇyaka, with an appendix on the Mahāvrata*. London, 1980CE.

Khaṭīb al-Baghdādī, Abū Bakr Aḥmad ibn ʿAlī, al-. *Tārīkh Baghdād*. Cairo, 1349.

——*al-Kifāya fī ʿIlm al-Riwāya*. 1357.

——*al-Riḥla fī Ṭalab al-Ḥadīth*. Ed. Nūr al-Dīn ʿItr, Damascus, 1395.

al-Khaṭīb, Muḥammad ʿAjjāj. *al-Sunna qabl al-Tadwīn*. Cairo, 1383.

Khoury, R. G., 'L'importance d'Ibn Lahiʿa et de son papyrus conservé à Heidelberg dans la tradition musulmane du deuxième siècle de l'hégire,' *Arabica*, XXII (1975CE), 6–14.

Kindī, Abū ʿUmar Muḥammad ibn Yūsuf, al-. *al-Wulāt wa'l-Quḍāt*. Leiden, 1912CE.

Lings, M. *Muhammad: His Life based on the Earliest Sources*. Revised ed. Cambridge (U.K.), 1991CE.

Loth, O. *Das Classenbuch des Ibn Sa'd*. Leipzig, 1869CE.

——'Ursprung und Bedeutung der Tabaḳāt,' *ZDMG*, XXIII, 593–614.

Makdisi, G. *The Rise of Colleges*. Edinburgh, 1983CE.

Mālik ibn Anas. *al-Muwaṭṭa'*. tr. Aisha Bewley. London, 1989CE.

Maqqarī, Aḥmad al-Maghribī, al-. *Nafḥ al-Ṭīb min dhikr al-Andalus al-Ḥabīb*. Cairo, 1302.

Margoliouth, D. S. *Lectures on Arabic Historians*. Calcutta, 1930.

Mingana, A. 'An Important Ms. of Bukhārī's *Ṣaḥīḥ*' *JRAS* (1936CE), 287–92.

Mizzī, *Tahdhīb al-Kamāl*. Beirut, 1403.

Mubārakfūrī, ʿAbd al-Raḥmān, al-. *Tuḥfat al-Aḥwadhī Sharḥ Sunan al-Tirmidhī*. Delhi, 1346–53.

Mubarrad, Abū'l ʿAbbās Muḥammad ibn Yazīd, al-. *al-Kāmil*. Ed. W. Wright. Leipzig, 1864CE.

al-Mufaḍḍalīyāt. Ed. Sir Charles J. Lyall. Oxford, 1918–21CE.

Muir, W. *Life of Mahomet*. Ed. T.H. Weir. Edinburgh, 1912CE.

Mullā ʿAlī al-Qārī. *al-La'ālī al-Maṣnūʿa fi'l-Aḥādīth al-Mawḍūʿa*. Beirut, 1406.

Munajjid, Ṣalāḥ al-Dīn, al-. 'Ijāzat al-Samāʿ fī al-Makhṭūṭāt al-Qadīma.' *Journal of the Institute of Arabic Manuscripts*. I/II. Cairo, 1375/1955, 232ff.

Muslim ibn al-Ḥajjāj al-Qushayrī. *Ṣaḥīḥ*. Delhi, 1309.

——*Kitāb al-Tamyīz*. Ed. M.M. al-Aẓamī. Riyadh, 1395/1975.

Nadwī, Sayyid Sulaymān. *Sīrat-i ʿĀ'isha*. Lucknow, 1340.

Nasā'ī, Aḥmad ibn Shuʿayb, al-. *Kitāb al-Ḍuʿafā' wa'l-Matrukīn*. Ed. Būrān al-Ḍannāwī and Kamāl al-Ḥūt. Beirut, 1405/1985.

Nawawī, Abū Zakarīyā Yaḥyā, al-. *Tahdhīb al-Asmā' wa'l-Lughāt*. Ed. F. Wüstenfeld. Göttingen, 1842–47CE.

——*al-Minhāj fī Sharḥ Ṣaḥīḥ Muslim ibn al-Ḥajjāj*. Cairo, 1347.

Nicholson, R. A. *A Literary History of the Arabs*. Cambridge, 1930CE.

Nuʿmānī, Shiblī. *Al-Fārūq*. Lucknow, 1898CE.

O'Neill, Maura. *Women Speaking, Women Listening*. Maryknoll, 1990CE.

Patai, R. *Ignaz Goldziher and his Oriental Diary. A Translation and Psychological Portrait*. Detroit, 1987CE.

Patton, W. M. *Ahmad ibn Hanbal and the Mihna*. Leiden, 1897CE.

Pfannmüller, D. G. *Handbuch der Islam Literatur*. Berlin and Leipzig, 1923CE.

Pouzet, *Une Herméneutique de la tradition islamique. Le Commentaire des Arbaʿūn al-Nawawīya de Muḥyī al-Dīn Yaḥyā al-Nawawī*. Beirut, 1982CE.

Qasṭallānī, Aḥmad ibn Muḥammad, al-. *al-Mawāhib al-Ladunnīya*. With commentary of Muḥammad ibn ʿAbd al-Bāqī al-Zurqānī. Cairo, 1291.

——*Irshād al-Sārī ilā Ṣaḥīḥ al-Bukhārī*. Cairo, 1285.

Qazwīnī, ʿUmar ibn ʿAbd al-Raḥmān, al-. *Mukhtaṣar Shuʿab al-īmān.* English translation by Abdal Hakim Murad as *The Seventy-Seven Branches of Faith.* Dorton (U.K.), 1990CE.

Rāzī, Ibn Abī Ḥatīm, al-. *al-Jarḥ wa'l-Taʿdīl.* Hyderabad, 1360–73.

Robson, J. *An Introduction to the Science of Tradition, being* Al-Madkhal ilā maʿrifat al-Iklīl *by Al Ḥākim Abū ʿAbdallāh Muḥammad b. ʿAbd Allāh al-Naisābūrī.* London, 1953CE.

——'The Isnād in Muslim Tradition.' Reprinted from *Transactions of the Glasgow University Oriental Society,* XV (1965), pp.15–26.

——'Ibn Iṣhāq's Use of Isnād'. *Bulletin of the John Rylands Library,* 38:2. (March 1965), 449–65.

——'Standards Applied by Muslim Traditionists', *Bulletin of the John Rylands Library,* XLIII (1961), 459–79.

——'Muslim Traditions—the Question of Authenticity.' *Memoirs and Proceedings, Manchester Literary and Philosophical Society,* XCIII (1951), no.7.

Rosenthal, F. *History of Muslim Historiography.* Leiden, 1952CE.

Sāʿātī, al-. *Minḥat al-Maʿbūd fī tartīb Musnad al-Ṭayālisī Abū Daūd.* Cairo, 1371.

Sakhāwī, Shams al-Dīn Muḥammad, al-. *Fatḥ al-Mughīth.* (Commentary on the *Alfiya* of Zayn al-Dīn al-ʿIrāqī.) Lucknow, n.d.

——*al-Ḍaw' al-Lāmiʿ li-Ahl al-Qarn al-Tāsiʿ.* Cairo, 1353–55.

Samʿānī, ʿAbd al-Karīm ibn Muḥammad, al-. *al-Ansāb.* Leiden, 1912CE.

Schacht, Joseph. *The Origins of Muhammadan Jurisprudence,* Oxford, 1959CE.

Sezgin, F. *Geschichte des arabischen Schrifttums.* Vol. I. Leiden, 1967CE.

——Sezgin, M. F., *Buhârî'nin Kaynakları hakkında araştırmalar.* Istanbul, 1956CE.

Shāfiʿī Muḥammad ibn Idrīs, al-. *al-Risāla.* Cairo, 1312.

Shawkānī. *al-Fawā'id al-Majmūʿa fī bayān al-Aḥādīth al-Mawḍūʿa.* Lahore, 1223 (?1323).

Sibāʿī Muṣṭafā, al-. *al-Sunna wa-Makānatuhā fi'l-Tashrīʿ al-Islāmī.* Cairo, 1381/1961.

Siddiqi, M. Z. *Studies in Arabic and Persian Medical Literature.* Calcutta, 1959CE.

Sprenger, A. 'On the Origin and Progress of Writing Down Historical Facts among the Musalmans.' *JASB* (1st series) XXV, 303–29, 375–81.

——'Notes on Alfred von Kremer's edition of Wakidi's Campaigns.' *JASB* (1st series) XXV, 53–74.

——*Das Leben und die Lehre des Muḥammad.* Berlin, 1869.

Subkī, Tāj al-Dīn ʿAbd al-Wahhāb, al-. *Ṭabaqāt al-Shāfiʿīya al-Kubrā*. Cairo, 1324.

Suyūṭī, Jalāl al-Dīn, al-. *Tadrīb al-Rāwī*. (Commentary on al-Nawawī's *al-Taqrīb wa'l-Taysīr*. Cairo, 1307.

——*Ṭabaqāt al-Ḥuffāẓ*. Ed. G. Wüstenfeld. Göttingen, 1833CE.

Ṭabarānī, Sulaymān ibn Aḥmad, al-. *al-Muʿjam al-Kabīr*. Ed. Ḥamdī al-Salafī. Baghdad, 1978 CE.

——*al-Muʿjam al-Ṣaghīr*. Cairo, 1388.

Ṭabarī, Abū Jaʿfar Muḥammad ibn Jarīr, al-. *Tārīkh al-Rusul wa'l-Mulūk*. Ed. Th. Nöldeke *et al*. Leiden, 1888CE.

Tabrīzī, Walī al-Dīn Muḥammad ibn ʿAbd Allāh, al-. *Mishkāt al-Maṣābīḥ*. Lucknow, 1326.

Ṭaḥḥān, Maḥmūd, al-. *Uṣūl al-Takhrīj wa-Dirāsat al-Asānīd*. Cairo, n.d.

Ṭayālisī, Abū Daūd, al-. *al-Musnad*. Hyderabad, 1321.

Thaʿālibī, Abū Manṣūr ʿAbd al-Malik, al-. *Yatīmat al-Dahr*. Cairo, 1352.

Tirmidhī, Abū ʿĪsā Muḥammad ibn ʿĪsā, al-. *Jāmiʿ al-Tirmidhī*. With *Kitāb al-Shamā'il* and *Kitāb al-ʿIlal* of the same author. Delhi, 1315.

ʿUmari, Ṣāliḥ ibn Muḥammad, al-. *Qiṭf al-Thamar*. Hyderabad, 1328.

Vajda, G. *Les certificats de lecture et de transmission dans les manuscrits arabes de la Bibliothèque nationale de Paris*. Paris, 1956CE.

von Denffer, Ahmad. *Literature on Hadith in European Languages: a bibliography*. Leicester, 1981CE.

von Kremer., A. *The Orient under the Caliphs*. Translation of *Culturgeschichte des Orients*. Tr. S. Khuda Bakhsh. Calcutta, 1920CE.

Watt, W. Montgomery. *Muḥammad at Mecca*. Oxford, 1953CE.

——*Muḥammad at Medina*. Oxford, 1956CE.

Wensinck, A. J., *et al. Concordance et indices de la tradition musulmane*. Leiden, 1936–88CE.

Wellhausen, J. *Reste arabischen Heidentums*. Berlin, 1897CE.

Winternitz. *A History of Indian Literature*. Calcutta, 1927CE.

Wüstenfeld, F. *Genealogische Tabellen der Arabischen Stämme und Familien*. Accompanied by the *Register zu den GT*. Göttingen, 1852–53CE.

——*Der Imām el-Schāfiʿī: seine Schüler und Anhänger bis zum J. 300 d.H.* Göttingen, 1890CE.

Yāqūt, Abū ʿAbd Allah. *Muʿjam al-Udabā'* Ed. D. S. Margoliouth. 2nd ed. London, 1923–25CE.

Zurqānī, ʿAbd Allāh al-. *Sharḥ al-Zurqānī ʿalā al-Manẓūma al-Bayqūnīya fi'l-Muṣṭalaḥ*. Ed. Nabīl al-Sharīf. Beirut, 1405/1985.

——*Sharḥ Muwaṭṭa' Malik*. Cairo, 1310.

INDEX